MW01285365

The Gospel of Pseudo-Matthew
and the Nativity of Mary

TOOLS AND TRANSLATIONS

The Westar Tools and Translations series provides critical tools and fresh new translations for research on canonical and non-canonical texts that survive from the earliest periods of the Christian tradition to the Middle Ages. These writings are crucial for determining the complex history of Christian origins. The translations are known as the Scholars Version. Each work, whether a translation or research aid, is accompanied by textual notes, translation notes, cross references, and an index. An extensive introduction also sets out the challenge a text or research aid addresses.

EARLY CHRISTIAN APOCRYPHA

Editorial Board:
TONY BURKE
BRENT LANDAU
JANET SPITTLER

Translations of non-canonical texts out of the Christian tradition are offered as part of the Westar Tools and Translations series in cooperation with the North American Society for the Study of Christian Apocrypha (NASSCAL). The Early Christian Apocrypha series features fresh new translations of major apocryphal texts that survive from the early period of the Christian church. These non-canonical writings are crucial for determining the complex history of Christian origins. The series continues the work of Julian V. Hills, who edited the first six volumes of the series for Polebridge Press.

Volume 1: *The Acts of Andrew*
Volume 2: *The Epistle of the Apostles*
Volume 3: *The Acts of Thomas*
Volume 4: *The Acts of Peter*
Volume 5: *Didache*
Volume 6: *The Acts of John*
Volume 7: *The Protevangelium of James*
Volume 8: *The Gospel of Pseudo-Matthew and the Nativity of Mary*

The Gospel of Pseudo-Matthew
and the Nativity of Mary

Brandon W. Hawk

CASCADE *Books* • Eugene, Oregon

THE GOSPEL OF PSEUDO-MATTHEW AND THE NATIVITY OF MARY

Early Christian Apocrypha 8

Copyright © 2019 Brandon W. Hawk. All rights reserved. Except for brief quotations in critical publications or reviews, no part of this book may be reproduced in any manner without prior written permission from the publisher. Write: Permissions, Wipf and Stock Publishers, 199 W. 8th Ave., Suite 3, Eugene, OR 97401.

Cascade Books
An Imprint of Wipf and Stock Publishers
199 W. 8th Ave., Suite 3
Eugene, OR 97401

www.wipfandstock.com

PAPERBACK ISBN: 978-1-5326-3713-1
HARDCOVER ISBN: 978-1-5326-3714-8
EBOOK ISBN: 978-1-5326-3715-5

Cataloging-in-Publication data:

Names: Hawk, Brandon W., author.

Title: The Gospel of Pseudo-Matthew and the Nativity of Mary / Brandon W. Hawk.

Description: Eugene, OR: Cascade Books, 2019. | Early Christian Apocrypha 8. | Includes bibliographical references and index.

Identifiers: ISBN 978-1-5326-3713-1 (paperback). | ISBN 978-1-5326-3714-8 (hardcover). | ISBN 978-1-5326-3715-5 (ebook).

Subjects: LCSH: Apocryphal Gospels. | Mary—Blessed Virgin, Saint—Legends. | Jesus Christ—Apocryphal and legendary literature.

Classification: BS2831 H39 2019 (print). | BS2831 (epub).

Manufactured in the U.S.A.   06/10/19

To those who have gone before:
Constantin von Tischendorf, Jan Gijsel, and Rita Beyers

Contents

Acknowledgments

My interest in the *Gospel of Pseudo-Matthew* began nearly ten years ago, and it has held my fascination ever since. In my work on this translation and commentary, I have had much help that I am happy to acknowledge here. I am especially thankful to Tony Burke, who invited me to contribute this volume to the Early Christian Apocrypha series, and who has been an excellent editor along the way; my work is all the better for his guidance, comments, and editorial shepherding. I am indebted to Janet Spittler, who meticulously checked my translations, offered valuable suggestions, and puzzled through the linguistic oddities of these texts with me in various conversations—which were always helpful and stimulating. My father, Timothy Hawk, read through the manuscript, caught errors, and posed questions for clarification, for which I am appreciative. Any remaining mistakes are, of course, my own. It is a pleasure to express my gratitude to the librarians at the James P. Adams Library of Rhode Island College who have worked to obtain many books and articles via interlibrary loans to aid in my research for this project; foremost, I am thankful to Lisa Maine and Leigh Mournighan. I received support from Rhode Island College for work on this volume in fall 2016, and for this I am grateful to Daniel Scott (Chair of the English Department), Earl Simson (Dean of the Faculty of Arts and Sciences), and Ron Pitt (Vice President for Academic Affairs at the time). I also want to thank Judy, my wife, and Catie, my daughter, for their personal support and encouragement. Many thanks go to the staff at Wipf & Stock, especially Matthew Wimer, Ian Creeger, and K. C. Hanson, for seeing this volume through production.

Finally, I owe a debt of gratitude to those who have previously worked on the *Gospel of Pseudo-Matthew*, the *Nativity of Mary*, and their medieval histories. This is especially true of Constantin von Tischendorf,

Jan Gijsel, and Rita Beyers, whose editions and studies remain founda-
tional, as the pages of this volume will attest. It is therefore my pleasure
to dedicate this book to these three scholars.

Brandon W. Hawk
Feast of Gregory the Great, 2018

Abbreviations

Ancient

Ambrose of Milan

    Enarrat. Ps.   *Enarrationes in XII Psalmos Davidicos*

    Exp. Luc.   *Expositio Evangelii secundum Lucam*

    Parad.   *De paradiso*

    Vid.   *De viduis*

    Virg.   *De virginibus*

    Virginit.   *De virginitate*

Apoc. Paul   *Apocalypse of Paul*

Arab. Gos. Inf.   *Arabic Infancy Gospel*

Arm. Gos. Inf.   *Armenian Infancy Gospel*

Augustine

    Bon. conj.   *De bono conjugali*

    Civ.   *De civitate Dei*

    Contin.   *De continentia*

    Enarrat. Ps.   *Enarrationes in Psalmos*

    Epist.   *Epistulae*

    Fel.   *Contra Felicem*

    Gen. Imp.   *De Genesi ad litteram imperfectus liber*

Nat. grat.	*De natura et gratia*
Serm.	*Sermones*
Vid.	*De bono viduitatis*
Virginit.	*De sancta virginitate*

2 Bar   2 Baruch

Clement of Alexandria

Strom.	*Stromateis*

Dorm. Vir.   *Dormition of the Virgin*

Gregory of Nyssa

Virginit.	*De virginitate*

Herm. *Vis.*   Shepherd of Hermas, *Vision(s)*

Hist. Jos. Carp.   *History of Joseph the Carpenter*

Inf. Gos. Thom.   *Infancy Gospel of Thomas*

Jerome

Comm. Am.	*Commentariorum in Amos libri III*
Comm. Matt.	*Commentariorum in Matthaeum libri IV*
Comm. Os.	*Commentariorum in Osee libri III*
Epist.	*Epistulae*
Helv.	*Adversus Helvidium de Mariae virginitate perpetua*
Ruf.	*Adversus Rufinum libri III*
Tract. Ps.	*Tractatus in Psalmos*

Josephus

B.J.	*Bellum judaicum*

Justin Martyr

Dial.	*Dialogue with Trypho*

Nat. Mary   *Nativity of Mary*

Origen

Cel.	*Contra Celsum*

Comm. Matt.	*Commentarium in evangelium Matthaei*

Pliny the Elder

Nat.	*Naturalis historia*
Prot. Jas.	*Protevangelium of James*
Ps.-Mt.	*Gospel of Pseudo-Matthew*

Pseudo-Rufinus

Hist. mon.	*Historia monachorum in Aegypto*
RB	*Rule of Benedict*
RM	*Rule of the Master*

Tertullian

Exh. cast.	*De exhortatione castitatis*
Mon.	*De monogamia*
Ux.	*Ad uxorem*
Virg.	*De virginibus velandis*

Virgil

Aen.	*Aeneid*
Vis. Theo.	*Vision of Theophilus*

Modern

AJP	*American Journal of Philology*
BJRL	*Bulletin of the John Rylands Library*
CCSA	Corpus Christianorum: Series Apocryphorum
ETR	*Études théologiques et religieuses*
JECS	*Journal of Early Christian Studies*
MS	*Mediaeval Studies*
NTTS	New Testament Tools and Studies
OECS	Oxford Early Christian Studies
RBén	*Revue Bénédictine*

RTAM	*Recherches de théologie ancienne et médiévale*
SacEr	*Sacris Erudiri*
Spec	*Speculum*
WUNT	Wissenschaftliche Untersuchungen zum Neuen Testament

Conventions

LXX	Septuagint
Vul.	Vulgate

Manuscripts and Sigla

A^1a2	Rheims, Bibliothèque municipale 1395 (ca.850), the model for branch A^1a [Gijsel's A]
A^1a1	Vienna, Österreichische Nationalbibliothek 550 (10th cent.)
A^1c1	Paris, Bibliothèque nationale de France, lat. 5327 (10th cent.), the model for branch A^1c [Gijsel's C]
A^1e4	Oxford, Bodleian Library, Rawlinson D 1236 (14th cent.)
A^2a1	London, British Library, Add. 11880 (ca. 820)
A^2b1	Einsiedeln, Stiftsbibliothek 250 (12th cent., before 1150), the model for branch A^2b [Gijsel's H]
A^3a1	Budapest, Széchényi Bibliothek National, Clmae 316 (9th cent.)
A^3a3	Vienna, Österreichische Nationalbibliothek 289 (10th cent.)
A^4a2	Bibliothèque nationale de France, lat. 1772 (11th cent.)
A^4a4	Leiden, Bibliotheek der Rijksuniversiteit, Voss. lat. Q 28 (12th cent.)
A^4a8	Berkeley, University of California, UCB 20 (12th cent.)

A^4c1	Berlin, Staatsbibliothek Preußischer Kulturbesitz, Phillipps 1675 (early 12th cent.), the model for branch A^4c [Gijsel's L]
b	Common model reconstructed for branch A^1b
e	Common model for branch A^1e
g	Common model reconstructed for branch A^2a
j	Common model reconstructed for branch A^3b
Ja1	Montpellier, Bibliothèque de la Faculté de médicine 55 (ca. 800) [also M^1]
k	Common model reconstructed for branch A^4a
P^1b3	Paris, Bibliothèque nationale de France, nouv. acq. lat. 1605 (9th cent.)
P^1c1	Vatican, Biblioteca Apostolica Vaticana, Pal. lat. 430 (ca. 840)
P^1y1	Karlsruhe, Badische Landesbibliothek, Fragmentum 94 (Aug. 248) (ca. 850)
P^2a3	Paris, Bibliothèque nationale de France, lat. 5559 A (14th cent.) [Tischendorf's C]
P^3a2	Paris, Bibliothèque nationale de France, lat. 1652 (15th cent.) [Tischendorf's D]
Q^1a1	Vatican, Biblioteca Apostolica Vaticana, Reg. lat. 648 (12th cent.)
Q^4b5	Paris, Bibliothèque nationale de France, lat. 11867 (13th cent.)
Q^4a1	Cambridge, Corpus Christi College 288 (12th/13th cent.)
Q^4a2	Vatican, Biblioteca Apostolica Vaticana, lat. 4578 (14th cent.) [Tischendorf's A]
Q^6b6	Paris, Bibliothèque nationale de France, lat. 2688 (ca. 1270, Italy)
R^1b4	Berlin, Staatsbibliothek, Preußischer Kulturbesitz, Theol. lat. qu. 369 (13th cent.)

R^2b1 Florence, Biblioteca Medicea Laurenziana, Gaddi 208 (14th cent.) [Tischendorf's B]

R^2c1 Paris, Bibliothèque nationale de France, lat. 5560 (13th/14th cent.)

Introduction

THE *GOSPEL OF PSEUDO-MATTHEW* (*Ps.-Mt.*) is one of the most important witnesses in the Latin West to apocryphal stories about the lives of Mary, Joseph, Jesus, and Mary's parents, Anna and Joachim. Among apocryphal gospels in medieval Western Europe, this apocryphon was second in popularity only to the more widely attested *Gospel of Nicodemus*, revealing *Ps.-Mt.* to be a bestseller of mainstream Christianity in the Middle Ages. In many ways, the origins and transmission of the Latin *Ps.-Mt.* are tied up with its source, the Greek *Protevangelium of James* (*Prot. Jas.*), and the transmission of related apocrypha in medieval Western Europe. As an adaptive translation and expansion of *Prot. Jas.*, the Latin apocryphon is a keystone in the explosion of apocryphal literature in the Middle Ages, including competing translations of *Prot. Jas.* as well as rewritings, excerptions, expansions, and translations of *Ps.-Mt.* from the ninth century onward.

Despite its apocryphal status—and medieval writers did acknowledge it to be extrabiblical—*Ps.-Mt.* remained both popular and influential throughout the Middle Ages and into the early modern period. Its popularity and influences may be traced in many pieces of Christian literature (in Latin and vernacular languages), visual arts, liturgy, and theological perspectives still revered by Roman Catholic theologians. *Ps.-Mt.* is also a significant work for considering the history of monasticism and the cult of the Virgin Mary. All of these developments provide evidence for the endurance of both *Prot. Jas.* and *Ps.-Mt.* as a major part of mainstream Christianity in Western Europe during the medieval period.

Summary

After some prefatory material (which varies in the manuscripts: see below), *Ps.-Mt.* begins by introducing Joachim and Anna, who live according to Israelite law but have no children after twenty years of marriage. When Joachim makes a pilgrimage to the temple to offer a sacrifice, a scribe rebukes him and rejects his offering because of his infertility. In shame, Joachim leaves but does not return home; instead, he assumes a self-exile in the mountains as a shepherd for five months. Meanwhile, Anna is left alone at home, ignorant of what has happened to Joachim and believing that he might be dead. In response to her lamentation, an angel visits her and promises that she will bear a child destined for greatness. Around the same time, this angel visits Joachim disguised as a boy and urges him to return home, telling him that Anna will have a daughter who will be blessed above all women. Joachim offers a sacrifice to the angel, who demurs, and at the angel's insistence instead makes his sacrifice to God. After Joachim's companions hear about the angel's visit and announcement, they insist that he return home, but Joachim still hesitates. Again, the angel visits him, this time in a dream, and tells him to return home. Finally, at the shepherds' continued urging, Joachim leaves the mountains to be reunited with Anna.

Nine months later, Mary is born and her parents raise her at home. At the age of three, Anna and Joachim take Mary to the temple and dedicate her to God, leaving her to live in a community of female virgins in an ascetic lifestyle. Mary is specifically singled out for her special status as the most holy of these virgins. The temple priests become anxious when she reaches fourteen years old, so they arrange to have her betrothed, through a ceremony in which they ask God to reveal the most suitable husband among the single men in Israel. Despite his hesitancy—because he is an older widower and has children from a previous marriage—Joseph is selected to be Mary's husband and she is betrothed to him. An angel visits Mary (as with Anna before, while her husband is away) and announces that she will give birth to a son through a miracle of God. When Joseph learns of this he considers quietly divorcing her, but an angel also appears to him (as with Joachim before) and reassures him that Mary is pure. Yet the rumor of Mary's pregnancy spreads, and the temple priests summon Mary and Joseph to appear before them and submit to a test of their purity. After undergoing this trial, they are exonerated of any sins.

Later, Mary and Joseph travel to Bethlehem for Caesar Augustus' census, but along the way Mary has a prophetic vision of two peoples and shortly afterward goes into labor. Joseph finds a cave for Mary, where she gives birth to Jesus. Joseph brings a midwife named Zahel to Mary, who inspects her postpartum and declares her to be still a virgin. Another midwife, Salome, hears of this, doubts that this could be true, and inspects Mary for herself; as a result, her hand withers, and an angel appears, instructing her to seek healing by touching the baby's swaddling cloths. A series of episodes follow, the point of each one to present the fulfillment of prophecy in the Hebrew Bible. Joseph then takes Jesus to the temple for his circumcision and to offer a sacrifice.

Two years later, three magi visit Jerusalem in search of a new-born king. Fearing that the baby is the king heralded by earlier prophecy, Herod commands that all children in Israel age two and under shall be killed. Joseph is warned in a dream about Herod's command and he flees to Egypt with Mary and Jesus. A series of miracles occur along the way, including Jesus subduing a group of dragons, wild animals venerating Jesus along the road, a palm tree bending to allow Mary to eat its fruit, Jesus creating a shortcut to shorten a thirty-day journey to one day, and Jesus being venerated by the idols of pagan gods and the governor in an Egyptian temple. The gospel in its original form ends at this point.

Over time, the narrative of *Ps.-Mt.* did not remain static. In fact, it is apparent from the manuscript evidence that the text of this apocryphon was dynamic throughout the medieval period—probably due, in large part, to its popularity. The core remained the same, but later compilers and scribes continued to expand the contents with more material about Jesus' childhood. Such expansions are most evident in additions made in the twelfth century, as well as later episodes further appended by the end of the thirteenth century. These will be discussed in the section about Later Transmission and Additions, and are included in this translation to demonstrate the evolution of the textual tradition throughout the Middle Ages.

Transmission and Survival

Transmission of *Ps.-Mt.* was widespread and long-lasting. The manuscript evidence ranges from the turn of the ninth century to the sixteenth century, with origins or provenances as far-flung as modern-day France,

Spain, Ireland, Britain, Iceland, Sweden, Denmark, Netherlands, Belgium, Germany, Austria, Switzerland, Italy, Austria, Czech Republic, Poland, and Slovenia. In his 1997 critical edition for the Corpus Christianorum Series Apocryphorum, Jan Gijsel identifies 190 manuscript witnesses, and in a follow-up article he identifies another seven.[1] These manuscripts are divided into four major family recensions: A, P, Q, and R. Within the four major textual families, further distinctions may be made, and some of the manuscripts contain hybrid versions. Gijsel also discusses forty witnesses that are either too fragmentary or have too much of a hybrid form to be conclusively classified. For the most part, the A-text takes precedence in this introduction and the following translation, although it is also useful to consider the P-text in establishing the early form of the apocryphon, and the Q and R texts reveal important aspects of its later transmission.

The A-text represents a version of *Ps.-Mt.* closest to the original, though revised around the year 800 with some slight grammatical changes. The earliest manuscript of the A family was created just a few decades later: London, British Library, Add. 11880, copied around 820 in Regensburg, Germany. Other early manuscripts of the A family include:

Budapest, Széchényi Bibliothek National, Clmae 316 (9th cent., Salzburg)

Paris, Bibliothèque nationale de France, lat. 5327 (10th cent., Saint-Amand-les-Eaux)

Rheims, Bibliothèque municipale 1395 (ca. 850, Rheims)

Vienna, Österreichische Nationalbibliothek 550 (10th cent., Northern France)

Vienna, Österreichische Nationalbibliothek 289 (10th cent., Salzburg)

The P-text also developed around 800, from the same antecedent version that lies behind the A-text. The earliest manuscripts of the P family include:

Paris, Bibliothèque nationale de France, nouv. acq. lat. 1605 (9th cent., Orleans)

---

1. See manuscript descriptions in Gijsel, *Libri de nativitate Mariae*, 108–217, and full "Listes des manuscrits *Pseudo-Matthieu*" in various groupings at 483–515; see also Gijsel, "Nouveaux témoins."

Vatican, Biblioteca Apostolica Vaticana, Pal. lat. 430 (ca. 840, South-
Western Germany)

Of the manuscripts that Gijsel found impossible to classify by family, or
for which only tentative classification is possible, particularly noteworthy
is Karlsruhe, Badische Landesbibliothek, Fragmentum 94 (Aug. 248),
copied around 850 in Reichenau, Austria. Because this manuscript is
fragmentary (containing only part of chap. 8) and due to its variant text
form, its precise relationship to the A and P recensions is indeterminate,
but it remains one of the earliest witnesses to *Ps.-Mt.*

Although the A and P text types share a common ancestor, P exhib-
its features of more profound revision with both grammatical and sub-
stantive changes. Such differences have even led commentators to deride
the author of the original text and uphold P as an improved revision.
Recently, for example, Ehrman and Pleše followed the general assessment
of scholars (including Gijsel) in claiming that the author "was not a particularly gifted writer, hence the rough and occasionally slovenly character of the older A recension, in contrast to the more refined P."[2] Yet Rita
Beyers has refuted these criticisms through a comparative examination
of the lexicographical styles of both A and P, especially calling attention
to several uncommon words or rare uses in A that signal some amount
of sophistication.[3] Indeed, as she says elsewhere about the apocryphon,
"le *Pseudo-Matthieu* possède une unite de structure et une richesse de
sentiments" ("*Pseudo-Matthew* has a unity of structure and a richness of
sentiment") to be appreciated.[4]

Around the middle of the twelfth century, the Q-text emerged. The
earliest surviving witnesses are Vatican, Biblioteca Apostolica Vaticana,
Reg. lat. 648 (12th cent., Rheims) and Cambridge, Corpus Chisti College
288 (12th/13th cent., Cambridge). This family of witnesses derives from
P, although some of the manuscripts also demonstrate affinities with A in
certain details. The Q-text also incorporates some innovative revisions,
especially with major additions to the main narrative: at the beginning,
a text now known as the *Trinubium Annae* and, at the end (as chaps.
26–42), a Latin version of the *Infancy Gospel of Thomas* (*Inf. Gos. Thom.*)
commonly referred to as the *pars altera*, or "other part" of the text. While

---

2. See Gijsel, *Libri de nativitate Mariae*, 88–89; and Ehrman and Pleše, *Apocryphal Gospels*, 75.

3. Beyers, "Transmission of Marian Apocrypha," 130–33.

4. Beyers, *Libri de nativitate Mariae*, 20.

this *pars altera* is now recognized as an addition to *Ps.-Mt.*, earlier editors and scholars believed it to be part of the original compilation, though from a separate source.[5]

Only some decades later, around the turn of the thirteenth century, the R-text was created, derived directly from Q. The earliest surviving witnesses are Berlin, Staatsbibliothek, Preußischer Kulturbesitz, Theol. lat. qu. 369 (13th cent., Northern France) and Paris, Bibliothèque nationale de France, lat. 5560 (13th/14th cent.). The R-text represents a further process of revision and, as Gijsel observes, "témoigne d'un effort constant de réécriture, qui ne porte pas seulement sur le style" ("witnesses to a constant effort to rewrite, which is not solely about the style").[6] The composer of R also worked with a variety of other sources to create a newly compiled narrative;[7] these sources include the *Nativity of Mary* (*Nat. Mary*), which had been written by about the year 1000 as an independent adaptation of *Ps.-Mt.* Finally, some manuscripts of this new revision end with an epilogue in the form of a prayer to Mary:

> intercedente sanctissima matre tua ad resurrectionis gloriam peruenire mereamur, ut te laeti facie ad faciem uideamus dominum nostrum Iesum Christum cum patre et spiritu sancto qui regnas deus per infinita saecula. Amen.

> Through your intercession, most holy Mother, may we deserve to attain the glory of resurrection, so that face to face with you we might joyfully see our Lord Jesus Christ with the Father and the Holy Spirit, who reigns as God forever into infinity. Amen.[8]

This intercessory doxology highlights the associations that had grown up between *Ps.-Mt.* and the cult of Mary from the tenth century onward.

Two other apocryphal texts may be brought to bear upon the history of the transmission of *Ps.-Mt.*: the so-called "J Compilation" and the *Liber de nativitate Salvatoris* ("Book of the Nativity of the Savior"). The J Compilation contains several sources pieced together into a single narrative: a Latin version of *Prot. Jas.*, *Ps.-Mt.*, a lost infancy gospel given the

---

5. For more details on these additions, see the section on "Later Transmission and Additions" below.

6. Gijsel, *Libri de nativitate Mariae*, 96.

7. For more details on these additions, see the section on "Later Transmission and Additions" below.

8. Gijsel, *Libri de nativitate Mariae*, 97.

name the *Liber de nativitate Salvatoris*,[9] and the Latin version of *Inf. Gos. Thom.* (the *pars altera*), though the latter was likely added later in the compilation's transmission. In total, seven manuscripts of this compilation have been identified, grouped into two types known as the Arundel and Hereford forms (based on the first identified manuscripts). The later Hereford version also incorporates, as in the Q-text, portions of *Nat. Mary*, and a Pseudo-Augustinian homily on the Annunciation (*Serm.* 195). Gijsel notes and describes these witnesses in his edition of *Ps.-Mt.* (nine manuscripts to which he assigns the designation J) but does not use them for his collation.[10] Jean-Daniel Kaestli and Martin McNamara edited both forms in a parallel edition in 2001.[11] The most significant manuscript of J is Montpellier, Bibliothèque de la Faculté de médicine 55, copied around the year 800 at Metz or in a scriptorium with similar writing style (possibly Worms). It contains only part of the J Compilation (perhaps an early form of its development), made up of an interweaving of a Latin translation of *Prot. Jas.* 1:1—7:3 and *Ps.-Mt.* 1–4. The text (though not the manuscript as a whole) also has certain features that might point to Irish or Hiberno-Latin associations, although Kaestli and McNamara provided no solid conclusions. This manuscript represents the earliest identified witness to the text of *Ps.-Mt.* in any of its extant forms.[12]

The contents of the *Liber de nativitate Salvatoris* have been reconstructed based on later texts that seem to share this source, including the J Compilation, the Irish *Liber Flavus Fergusiorum*, and an Irish "gospel history" found in the *Leabhar Breac* and other manuscripts.[13] The contents that Kaestli and McNamara have reconstructed based on these later texts include: Mary and Joseph's journey to Bethlehem; the birth of Jesus

9. M. R. James first titled this text the "New Source" in his 1927 edition of the J Compilation in *Latin Infancy Gospels*; it has since been named the "Source" or "Special Source" (as in Kaestli and McNamara, "Latin Infancy Gospels"); Kaestli proposed the title *Liber de nativitate Salvatoris* in "Mapping an Unexplored Second Century Apocryphal Gospel."

10. Gijsel, *Libri de nativitate Mariae*, 108–217 and 483–515.

11. Kaestli and McNamara, "Latin Infancy Gospels."

12. Kaestli and McNamara, "Latin Infancy Gospels," 650–54. Montpellier 55 is also significant because it includes a Latin translation of *Prot. Jas.* 8–25 with interpolations from the canonical Gospels; this Latin version of *Prot. Jas.* and the J Compilation do not belong together, as they are in different sections of the manuscript and thus present witnesses to two different Latin versions of *Prot. Jas.*

13. See Kaestli and McNamara, "Latin Infancy Gospels."

and testimony of the midwife about Mary's perpetual virginity; as well as the visit of the shepherds, the visit of the magi, and their encounter with Herod.[14] Kaestli and McNamara also concede the possibility (without further evidence one way or the other) that the original text of the *Liber de nativitate Salvatoris* may have also included the flight into Egypt and Jesus' childhood miracles along the way, since these are attested in the *Leabhar Breac*.[15] Kaestli claims that this *Liber de nativitate Salvatoris* should be identified with a work called the *Liber de natiuitate Saluatoris et de Maria uel obstetrice* ("Book on the Nativity of the Savior and on Mary and the Midwife") in a list of apocrypha in the *Pseudo-Gelasian Decree* (6th cent.).[16] Evidence suggests that this apocryphon was composed before 800, since it was incorporated into the J Compilation that was in circulation by this date. Kaestli further argues that the episode of the midwife in the *Liber de nativitate Salvatoris* is independent of and potentially even older than the corresponding episode in *Prot. Jas.*[17] If his suggestions are correct, the *Liber de nativitate Salvatoris* was likely composed in the second century.

A brief history of editions and printings of *Ps.-Mt.* made prior to Gijsel's critical edition is useful for demonstrating some of the issues surrounding the different text types and what they reveal about the transmission of the apocryphon.[18] The earliest printing occurred in Rome only a few decades after Johannes Gutenberg set up his printing press. In 1468 (in fact, the year Gutenberg died), Giovanni Andrea Bussi included fragments of the gospel among the *editio princeps* of Jerome's *Epistulae* (*Letters*) printed by Conrad Sweynheym and Arnold Pannartz.[19] In England, around 1477, William Caxton printed a version of *Ps.-Mt.* focused on the life of Jesus and omitting the parts before the Nativity.[20] Titled *Infantia salvatoris*, this version includes chaps. 13–24, the *pars altera*, and a handful of other added episodes, presumably from a late medieval manuscript

---

14. Kaestli and McNamara, "Latin Infancy Gospels," esp. 64–102.

15. Kaestli and McNamara, "Latin Infancy Gospels," 67.

16. Kaestli, "Mapping an Unexplored Second Century Apocryphal Gospel."

17. Kaestli, "Recherches nouvelles" and "Mapping an Unexplored Second Century Apocryphal Gospel."

18. See Gijsel, *De nativitate Mariae*, 37–48.

19. Jerome, *Epistolae et Tractatus*.

20. Caxton, *Infantia salvatoris*.

exemplar. Unfortunately, Caxton's book has remained largely overlooked in studies of *Ps.-Mt.*'s reception.[21]

A full printing of *Ps.-Mt.* in its now-familiar form did not appear until more than 350 years after the publication of Caxton's text. In 1832, Johann Karl Thilo printed the *editio princeps* in his Christian apocrypha collection titled *Codex apocryphus Novi Testamenti*.[22] Here Thilo printed *Ps.-Mt.* following *Prot. Jas.* and *Nat. Mary* (because he thought this was older than *Ps.-Mt.* and not based on it), thus solidifying an identified relationship between the three texts. Thilo's text relies on two manuscripts of the P recension: Paris, Bibliothèque nationale de France, lat. 5559 A (14th cent.) and lat. 1652 (15th cent.). In 1852, J. A. Giles reprinted Thilo's text in his collection of *The Uncanonical Gospels and Other Writings*.[23]

Before Gijsel's critical edition, the most important edition was that of Constantin von Tischendorf, included in his *Evangelia Apocrypha* (1853).[24] To the manuscripts used by Thilo, Tischendorf added two others: Vatican, Biblioteca Apostolica Vaticana, lat. 4578 (14th cent.) of the Q recension, and Florence, Biblioteca Medicea Laurenziana, Gaddi 208 (14th cent.) of the R recension. Because these two provided witnesses to different text types, they significantly contributed to knowledge about the textual tradition of *Ps.-Mt.* In another major development for modern study, Tischendorf's edition included, for the first time, the *pars altera*. While he acknowledged that this section diverges from the rest of the text, and derives from a separate source (*Inf. Gos. Thom.*), he did not come to the more recent conclusion that these episodes were a later addition to the original narrative of *Ps.-Mt.* After the first edition of Tischendorf's collection, in 1869 Oscar Schade edited the A-text as found in Stuttgart, Württembergische Landesbibliothek, Cod. theol. phil. 8° 57 (12th cent., Zwiefalten Abbey), although he also consulted Paris 5559.[25] Schade's edition proved influential to German scholarship, and Tischendorf used the Stuttgart manuscript for his second edition of *Evangelia apocrypha* (1876). Tischendorf's edition remained a significant contribution to scholarship, and indeed the sole authoritative text, until it was

21. See Dzon, *Quest for the Christ Child*, with summary at 253–55; and translation in *Middle English Poems*.

22. Thilo, *Codex apocryphus Novi Testamenti*, 337–400.

23. Giles, *Uncanonical Gospels*, 1:66–89.

24. Tischendorf, *Evangelia Apocrypha*, 52–112.

25. Schade, *Liber de infantia Mariae et Christi*. On Schade's reliance on Paris 5559, see Elliott, *Apocryphal New Testament*, 83 n. 5.

superceded by Gijsel's full critical edition. *Evangelia Apocrypha* remains the only edition to include the full *pars altera*; a new critical edition of this material would be a benefit to the study of this text.

Title

Although the "Gospel of Pseudo-Matthew" is the common title assigned to this apocryphon, it comes from modern convention rather than medieval tradition. Indeed, medieval scribes had altogether different ideas about the title. The oldest manuscript witnesses fall into two types: either they lack a title completely or they offer a title showing interest in the birth of Mary. For example, there is no title at all in early witnesses to A—such as Budapest, Clmae 316 and Vienna, ÖNB 550—nor in the oldest manuscript of Q: Vatican, Reg. Lat. 648. On the other hand, the oldest witnesses that do have titles use variations on the name *Natiuitas sanctae Mariae* ("Nativity of Saint Mary"), some adding *uirginis* ("virgin," like Rheims 1395 and Paris, nouv. acq. lat. 1605) and others adding *incipit* or *historia* ("beginning" or "history"). Over time, scribes expanded the title beyond a focus on Mary, often adding a phrase like *atque infantiam Iesu Christi* ("and the infancy of Jesus Christ") or *atque infantia nostri Saluatoris* ("and the infancy of our Savior"). By the later Middle Ages, the expanded text with the *pars altera* was often known as the *(Liber de) Infantia salvatoris* ("Book of the Infancy of the Savior"), as in Caxton's version.[26] As Gijsel demonstrates, the evolution of titles is especially linked with the history of the text: the titles generally reflect the concerns of the revisions found in each family. Thus, the expansion of the title to include more information about Jesus appears alongside the addition of the *pars altera* relating more of Jesus' childhood miracles in Q and R, shifting the focus of both text and title to include as much about the Christ child as about the Virgin Mary.

Formal elements also influenced the title and its evolution. A set of spurious correspondence purportedly between bishops Chromatius (died ca. 406/407) and Heliodorus (ca. 330–ca. 390) and Jerome (ca. 347–420), appended to manuscripts of the A-text as a preface, provide further evidence. The first letter attributed to the bishops mentions the text as "ortus Mariae et natiuitas atque infantia" ("the birth of Mary and

---

26. Caxton, *Infantia salvtoris*; see Dzon, "Cecily Neville and the Apocryphal *Infantia salvatoris*"; *Quest for the Christ Child, passim*; and *Middle English Poems*.

also the nativity and the infancy [of Jesus]"), while the letter attributed to Jerome refers to it as a *libellus* ("little book") and discusses its content about *nostri saluatoris* ("our Savior")—all phrases that became adopted by various scribes who expanded the title. The history of the text's translation in the letter attributed to Jerome also contributes to the later perception of the title, as the pseudonymous author explains that it was first written in Hebrew by the evangelist Matthew; from this arises the modern title with its focus on the author rather than content. Curiously, the title never took on elements from the prologue taken from *Prot. Jas.* 25 (in the P manuscripts), with its attribution to the apostle James.

Another formal element that influenced the title concerns the transmission of *Ps.-Mt.* in collections of preaching texts like homiliaries, lectionaries, and legendaries.[27] One example is found in a branch of the A family that features extracts from *Ps.-Mt.* to be read for the Feast of Saint Anna; here the title is commonly given as *Lectiones de sancta Anna* ("Readings on Saint Anna"). In another manuscript of the A family (Berlin, Staatsbibliothek, Preuß. Kulturbesitz, theol. Lat. C. 256), the title is completely reworked as *Vita sanctae Annae et Ioachim et natiuitas sanctae [Mariae] et quomodo uixit in templo* ("The Life of Saints Anna and Joachim and the nativity of Saint [Mary] and how she lived in the temple"). Certain preaching collections include titles with additions like *exordium*, *sermo*, and *omilia* ("address," "sermon," and "homily"). All of these instances speak to the influence of *Ps.-Mt.* on liturgy and preaching during the medieval period.

Titles from the manuscripts carried over into print, where they underwent further developments by modern editors. In the *editio princeps*, Thilo uses the title *Historia de nativitate Mariae et de infantia Salvatoris* ("History of the nativity of Mary and the infancy of the Savior"), and he reproduces the manuscript rubric "Incipit Historia de Joachim et Anna et de nativitate beatae deigenitricis semperque virginis Mariae et de infantia Salvatoris" ("Beginning of the History of Joachim and Anna and of the nativity of the blessed Mother of God and perpetual virgin Mary and the infancy of the Savior"). The next development came about in Tischendorf's edition. Based on new manuscript witnesses, Tischendorf uses the heading "Incipit liber de ortu beatae Mariae et infantia salvatoris. A beato Matthaeo evangelista Hebraice scriptus et a beato Ieronimo presbytero in Latinum translatus" ("Beginning of the book of the birth of

---

27. See Gijsel, *Libri de nativitate Mariae*, 101–3.

blessed Mary and the infancy of the Savior. Written in Hebrew by blessed Matthew the Evangelist and translated into Latin by blessed Jerome the priest"), although in his table of contents and prolegomena he titles it *Pseudo-Matthaei evangelium*. This development occurred largely because Tischendorf's added witnesses include the Pseudo-Jerome correspondence, with its fabricated explanation about Matthew's authorship. From that point onward, the text retained its association with Matthew in traditional attribution and title.

Prefatory Matter

Ps.-Mt. is accompanied in the manuscripts by two different types of prefatory matter: one prologue is seemingly taken from the epilogue of *Prot. Jas.* 25, and the other is the spurious correspondence between Jerome and the bishops Chromatius and Heliodorus. These two prologues are distinguished by their association with the two earliest recensions, the P and A texts, respectively. While the A recension is presumably closer to *Ps.-Mt.*'s original form, it is the P recension that includes an authorial prologue. Both sets of prefatory material are translated together here for the first time, in order to represent the differing prologues in the manuscripts.

In P, the prologue begins "I James" ("Ego Iacobus") and provides a brief (spurious) identification of the author as the apostle James, "son of Joseph the carpenter" ("filius Joseph fabri"). This prologue generally has been read as an adaptation of the authorial colophon at the end of *Prot. Jas.*, but the two differ in their details. Nonetheless, the prologue follows the widespread tradition found in Christian apocrypha of establishing the author as an eye-witness to the events reported in the narrative. In this case, the author is to be identified with James, the brother of Jesus (as mentioned in Mark 6:3, Gal 1:19, and elsewhere), one of Joseph's children from a marriage previous to his relationship with Mary. For a text attributed to (pseudo-) Matthew, this may seem an odd authorial ascription, but it is consistent with the compiler's reliance on *Prot. Jas.* as the main source. This prologue also offers a glimpse into several themes in the apocryphon: a primary focus on the events surrounding the birth of Mary, a secondary interest in the birth of Jesus, and the association between these births and the typological fulfillment of prophecies in the Hebrew Bible.

In A's prefatory matter, the two bishops ask Jerome to translate the apocryphon from its original Hebrew into Latin, so that they may read it, and Jerome hesitantly accepts their request. These letters establish notions of secrecy and dangerousness often linked with apocrypha in the late antique and medieval periods, as well as the traditional idea that Matthew originally wrote his gospel (and, as is claimed, *Ps.-Mt.*) in Hebrew. It is presumably because of these letters that the text is now known by its modern title, since the letter attributed to Jerome cites the evangelist as the original author. It is not surprising that these letters would replace the original, rather than supplement it, since the differing attributions would be at odds with each other. The letters also allude to Manichaeus and Leucius, who are associated in patristic writings with apocrypha, signaling wider intertextual connections with apocryphal literature.

Sources

Infancy Gospels

As mentioned above, a full understanding of *Ps.-Mt.* requires some consideration of its relationship to the Greek *Prot. Jas.* This earlier infancy gospel is the primary source for *Ps.-Mt.*, though it is substantially reworked in the Latin apocryphon. The precise nature of the text of *Prot. Jas.* used by *Ps.-Mt.* remains unknown. Both Gijsel and Beyers maintain that the author of *Ps.-Mt.* should be more properly viewed as a compiler, who relied not on the Greek *Prot. Jas.* for a direct Latin translation, but on some form that had already undergone significant adaptations.[28] Without earlier forms of *Ps.-Mt.* to compare with the A and P texts, this view must remain a hypothesis until further evidence is assessed. Yet, as will be seen in the following discussion, there are also a number of other ways that *Ps.-Mt.* is a compilation of disparate sources.

The text of *Ps.-Mt.* certainly reveals a number of adaptations, additions, and omissions in its use of *Prot. Jas.* as a main source. Perhaps the most innovative and substantial adaptation is the depiction of Mary's life in the temple in chap. 6, which is significantly reworked with added details.[29] Two other changes concern names of individuals: while Anna's father is not mentioned in *Prot. Jas.*, he is named Issachar (Achar in P)

---

28. Gijsel, *Liber de nativitate Mariae*, 50–59 and 71–83; and Beyers, "Transmission of Marian Apocrypha," 126–27.

29. See the discussion below about the *Rule of Benedict* as a source.

in *Ps.-Mt.* 1:5; and while the High Priest presiding over the selection of Mary's husband is named Zechariah in *Prot. Jas.*, he is named Abiathar in *Ps.-Mt.* 7:1, 8, and 12:6 (although see 8:3 for a discrepancy).[30] Additions in *Ps.-Mt.* are more abundant: a mention of Joseph's sons and grandchildren, who are older than Mary (presumably because of a previous marriage), in 8:11; the visit from the shepherds (from Luke 2:8–20) and the star announcing Jesus' birth in 13:29–30; an ox and ass worshipping Jesus at his birth (thus fulfilling Isaiah 1:3) in 14:1–2; information about Jesus' circumcision in 15:1–3; and, in some manuscripts of the A-text, a reference to the purification of Mary in 15:2. Such changes seem to present uncertainties about the text in the manuscripts; these instances show some amount of textual instability in the early circulation of *Ps.-Mt.*

The compiler of *Ps.-Mt.* also omits certain material found in *Prot. Jas.* Most outstanding are the exclusions of three major episodes from *Prot. Jas.*: the first-person relation of miracles that Joseph sees when Jesus is born, often called the "catalepsys of nature" (*Prot. Jas.* 18); information about Mary's cousin Elizabeth and her son John the Baptist (*Prot. Jas.* 22–23); and the conflict between John's father Zechariah and Herod (*Prot. Jas.* 23–24). The latter two omissions present evidence that the compiler of *Ps.-Mt.* relied on *Prot. Jas.* only as far as chap. 20 (*Ps.-Mt.* 13). All of the material for *Ps.-Mt.* 13:29–17:3 is parallel to the accounts in Luke 2 and Matthew 2. Indeed, the episodes about the magi and Herod's slaughter of the innocents in *Ps.-Mt.* 16–17 are closer in details to Matthew 2, and even the wording of *Ps.-Mt.* presents several verbal parallels with the canonical gospel. *Prot. Jas.* includes a number of details not present in either Matthew or *Ps.-Mt.*: the narrative mentions that Joseph was about to depart for Judea when an uproar took place in Bethlehem in 21:1; Herod's questions to the high priests are quoted directly in 21:4; spoken dialogue between Herod and the magi is quoted in 21:7–8; and the magi find Jesus in the cave where he was born (not in a house, nor even a stable) in 21:10.

Conversely, both Matthew and *Ps.-Mt.* include details not present in *Prot. Jas.*: Micah 5 is quoted as evidence for Jesus' birth in Bethlehem in Matt 2:6 and *Ps.-Mt.* 16:5; and in relating Herod's slaughter of the innocents, both Matt 2:16 and *Ps.-Mt.* 17:1–2 mention Bethlehem and that

30. Historically, the actual High Priest at the time of Jesus' birth (ca. 4/3 BCE) is likely to have been either Joazar ben Boethus (4 BCE) or Eleazar ben Boethus (4–3 BCE), although the canonical Gospels mention only Joseph Caiaphas (18–36 CE) in relation to Jesus' death.

the age of children to be murdered was based on the timing of Herod's questioning of the magi. *Ps.-Mt.* also includes details not found in either Matt or *Prot. Jas.*: a transition sentence mentions that two years had passed between the birth of Jesus and the visit of the magi in 16:1; and the magi offer gold, frankincense, and myrrh along with each giving Jesus a piece of gold in 16:9. Questions remain about where the compiler gleaned these details, and it is possible that another source was used—possibly the same source on which chaps. 18–24 rely—or that they were invented for this text. Whatever the case, the evidence indicates that the compiler of *Ps.-Mt.* probably stopped relying on *Prot. Jas.* after the episodes with the midwives. Instead, the compiler of *Ps.-Mt.* relied on the canonical accounts in Luke 2 and Matthew 2 as major sources for 13:29—17:3.

After narrating the events up to Herod's slaughter of the innocents, *Ps.-Mt.* recounts a series of episodes about the flight into Egypt, including miracles performed by Jesus on the journey and when they arrive (chaps. 18–24). Any specific sources used for these chapters remain unidentified. Some clues are found in parallels from other texts that must rely on a common source, especially those in Irish and Hiberno-Latin literature. The Irish gospel history found in the *Leabhar Breac* and other manuscripts contains parallels to Jesus' childhood miracles on the way to Egypt, as well as the incidents with the Egyptian idols and Afrodisius (sections 126–29 and 133–36). The manuscript witnesses to this text are all from the fifteenth and sixteenth centuries, although the work they contain is in Middle Irish (in use ca. 900–ca. 1200) and was likely composed in the eleventh or twelfth century.[31] The flight into Egypt is also mentioned in an eighth-century Hiberno-Latin biblical commentary known as *De enigmatibus* (or the *Reference Bible*) in the section on Matthew, in which the cities "Helipolem" and "Sothinent" are mentioned (see *Ps.-Mt.* 22:4), as is the falling of idols in an Egyptian temple. However, there is no definitive evidence that this commentary relies on *Ps.-Mt.* for these details.[32] Finally, the incident of dragons venerating the holy family is also mentioned in an early eighth-century Hiberno-Latin *Glossa in Psalmos* (Vatican, Biblioteca Apostolica Vaticana, Pal. lat. 68) in a note on Psalm 148:7—the same psalm used in *Ps.-Mt.* 18:6. While it is possible that the gloss represents an allusion to *Ps.-Mt.*, it is different enough in

---

31. McNamara et al., "Infancy Narrative of the *Leabhar Breac*."

32. See McNamara, *Bible and the Apocrypha*, 587–88. My thanks to McNamara and Anthony Harvey for information about this source, in private correspondence.

details to warrant caution when drawing conclusions about its reliance on *Ps.-Mt.* rather than a common source.[33]

Other clues about any potential sources used for *Ps.-Mt.* 18–24 are parallels related specifically to the episode of the palm tree in chaps. 20–21. Again, one parallel is found in Irish literature, in an Old Irish translation of the *Dormition of the Virgin* 3–5.[34] This story also appears in an early version of the *Dormition*, the fourth- or fifth-century Ethiopic *Liber requiei* 5–9, and its close parallel in the fragmentary Georgian *Dormition* 1–11.[35] In all of these texts, Jesus appears to Mary and retells the story of the palm-tree as a testimony to his power and identity as Christ. A generally similar episode is related more abstractly in the Qur'an 19:23–26, in which Mary receives both water and dates from a palm tree in her solitude before Jesus' birth. Without an intermediary between these texts and *Ps.-Mt.*, we cannot come to any solid conclusions about the relationships that led to the similarities.

Parallels to chaps. 23–24 also pose especially intriguing possibilities concerning the sources of *Ps.-Mt.* Three infancy gospel narratives relate similar episodes: in the *Arabic Infancy Gospel* 10 (itself a translation of the East Syriac *History of the Virgin*), *Armenian Infancy Gospel* 15:13–16 and 16:4, and *Vision of Theophilus* (pp. 19–21 in Mingana's translation), Jesus causes pagan idols to fall down at his presence. Yet none of these episodes is particularly close to the events in *Ps.-Mt.* A few other sources also seem related to this episode. Pseudo-Rufinus mentions idols falling at Jesus' arrival in Egypt (with the name Hermopolis) and makes a connection to Isaiah 19:1 in the *Historia monachorum* 7. While it is possible that Pseudo-Rufinus is a source for *Ps.-Mt.*, the latter is greatly expanded. As already mentioned, the Hiberno-Latin *De enigmatibus* refers to the same episode and also notes that it is a fulfillment of Isaiah 19:1; the exact relationship between this text and *Ps.-Mt.* remains uncertain.

Finally, another Greek apocryphon posing parallels to *Ps.-Mt.* 23–24 is the *Legend of Aphroditianus* (the "Narrative of Events Happening in Persia on the Birth of Christ" falsely attributed to Julius Africanus). This pseudo-pagan text is meant to provide arguments for the truth

33. McNamara, *Bible and the Apocrypha*, 565–66.

34. A version from Oxford, Bodleian Library, Laud Misc. 610 is printed in Donoghue, *Testament of Mary*; another version from Dublin, Royal Irish Academy, 23 O 48 (the *Liber Flavus Fergusiorum*) is translated in Herbert and McNamara, *Irish Biblical Apocrypha*, 119–31. See Clayton, *Apocryphal Gospels of Mary*, 38–40 for discussion.

35. See Shoemaker, *Ancient Traditions*, esp. 290–97.

of Christianity to pagans, as it relates various events at Jesus' birth, including an explanation for the journey of the magi to see the child. In the earlier part of the narrative, one of the events at Jesus' birth is that a star descends to the Temple of Here, hovers over the statue of Pege, who represents Mary, and all of the other idols fall down in veneration of this figure. Plot parallels with *Ps.-Mt.* are striking, as are similarities between the names *Aphroditianus* and *Afrodisius* (as in *Ps.-Mt.* 24). Indeed, as Katharina Heyden has demonstrated, the titular name would have been readily available in authorial ascriptions for the *Legend* in the manuscripts.[36] This work survives primarily in Greek and Slavonic versions, and there is little evidence for its transmission in Western Europe. The nature of the relationship between the *Legend of Aphroditianus* and *Ps.-Mt.*, therefore, remains elusive but tantalizing. In a related way, there is also a striking similarity with the name of the city *Aphrodisias*, which was established in the second century BCE, associated with the goddess Aphrodite—now known as Geyre in modern-day Turkey.[37]

All of these examples of parallels to *Ps.-Mt.* 18–24 point to the likelihood that many of these texts share some source (or multiple sources). The possibility remains that the compiler of *Ps.-Mt.* relied on the same intermediate source used for the apocryphal narratives in the *Leabhar Breac*—that is, the lost *Liber de nativitate Salvatoris* ("Special Source"). Yet, since this apocryphon does not exist independent of later texts that rely on it, questions remain about this source and the various relationships between all of the seemingly related texts.[38] Gijsel argues that *Ps.-Mt.* 18–21 are not part of the original form of the text but were added before the earliest surviving manuscripts were copied, based on four claims.[39] First, there is no transition formula at the start of chap. 18. Second, the theological content is not the same as in earlier chapters—it shifts from a focus on Mary to stories about Jesus' childhood miracles. Third, the language and style are markedly different, with significantly more awkwardness. And fourth, the narrative in this portion contains contradictions or inconsistencies with the preceding section, such as differences between Jesus' age in chaps. 16 and 18. In addition, Gijsel also notes that one manuscript of the A family (Oxford, Bodleian Library,

---

36. Heyden, "Legend of Aphroditianus," 9 n. a.

37. See Reynolds, "Aphrodisias."

38. Some of these questions are summarized and discussed in Beyers, "Transmission of Marian Apocrypha."

39. Gijsel, *Die unmittelbare*, 15–17.

Rawlinson D 1236; 14th cent.)—which is generally a faithful witness to the A-text in many instances, despite its late date—includes a new title at the start of chap. 18: "Narratio Elysiodorii de factis Iesu Christi" ("Narrative of Elysiodorus on the acts of Jesus Christ").[40] These points, however, need not lead to Gijsel's conclusion that the chapters were added after the original compilation of *Ps.-Mt.*; they could also be explained by the compiler's clumsiness in turning to an altogether new source (or sources) for chaps. 18–24. Thus, the issue remains unresolved.

Omission of details from the last few chapters of *Prot. Jas.* (22–24) and the use of at least one other source for the flight into Egypt raise a number of questions concerning the original form of *Ps.-Mt.* I have already suggested that the compiler did not use *Prot. Jas.* following the birth of Jesus and incidents with the midwives (chap. 13). Nonetheless, relationships between *Ps.-Mt.* and its sources discussed so far leave some issues unaddressed. Many of these issues concern how to explain the shift in sources toward the end of the narrative. Why would the compiler of *Ps.-Mt.* ignore material from the primary source in *Prot. Jas.* following the nativity? One explanation presumes that the compiler had the entirety of *Prot. Jas.* but intentionally turned to other sources following the episode with the midwives. It is likely that two of these sources were the canonical accounts in Luke and Matthew, but some details also point to the possibility that the compiler of *Ps.-Mt.* turned to at least one other text. This explanation becomes more complicated when considering chaps. 18–24 (recounting the flight into Egypt), which could have been added at the time of its original compilation or (following Gijsel's claims) at a later stage.

A second explanation is that the compiler of *Ps.-Mt.* did not intentionally diverge from *Prot. Jas.* but lacked the ending and sought other sources to finish the narrative. This explanation helps to understand the divergences after 13:28 most cogently. It is true that *Ps.-Mt.* does not particularly remain faithful to the details in *Prot. Jas.*, but most of the adaptations of material from this source are additions, not wholesale omissions. This explanation also allows for accepting Gijsel's suggestions about chaps. 18–24, although it is not necessarily predicated upon his conclusions. For example, this explanation accords with the possibilities that the ending of *Ps.-Mt.* developed either at once or in stages. In

---

40. Gijsel, *Die unmittelbare*, 16–17; and Gijsel, *Libri de nativitate Mariae*, 115 n. 1. I have been unable to identify any other instance of the name *Elysiodorus* in patristic and apocryphal literature.

the former case, perhaps the inconsistencies pointed out by Gijsel were caused merely by weaving multiple sources together. In the latter case, materials from the gospels could have been added first (and perhaps another text for the other details), with other episodes added later from at least one other unknown source about the flight into Egypt.

Admittedly one potential complication to this hypothesis is the circulation of manuscripts in the P family with the Latin "Ego Iacobus" prologue based on *Prot. Jas.* 25. Gijsel has suggested that the *Prot. Jas.* epilogue was turned to a prologue and underwent adaptations in the Latin text of the *Prot. Jas.* before the compiler of *Ps.-Mt.* used it.[41] Gijsel's suggestion helps to support the likelihood that the *Ps.-Mt.* compiler lacked the ending of *Prot. Jas.* It is also feasible that the Latin prologue could have been added later by someone familiar with the source. The possibility of such a later addition helps to make sense of the stark differences between *Prot. Jas.* 25 and the "Ego Iacobus" prologue, as well as why this prologue does not circulate in manuscripts of the A family.

A final explanation (not exclusive of the others proposed) is that the original ending of *Ps.-Mt.* is lost, not having survived in any manuscript. In this case, Gijsel's judgments about the shifts around chap. 18 could still be accepted, as could the possibility that the compiler lacked the ending of *Prot. Jas.* With this hypothesis, a number of possibilities might be imagined. One is that the ending (whether or not *Ps.-Mt.* followed *Prot. Jas.* all the way through) was lost at an early stage of the text's transmission and replaced. Another is that an early copyist of the text (or multiple copyists) found the ending unsatisfactory and replaced it, either at once or in stages. This explanation could include all of chaps. 18–24, or only portions of it. At least part of this hypothesis is cogent, since it is difficult to reconstruct any coherent conclusion after the episode with Afrodisius (following 24:5) from the manuscript witnesses. In any case, it is imaginable that a compiler could have replaced or appended the ending before any of the earliest surviving manuscripts were copied, creating an exemplar on which both the A and P texts were based, as well as later developments in the Q and R texts.

Whatever the circumstances of developments from 13:29 to the end of *Ps.-Mt.*, both the A and P families are based on an archetype with a similar ending, though the problems of piecing together sources gave rise to some amount of textual fluidity. Many of the source problems

---

41. Gijsel, *Libri de nativitate Mariae*, 71–83.

discussed are due to the fact that *Ps.-Mt.* is—like many medieval apocrypha—a compilation of materials from a variety of sources. It may even
be the case that all of these problems are caused by modern assumptions
about textual coherence, and that the original compiler of *Ps.-Mt.* would
not have seen the same issues in the handling of apocryphal sources.

The Bible

Like its predecessor (*Prot. Jas.*) and other apocryphal gospels, *Ps.-Mt.*
naturally relies on the canonical Bible as a major source, as already discussed. Foremost among biblical sources are the Gospels of Luke and
Matthew, although occasional references also link the apocryphon to
Mark and John. In references to and reliance on Jewish beliefs, practices,
and rituals, it also relies on the Hebrew Bible: several passages directly
quote from Numbers, several allude to 1 Samuel, and a number of quotations connect Jesus' birth to prophecies in the Psalms, Isaiah, and Habakkuk. Some of these (Numbers and 1 Samuel) are also present in *Prot. Jas.*,
but *Ps.-Mt.* contains additions that emphasize fulfillments of the Hebrew
Bible in Jesus' life.

The lives of Anna and Joachim in many ways generally reflect
certain biblical stories. For example, there are parallels with Abraham
(Abram) and Sarah (Sarai) in Genesis: like Abraham, Joachim is a wealthy
shepherd; both couples remain childless for many years; they attempt to
deal with their situations on their own (Abraham with Hagar, Joachim
by fleeing Anna); and both couples are recipients of God's promises of
children through miraculous births. Many closer parallels may be found
also in the story of the prophet Samuel (1 Sam 1): his mother Hannah
is childless, his father Elkana offers a sacrifice at the temple, Hannah offers a prayer and promises her child to God, and Samuel is devoted as a
servant of God and later given to the temple. Similarly, Tobit is another
plausible model for Joachim, as both are presented as faithful in their piety and sacrifices at the temple, and Tobit's wife is named Anna. Notably,
in Greek additions to the Book of Daniel in the Septuagint, the husband
of the protagonist Susanna is a wealthy, righteous man named Joakim.
There are also notable parallels with the story of Elizabeth and Zechariah
in Luke 1. The author of *Ps.-Mt.* gains some of these echoes from *Prot.
Jas.*, but certain details (discussed in the commentary) also further ac-
centuate these associations.

Especially noteworthy are allusions to and direct quotations from Jewish practices in Numbers (mainly in chaps. 8 and 12). For example, the ritual of presenting rods for the selection of Mary's husband in chap. 8 is parallel to a similar practice in Numbers 17, and the testing of Joseph and Mary for sexual purity with holy water in chap. 12 is parallel to a similar practice in Numbers 5. The repeated phrase "As the Lord lives" (later "As the Lord of all hosts lives") also poses a direct use of biblical speech often found introducing affirmations and oaths throughout 1–2 Samuel, 1–2 Kings, 2 Chronicles, Jeremiah, and a number of other scattered verses. All of these echoes help to align the life of Mary, her marriage to Joseph, and her pregnancy with Jewish purity laws and practices, further emphasizing Mary's piety and virginity. In light of the earlier chapters focused on Anna and Joachim, this is a logical extension of the text's emphasis on the lineage of Mary and Jesus as well as an insistence about the piety of their family in Jewish tradition. Such emphasis on Jewish rituals and law as portrayed in the Hebrew Bible also serves to create greater contrast between Jewish and Christian concepts of soteriology.

Some of the key uses of the Bible in *Ps.-Mt.* constitute episodes that establish moments in Jesus' childhood as fulfillments of prophecies in the Hebrew Bible. A first mention is made in the "Ego Iacobus" prologue, which declares that the narrative culminates in Jesus' birth as "fulfillment through the twelve tribes of Israel"—an element not taken over from *Prot. Jas.* but original to *Ps-Mt.* Later in the gospel, different episodes are recounted and aligned with passages in the Hebrew Bible. Such fulfillments are included in 14:1–4 (Isa 1:3; Hab 3:2 LXX), 18:5–6 (Ps 148:7), 19:6–9 (Isa 65:25), 23:1–2 (Isa 19:1), and 39:3–9 (in the *pars altera*; Ps 64:10). In each case, the author introduces the biblical passage with the formula "Then was fulfilled. . ." ("Tunc adimpletum est. . ."), a technique found also in the canonical Gospels, most prominently in Matthew's infancy narrative (1:22–23; 2:5–6, 15, 17–18, 23).

Notably, variant readings in different biblical versions that circulated before major reforms in the Carolingian era are starkly demonstrated by discrepancies between the A and P families.[42] The A-text relies on Old Latin forms (based on the LXX) that circulated before Jerome's Latin translation and remained in use into the early Middle Ages. In some cases, Old Latin forms are necessary for the associations between verses in the Hebrew Bible and their perceived fulfillments in the narrative;

---

42. See Gijsel, *Libri de nativitate Mariae*, 90.

these same associations disappear in Jerome's translation from Hebrew. This use of Old Latin forms is one reason among others indicating the closer proximity of the A-text to the original text of *Ps.-Mt.* The P-text revision brought many of the biblical sources into conformity with the increasingly standardized Vulgate version of Jerome's translation. Vulgate forms from the P-text were carried over into the Q and R recensions. The reviser of the Q-text, in fact, further systematized biblical quotations to match the Vulgate through additional revisions.[43] This process in itself conforms to the more general trajectory of the standardization of the Latin Bible in the medieval period, which largely began with Alcuin (ca. 735–804) at the court of Charlemagne (r. 800–814) and continued in stages through the scholastic movements of the twelfth century. Much of this work on biblical reform was undertaken at Benedictine and other monastic centers, a milieu in which *Ps.-Mt.* took a prominent role during the same period.

Late Antique Literature

Among the Christian literature of late antiquity, one major source that lies behind *Ps.-Mt.* is the *Rule of Benedict* (RB), composed by Benedict of Nursia (ca. 480–ca. 547) between 529 and his death. Émile Amann first observed general parallels between the monastic life and the depiction of Mary's life among the young virgins in the temple in chap. 6.[44] The text relates that Mary lived "in contubernium uirginum" ("in the company of virgins," 4:3) and followed a "sibi. . . regulam statuerat" ("rule she had set for herself," 6:4). The rest of the chapter describes the details of her daily observances, including prayer and labor, within the general framework of devotion to God and asceticism. With this starting point in mind, Amann claims that the depiction relies on a similar daily routine established in the RB. Although he does not point to specific parallels, this association has been accepted by a number of scholars. As Gijsel observes, precise verbal echoes are difficult to demonstrate, although the description does seem to rely on a monastic rule, and parallels with the RB in particular are striking.[45] Nonetheless, in his commentary, Gijsel lists an assortment

43. Gijsel, *Libri de nativitate Mariae*, 91.

44. Amann, *Protévangile de Jacques*, 101–9, and his note on Mary's time in the temple in *Ps.-Mt.* 6, at 298–99.

45. Gijsel, *Libri de nativitate Mariae*, 66.

of parallels between *Ps.-Mt.* and the RB, some of which do feature verbal echoes, and I have demonstrated various parallels elsewhere.[46]

In turning to monastic precepts, however, the RB is not the only source with close parallels to *Ps.-Mt.* Both thematic and verbal parallels are also found in the older *Rule of the Master* (RM), likely composed in the sixth century. At first glance, one might conclude that themes and vocabulary from the RM found also in *Ps.-Mt.* have arrived via the RB, inasmuch as Benedict himself relied on the RM in compiling his own set of precepts. There are, however, certain parallels and even verbal echoes between *Ps.-Mt.* and RM that do not appear in RB. For example, the Greek loanword *heremus* used during the flight into Egypt (17:3 and 20:1) appears in the RM in close proximity to mention of Egypt; the rare, post-classical Latin word *exagilium* for "inheritance" used in *Ps.-Mt.* 21:2 also appears with the same sense in the RM in a passage about sons of nobles donating their possessions before entering a monastery; and this same precept about the division of nobles' possessions in the RM provides a parallel for the depiction of Joachim's tripartite division of his goods in *Ps.-Mt.* 1:3—a passage not reliant on any description in *Prot. Jas.* None of these specific details appear in the RB, and the accumulation of evidence points to the influence of the earlier RM on *Ps.-Mt.*[47]

Influences may be found also in patristic literature about virgin ascetics. Beyers has investigated such parallels, arguing that the depiction of Mary's life in the temple is based more on literary representations of virgin asceticism than on actual monastic life.[48] Analyzing chap. 6, she points to *De virginibus* by Ambrose (ca. 340–397) as a model for the type of "literary portrait" described in *Ps.-Mt.* In particular, she points to three elements in common between Ambrose's treatise and *Ps.-Mt.*: the emphasis on virtues for a sacred virgin, which became a popular idea during Ambrose's time; the use of gospel references highlighting these virtues; and an eschatological feature of the depiction of Mary. Another example that could be added to Beyers' comparison is Ambrose's mention of the dual crown of martyrdom and virginity (*aut martyr, aut virgo . . . corona*; *Virg.* 2.4.24), which Mary invokes regarding Abel (*Ps.-Mt.* 7:5–7). Preferring the perspective that both Ambrose and *Ps.-Mt.* provide representative depictions of virgin ascetic life rather than strict adherence

---

46. See Hawk, "*Gospel of Pseudo-Matthew.*"
47. See Hawk, "*Gospel of Pseudo-Matthew.*"
48. Beyers, "La règle de Marie."

to monastic rules, Beyers suggests a more circumspect consideration of sources than the view that the RB was the only major work on virginity evoked in the adaptations made in *Ps.-Mt.* 6.

Other late antique texts about virgins are also instructive for their influences on *Ps.-Mt.* A host of treatises on virginity share general similarities, though not all parallels with these texts are close enough to warrant calling them sources. Certainly the compiler of *Ps.-Mt.* drew on these types of texts in adapting *Prot. Jas.* as a source and presenting Mary as a model virgin ascetic. A variety of texts with general similarities are cited in the commentary, but a few cases with more specific correspondences are worth singling out. Michael Berthold has demonstrated that the text shares distinct verbal parallels with the Pseudo-Ambrosian *Life of Saint Agnes* for the description of Mary entering and illuminating a cave of darkness in *Ps.-Mt.* 13:8–11.[49] One specific treatise on virginity that stands out is Jerome's *Epist.* 22 (composed in 384) to Eustochium (ca. 368–419/420), a noblewoman and an ascetic (like her mother Paula), virgin, and Desert Mother. Jerome mentions several aspects of Mary's life that also appear in passages of *Ps.-Mt.* that do not rely on *Prot. Jas.* Most generally, he continually points to Mary as a model virgin and ascetic—just as she is represented throughout *Ps.-Mt.*—and discusses the Annunciation in this regard in chap. 38. Other examples of details held in common appear across the texts: Jerome discusses virgins as "vessels of the Lord's temple" ("uasa templi," 23) and further claims (drawing on 1 Cor 6:19) that, "no gold or silver vessel was ever so dear to God as is the temple of a virgin's body" ("neque enim aureum uas et argenteum tam carum deo fuit, quam templum corporis uirginalis," 23), just as this imagery is applied to Mary as a temple of God in *Ps.-Mt.* 3:6; he mentions the murder of Abel with the epithet "the just" ("iustus," 39), as Mary does in 7:5; and he uses the image of the crown of virginity throughout ("virginitatis coronam," esp. 15), as Mary mentions regarding Abel in 7:7. These last two parallels are not particularly rare in patristic literature (as noted above for the crown of virginity in Ambrose's *Virg.* 2.4.24), but all three details appearing together in Jerome's letter—which was widespread and famous in the medieval period—do point to the likelihood of direct influence on *Ps.-Mt.*

---

49. Berthold, "Datierung."

Date

The most solid information about the date of composition of *Ps.-Mt.* comes from manuscript evidence, which establishes a *terminus ante quem* for the text. As already indicated, the oldest surviving manuscripts of the two early recensions (A and P) were created around the first half of the ninth century: London Add. 11880 of the A family is dated to around 820 and Vatican Pal. lat. 430 of the P family is dated to around 840. A more important manuscript for dating *Ps.-Mt.*, however, does not belong to either of these families: Montpellier 55, containing the J Compilation, is dated to around 800. With the knowledge that none of these manuscripts is the archetype, and all of them must rely on previous exemplars, it is safe to assume that both the A and P recensions as well as the J Compilation were all created before 800. Yet, since all of these versions derive from an earlier form of the apocryphon, the date of composition of the original text remains an open question.

In seeking a *terminus post quem* for the composition of *Ps.-Mt.*, the compiler's reliance on sources presents valuable evidence. The most obvious starting point is the date of the main source, *Prot. Jas.* Unfortunately, this consideration does not help to narrow the range significantly, since *Prot. Jas.* was likely composed sometime before the end of the second century.[50] A few external sources help to date this apocryphon. In his *Stromateis*, Clement of Alexandria (ca. 150–ca. 215) discusses the midwife who attested to Mary's virginity (*Prot. Jas.* 19:16–18; *Strom.* 7.16.93), and a note about Jesus' brothers in the *Commentary on Matthew* by Origen (ca. 184/185–ca. 253/254) also indicates knowledge of the text (*Comm. Matt.* 10.17).

Other sources used by the author of *Ps.-Mt.* provide a more precise date of composition. For this determination, it is tempting to look toward Hiberno-Latin exegetical works containing similar apocryphal parallels, such as *De enigmatibus* (*Reference Bible*) or the *Glossa in Psalmos*. But there is, as yet, no definitive evidence that these texts rely on *Ps.-Mt.* rather than on a common source or traditions that circulated more generally in the late antique and medieval periods. Instead, conclusions about the date of *Ps.-Mt.* must rely on knowledge of direct influences from identifiable sources. One such source is the Pseudo-Ambrosian *Life of Saint Agnes*. While the date of this saint's life is not precise (assessments range from the fifth to seventh centuries), Berthold points out that

---

50. See Hock, *Infancy Gospels*, 11–12.

Aldhelm relied on it for his prose *De virginitate* around 690, meaning the *Life of Saint Agnes* was certainly composed before that date.[51] While this evidence narrows the possible date of *Ps.-Mt.*'s composition somewhat, given the unknown date of the *Life of Saint Agnes*, other evidence must be consulted.

Noteworthy conclusions have been posed based on the reliance of *Ps.-Mt.* on the RB for its depiction of Mary's ascetic life in the temple. Since Benedict composed his *Rule* while at Monte Cassino between 529 and his death in 547, the *terminus post quem* for *Ps.-Mt.* must be no earlier than the middle of the sixth century.[52] Gijsel has offered further speculations for a more specific date based on the representation of Joachim. Noting that Joachim's role is greatly amplified in *Ps.-Mt.*, he suggests that this depiction is meant to evoke the model figure for a Merovingian nobleman: rich, powerful, a good believer, and conscious of his social duty. He links this type of depiction specifically to the reign of Dagobert I (629–639).[53] Yet Gijsel presents little evidence for conclusions beyond generalities, and his suggestions remain only speculations without substantiation.[54] What can be said is that a date range for the composition of *Ps.-Mt.* may be set between about 550 and 800, likely in the seventh century.

Theological and Thematic Content

One of the most remarkable theological themes of *Ps.-Mt.* is its special emphasis on purity. Through the first part of the narrative, focusing on Anna and Joachim, the concept of purity is broadly defined by Jewish law, but after Mary's birth it is represented also by virginity and asceticism. Much of this emphasis derives from the main source, *Prot. Jas.*, which intentionally highlights Anna and Joachim as righteous Jews and Mary's sexual purity as a virgin. Yet many of the adaptations in *Ps.-Mt.* expand these concepts, emphasizing them in exaggerated ways. For example, the descriptions of Anna and Joachim at the start not only depict them as righteous Jews but also link them more closely with associations in the Hebrew Bible than we see in *Prot. Jas.* Much is conveyed through added, explicit references to the twelve tribes of Israel (in the "Ego Iacobus"

---

51. Berthold, "Datierung."

52. Gijsel, *Libri de nativitate Mariae*, 67.

53. Gijsel, *Libri de nativitate Mariae*, 66–67 and 288 n. 1.

54. cf. criticism by Beyers, "Règle de Marie," 83 n. 124.

prologue), Joachim's genealogy in the tribe of Judah, and Anna's genealogy in the tribe of David. In the latter part of the narrative, Mary's speech
to the temple priests aligns her own purity with the Hebrew Bible, and
the testing of Mary and Joseph align the couple's purity with Israelite rituals of purity. Other added biblical references (including allusions, geographical references, and prophecy fulfillments) continually emphasize
the link between the Hebrew Bible and this gospel.

The depiction of Mary as virgin ascetic brings the theme of purity
into sharper focus. As already seen, the sources used for this description
highlight the late antique and medieval Christian view that virginity is
both an exceptional and superior lifestyle. Such an emphasis is consistent
with concerns of Benedictine monasticism, which are fundamentally
linked to the contexts of the composition and early circulation of *Ps.-Mt.*
There is no doubt, based on the origins and provenances of the oldest
witnesses, that Benedictine monastic houses played a major role in the
transmission, circulation, and reception of *Ps.-Mt.*, from the early period
into the high Middle Ages. Indeed, the connection to monasticism is a
central part of the text itself. This is seen most explicitly in the description
of Mary's ascetic life among the temple virgins in chap. 6, but there are
also other influences of monastic life and writings on the text. A number
of these have already been discussed in the section on sources: Ambrose's
De virginibus and Jerome's *Epist.* 22 as treatises on the virgin life, the
Pseudo-Ambrosian *Life of Saint Agnes* as a model of female virginity, and
the RM and RB as codified precepts. All of these were valued works in
medieval Benedictine monasticism.

Much of the emphasis on Mary's virginal purity is brought to the
foreground of the narrative surrounding the birth of Jesus. This is not
altogether surprising, given the traditions that developed about Mary's
perpetual virginity, but this legacy had not taken hold as firmly in the
early Middle Ages as it would in the following centuries. *Ps.-Mt.* is thus
an early witness to, model of, and influence on the emergence of the
veneration of Mary as perpetual virgin in the medieval West. Like other
themes, Mary's purity is already a preeminent concern in the *Prot. Jas.*,
as Lily Vuong has most extensively discussed,[55] and *Ps.-Mt.* once again
further highlights this theme. The most obvious instance appears in
13:12–25, after the birth of Jesus, when the midwives inspect Mary. In
Prot. Jas. 19:2, the first (unnamed) midwife does not inspect Mary; nor

---

55. Vuong, *Gender and Purity.*

does she mention Mary's virginity until she meets Salome (the second midwife) and tells her about the incident, after which Salome inspects Mary to verify her virginity.[56] In contrast, in *Ps.-Mt.* 13:17–20, Zahel (the first midwife) inspects Mary and declares her virginity with expanded and more direct statements. Salome's second inspection in 13:21–23 thus further solidifies the claims to Mary's virginity already established with Zahel's assertion. While they are redundant, these dual declarations provide special emphasis on a key feature of Mary's purity. In fact, Zahel's initial declaration that "A virgin has given birth and after giving birth she has remained a virgin" (13:20) is parallel with similar formulas that developed after Mary's perpetual virginity was defined at the Lateran Council of 649—showing *Ps.-Mt.* to be a vital part of emerging Marian traditions in Western Christianity.

Notions of purity and Mary's virginal status also relate to the prominent roles given to women in *Ps.-Mt.* It is worth noting that the text emphasizes interactions between women on a few occasions: when Anna and her maidservant speak about Anna's infertility (2:11–13), it is implied in the depiction of Mary's temple community (chap. 6), and when Zahel and Salome speak about Mary's virginity to each other and to Mary (chap. 13). This is not to negate the fact that men often have the upper hand, as is most explicit in the control of Mary's body by the priests and men of Israel in chaps. 8 (when Joseph is chosen as her husband) and 12 (when she is tested for her purity). Yet strong female presences appear throughout this apocryphon. From the start, Anna's role is central, as she is not only the wife of Joachim, from the tribe of Judah, but also a descendant of David. Following the rejection of Joachim's sacrifice, there are constant narrative shifts between the perspectives of Joachim in the wilderness and Anna at home (chaps. 2–3). Episodes of both characters based on *Prot. Jas.* are expanded with equal justice, and Anna remains a major figure without being overshadowed by Joachim.

Most strikingly, *Ps.-Mt.* is unlike many so-called "apocryphal infancy gospels" because so much of the narrative attention is placed on Mary: the main concern is with the events leading up to Mary's birth, Mary's childhood, and her role as the mother of Jesus. At the heart of the narrative, Mary becomes the main character until Jesus' birth. Even Joseph remains secondary through most of the gospel. As with Joachim and Anna in chaps. 2–3, the story alternates between the perspectives of

56. On this passage, see esp. Vuong, *Gender and Purity*, 148–91; and Lillis, "Paradox *in Partu.*"

Mary and Joseph as they learn about the pregnancy (chaps. 9–11). Jesus does not appear until chap. 13, in which Mary's role is still the focal point, before the narrative shifts to the events of Jesus' life more directly in chap. 14. The birth story also features the midwives Zahel and Salome, women who are, again, placed in prominent roles—and their presence bolsters the centrality of Mary. Even in the later episodes, Mary's role remains significant (more so than Joseph's). One telling example is the bending of the palm tree, which only comes about because of Mary's request for fruit, and which demonstrates even Jesus' veneration and respect for his mother. It is worth pointing out that medieval scribes noticed these characteristics too, as many of the titles in the manuscripts (previously discussed) emphasize Mary, at times more than Jesus. While *Ps.-Mt.* is seemingly an apocryphal gospel culminating in Jesus' childhood, it places Mary in a central role throughout the whole of the narrative.

A few notable themes also appear in later additions to *Ps.-Mt.*, such as the *pars altera* based on *Inf. Gos. Thom.* Episodes about Jesus' childhood miracles and his education (or, more accurately, his teachings) raise significant theological questions about the nature of his humanity and divinity. This was, of course, a hotly debated topic in the early centuries of Christianity, before consensus formed around the belief that he was both fully human and fully divine. Despite the development of consensus, questions remained about when Jesus' powers manifested, or how Jesus understood his own divinity—concerns largely unaddressed in the canonical Gospels. As Mary Dzon has shown, questions like these emerged again in the twelfth century, and the additions to *Ps.-Mt.* played a part in ongoing debates about the nature of Christ in the late Middle Ages.[57]

Other less prominent themes also emerge in these additions. For example, anti-Judaism manifests in these episodes through explicit references to the Jewish people (as crowds) or Jewish characters (such as priests and teachers) as antagonists toward Jesus, Mary, and Joseph. Many of the specific references to these antagonists as "Jews" have been added to the stories by medieval redactors. Both Pamela Sheingorn and Dzon have discussed this issue in *Ps.-Mt.* as well as related medieval texts and images.[58] Less insidious are various references to biblical geography—again, not derived from *Inf. Gos. Thom.* but added by medieval redactors. As Dzon mentions, in the late medieval period "all the places in

57. Dzon, *Quest for the Christ Child.*

58. Sheingorn, "Reshapings of the Childhood Miracles of Jesus"; and Dzon, *Quest for the Christ Child, passim* (esp. 174–81).

the Holy Land—where Christ was born, lived, suffered, and died—were highly venerated."[59] While some of these place names, their locations, and explanations about them are questionable or confusing to modern readers, they would have lent a certain amount of authority to the text. Medieval readers seeking connections between Jesus' childhood miracles and other biblical subjects would have found a wealth of associations in the additions to *Ps.-Mt.*

Later Transmission and Additions

As already indicated, *Ps.-Mt.* underwent many adaptations throughout the Middle Ages. A significant development in its medieval afterlife is the revision in *Nat. Mary*. In large part, the changes undertaken in composing this text comprise an abbreviation of the narrative and revision of the details to conform to ideas that had emerged as "orthodox" theology. Much of this revision was made in reaction to Mariological and Christological controversies in the early medieval period, especially in the ninth century. While it is difficult to date precisely, *Nat. Mary* appears to have been composed by about the year 1000; the earliest external reference to it is in a sermon on the Nativity of Mary by Fulbert of Chartres (ca. 960–1028), and it was certainly known in Winchester, England by the eleventh century.[60]

Another later apocryphon related to the same traditions as *Ps.-Mt.* is the *Trinubium Annae*, concerning Mary's parentage and familial relationships to other biblical and apocryphal figures.[61] This brief text explicates the tradition surrounding Anna's marriages to three different men known as Joachim, Cleopas (Clopas), and Salome, and of her three children from these marriages, all named Mary. An explanation for this situation was needed in part because of details about Anna in apocryphal gospels like *Prot. Jas.* and *Ps.-Mt.*, as well as the dual necessity of clarifying biblical references to the apostle James as the "brother" of Jesus (as in Mark 6:3 and Gal 1:19) and of distinguishing him from James the son of Zebedee.

The major source of the *Trinubium* is Haymo of Auxerre's (died ca. 865) *Epitome of Sacred History*, a synthesis of earlier narratives largely

59. Dzon, *Quest for the Christ Child*, 36–37.

60. Beyers, *Libri de nativitate Mariae*, 32–33; and Clayton "De Nativitate Mariae."

61. See Hall, "Earliest Anglo-Latin Text of the *Trinubium Annae*."

reliant on Rufinus' Latin translation of Eusebius' Greek *Ecclesiastical History* and other materials related to biblical subjects. Haymo draws on these various traditions to construct a coherent account to explain various earlier references to Anna's marriages and her children's names. This explanation suggests that Anna first married Joachim, with whom she gave birth to Mary the wife of Joseph and mother of Jesus; then she married Cleopas (Clopas), with whom she gave birth to Mary the wife of Alphaeus and mother of the apostle James the Lesser; finally, she married a man named Salome,[62] with whom she gave birth to Mary the wife of Zebedee and mother of John the Evangelist and the apostle James the Greater.

By the end of the eleventh or the beginning of the twelfth century, a version of the passage from Haymo's *Epitome* began circulating independently as the *Trinubium Annae*. While the *Trinubium* is heavily dependent on Haymo's explanation—even verbatim in much of its content—it also adds some information and amplifies certain aspects. For example, it begins by discussing Anna's sister Emeria, the mother of Elizabeth, who in turn was the cousin of the Virgin Mary and mother of John the Baptist. This detail appears to be unique to the *Trinubium*. The new apocryphon also places special emphasis on Anna's adherence to Jewish law, in many ways an extension of the same concerns about the purity of women found in *Prot. Jas.* and *Ps.-Mt.*

The earliest surviving copy of the *Trinubium* appears as an addition in Cambridge, St. John's College 35, a manuscript of Gregory the Great's *Homilies on Ezekiel* produced at the end of the eleventh century at Bury St. Edmunds, England. Based on the extant manuscript evidence, Thomas N. Hall has suggested that the adaptation of Haymo's explanation into an independent text was an English innovation. It soon circulated more widely, and further recensions of the text developed.[63] The *Trinubium* participated in the development of the cult of Anna in the medieval West, which followed on the heels of the cult of Mary to blossom in the twelfth century. By the end of the twelfth century, the text enjoyed enough cir-

62. Salome is more commonly a woman's name, as with the daughter of Herod II (though not named, in Mark 6:21–29//Matt 14:6–11), the woman at Jesus' Crucifixion in Mark 15:40, and the midwife in *Ps.-Mt.* The second of these women is identified with the third Mary here, traditionally known as Mary Salome because of her father's name.

63. See, for example, the edition based on Q manuscripts of *Ps.-Mt.* in Gijsel, *Libri de nativitate Mariae*, 93; and the version from Paris, Bibliothèque Saint-Geneviève 2787 (13th cent.), discussed and printed in Beyers, "Latin Translation."

culation and prominence that the compiler of the Q-text added it to the beginning of this revision.[64] A translation of the *Trinubium Annae* from St. John's College 35 is included in this volume.

Other extrabiblical sources were incorporated into later adaptations and expansions of *Ps.-Mt.* as its transmission took greater hold and newer forms proliferated. As already mentioned, the mid-twelfth-century Q revision adds new material: to the beginning, the *Trinubium Annae*, and to the end, the so-called *pars altera* adapted from a Latin translation of *Inf. Gos. Thom.* made some time before the fifth century, extending the scope of the apocryphon to include further episodes and miracles of Jesus' childhood.[65] Within the *pars altera*, chaps. 24–34 and 37–39 consist of translations of *Inf. Gos. Thom.* 2–9, 11–12, and 13–15, while chaps. 35–36, 40, and 42 are unique to the Latin text. The earliest surviving manuscript with both *Ps.-Mt.* and the Latin version of *Inf. Gos. Thom.* is Paris, Bibliothèque nationale de France, lat. 1772 (11th cent., Reichenau). This manuscript belongs to the A family of manuscripts, but here the *pars altera* (followed by three versions of the *Trinubium Annae*) is rubricated with a new title and not coherently incorporated into the preceding text as in manuscripts of the Q family.

Later still, *Ps.-Mt.* was expanded in other ways to cover more of Jesus' life. One example is a reworked and expanded version of the text (part of the Q family) included in Paris, Bibliothèque nationale de France, lat. 11867 (13th cent., Marmoutier). This text is titled *De infantia Saluatores* and was published from the Paris manuscript in a transcription by Catherine Dimier-Paupert.[66] The text begins with the *Trinubium Annae*, proceeds to tell the narrative of *Ps.-Mt.*, includes the *pars altera*, and ends with a further series of Jesus' childhood miracles. Many of these episodes (chaps. 55 and 59–63) are reworked from a later medieval Latin version of *Inf. Gos. Thom.* (designated LT and translated from the Greek D recension of the text) not related to the earlier translation used in the

64. Gijsel, *Libri de nativitate Mariae*, 92–94.

65. The earliest evidence for this Latin version of *Inf. Gos. Thom.* is a fragment (often designated LV) found in a fifth-century palimpsest in Vienna (Österreichische Nationalbibliothek, lat. 563). Also related is a translation into Irish verse dated to ca. 800 and extant in a single manuscript: Dublin, National Library of Ireland, MS G 50. See Voicu, "Verso"; Voicu, "La tadition latine des *Paidika*"; and Burke, *De infantia Iesu euangelium Thomae graece*, 144–49.

66. Dimier-Paupert, *Livre de l'Enfance du Sauveur*.

pars altera.[67] Several other manuscripts feature this same combination; two of them (Paris, Bibliothèque nationale de France, lat. 1652, and Florence, Biblioteca Medicea Laurenziana, Gaddi 208) were used in Tischendorf's edition.[68] Additional chapters in Dimier-Paupert's text (53–54, 56–58, and 64) derive from unknown sources. Parallels to two of these episodes appear in a thirteenth-century Irish poem relating Mary's birth (based on *Ps.-Mt.* 15–32). Following accounts of the Annunciation and the Visitation, the poem adds an episode about Jesus visiting a well and restoring the broken pitchers of his companions (parallel to chap. 64), and another in which he heals a child who has attempted to follow him in leaping between two peaks (parallel to the episode about the sunbeam in chap. 58).[69] In some ways, the episode of the broken pitchers is similar to *Inf. Gos. Thom.* 11, but the details are not altogether analogous. Parallels to the episode about the sunbeam also occur in the *Armenian Infancy Gospel*, Ethiopic *Inf. Gos. Thom.*, and some Slavonic manuscripts. Nonetheless, these associations offer only clues to common traditions, not clear answers about sources and how they were incorporated into late medieval manuscripts as expansions of *Ps.-Mt.*

The text that Caxton printed as *Infantia salvatoris* represents another type of late medieval adaptation, in which *Ps.-Mt.* is both condensed and expanded with materials from other apocrypha.[70] The text omits chaps. 1–12 and begins with the journey of Mary and Joseph to Bethlehem, covering the narrative from chap. 13 to the end of *Ps.-Mt.* proper (Caxton's chaps. 1–14). This version also includes the *pars altera*, interspersed and expanded with other episodes—some parallel to those in Paris 11867, while others must derive from apocrypha like the *Arabic Infancy Gospel* and other unidentified sources (Caxton's chaps. 15–35). It is likely that

67. This version was published by Tischendorf (*Evangelia Apocrypha*, 164–80) based on Vatican, Biblioteca Apostolica Vaticana, lat. 4578, and is extant in numerous other manuscripts; see Burke, *De infantia Iesu euangelium Thomae graece*, 149–53.

68. See the descriptions of their contents in Burke, *De infantia Iesu euangelium Thomae graece*, 156–59, and the R family manuscripts in Gijsel, *Libri de nativitate Mariae*, 179–86. Voicu ("La tadition latine des *Paidika*") discusses the mixed text in some detail and draws attention also to one additional mixed-text manuscript of the P family (Cambridge, University Library, Ff.VI.54).

69. See discussion by Ó Cuív, "Thirteenth-Century Irish Poem," with the poem at 500–13.

70. Caxton, *Infantia salvatoris*; see also Dzon's summary in *Quest for the Christ Child*, 253–55; and translation in her *Middle English Poems*.

Caxton himself did not arrange the text this way, but printed it from a late medieval redaction of *Ps.-Mt.*

Because of the complex nature of the sources used for *Ps.-Mt.* and the accretions of content attached to the apocryphon over time, it is helpful to provide a table summarizing the sections and main sources.[71]

Pseudo-Matthew	Source
Prefatory letters	
Prologue	*Prot. Jas.* 25
Mary's genealogy (12th cent. addition)	*Trinubium Annae*
1–13:28	*Prot. Jas.* 1–20
13:29–15:12	Luke 2:8–38 (Unknown Source?)
16–17	Matt 2:1–16 (Unknown Source?)
18–24	Unknown Source(s)
25–34 (*pars altera*, 12th cent. addition)	*Inf. Gos. Thom.* 2–9, 11–12
35–36 (*pars altera*, 12th cent. addition)	Unknown Source(s)
37–39 (*pars altera*, 12th cent. addition)	*Inf. Gos. Thom.* 13–15
40 (*pars altera*, 12th cent. addition)	Unknown Source
41 (*pars altera*, 12th cent. addition)	*Inf. Gos. Thom.* 16
42 (*pars altera*, 12th cent. addition)	Unknown Source(s)
53–54 (additional supplements)	Unknown Source(s)
55 (additional supplements)	*Inf. Gos. Thom.* (LT) 12
56–58 (additional supplements)	Unknown Source(s)
59–60 (additional supplements)	*Inf. Gos. Thom.* (LT) Prol. 3–7
61–63 (additional supplements)	*Inf. Gos. Thom.* (LT) 4–5, 9–10
64 (additional supplements)	Unknown Source (cf. *Inf. Gos. Thom.* 11)

All of the added episodes from the *pars altera* and *De infantia Saluatores* in Paris 11867 are translated in this volume to demonstrate the expansion of *Ps.-Mt.* through the Middle Ages.

71. Note the shift in chapter numbering from 42 to 53. This is due to the expanded nature of the compilation in Paris 11867. In order to facilitate cross-references for these additions, I follow the numbering in Dimier-Paupert, *Livre de l'Enfance du Sauveur*.

Influences

It is impossible to account for all of the influences that this apocryphal gospel had on medieval culture, but the following discussion covers some significant patterns. From about the ninth century onward, authors began to adapt *Ps.-Mt.* into other forms, in both Latin and vernacular languages. Worth mentioning in this regard is the tenth- or eleventh-century *Nat. Mary*, previously discussed. Passages of *Ps.-Mt.* were also excerpted in collections of preaching texts like homiliaries and legendaries from the ninth century onward.[72] Because of these afterlives, parts of *Ps.-Mt.* were translated into Old English for use as sermons in the tenth and eleventh centuries, thereby contributing to the growth of Marian devotion, as Mary Clayton has discussed.[73]

In the high and late Middle Ages (from the eleventh through fifteenth centuries), the uses of *Ps.-Mt.* exploded in various media. One major point of influence appears in the liturgy for the Feast of the Nativity of Mary (September 8).[74] Montpellier 55 is a useful example of such use, since the J Compilation that incorporates *Ps.-Mt.* found in that manuscript is a legendary containing readings about the lives of saints meant to be used for liturgical and devotional purposes. This witness demonstrates the development of the cult of Mary and the emergence of new liturgical materials during the Carolingian period. Among the surviving manuscripts of *Ps.-Mt.*, many are collections of saints' lives, sermons, and other texts related to liturgy. Margot Fassler has demonstrated that such developments for the Nativity of Mary continued apace in the medieval West, and flourished especially around the year 1000.[75] There is also a close association with these developments and the composition of *Nat. Mary*, which began to flourish in the eleventh century in contexts particularly related to the liturgy.[76]

Dzon has studied many of the influences of *Ps.-Mt.* and other infancy gospels in the later medieval period, tracing medieval knowledge of it in many media forms (textual and visual), in both intellectual and

---

72. See Hawk, "'Cherries at Command,'" 209–11; and Hawk, *Preaching Apocrypha in Anglo-Saxon England.*

73. See Clayton, *Cult of the Virgin* and *Apocryphal Gospels of Mary*; and Hawk, "'Cherries at Command.'"

74. See Fassler, "Mary's Nativity."

75. Fassler, "Mary's Nativity."

76. For details, see Fassler, "Mary's Nativity."

popular domains. The Old English sermons already mentioned were only the earliest translations in a long history of adapting *Ps.-Mt.* into vernacular languages. From about the twelfth century onward, authors used the apocryphal gospel and additions that accrued to it for composing texts in languages like French,[77] German,[78] and Middle English (to name only a few).[79] The transmission and popularity of *Ps.-Mt.* may be seen in works by figures such as Aelred of Rievaulx (1110–1167), Francis of Assisi (1184–1226), Thomas Aquinas (1225–1274), Birgitta of Sweden (1303–1373), and a host of English authors writing in the vernacular— some explicitly using the apocryphon, others doing so more subtly, while still others responding to it with skepticism.[80] Influences may be seen also in anti-Christian Jewish works from the medieval period, such as the *Toledot Yeshu* ("Chronicles of Jesus"), a life of Jesus (probably written in Aramaic) meant to slander his reputation, and the thirteenth-century polemical text *Sefer Nizzahon Yashan* ("Old Book of Victory"), a Hebrew apologetic text from Germany that refutes Christianity.[81] In some instances, authors used the apocryphon wholesale, or large parts of it; in other instances, they used only specific episodes from *Ps.-Mt.* or additions derived from *Inf. Gos. Thom.*[82]

Visual arts based on *Ps.-Mt.* appear in many manuscripts and on objects in the medieval period.[83] Scenes of the Nativity—even up to contemporary times—frequently incorporate the ox (14:1); similarly, the midwives Zahel (13:13–20) and Salome (13:21–28) feature in many of these same depictions.[84] Representations of Anna and Joachim reunited at the Golden Gate (3:25–28) also became a popular artistic motif in many late medieval manuscripts. One example of an illustrated text is Paris, Bibliothèque nationale de France, lat. 2688 (ca. 1270), which contains the Q recension of *Ps.-Mt.*, including the *pars altera* and other

---

77. See Boulton, *Sacred Fictions of Medieval France.*

78. See Reinsch, *Die Pseudo-Evangelien.*

79. For an overview, especially focused on Middle English, see Dzon, *Quest for the Christ Child*; and Dzon, *Middle English Poems.*

80. Dzon, *Quest for the Christ Child.*

81. Dzon, *Quest for the Christ Child*, 154–56.

82. For a few examples, see Dzon, "Jesus and the Birds" and "Out of Egypt, into England"; and Hall, "Miracle of the Lengthened Beam."

83. For a selection of images available online, see Hawk, "Gospel of Pseudo-Matthew in Images."

84. For one example, see Hawk, "'Cherries at Command.'"

additions, with a series of fifty-two miniatures illustrating events from Jesus' childhood.[85] Other images from the apocryphon and later expansions also permeate late medieval depictions on a variety of media.[86] For example, a series of fourteenth-century tiles from the parish church at Tring, Hertfordshire in England depict episodes from the *pars altera* and other additions such as those found in Paris 11867.[87]

Some of the most prominent images related to *Ps.-Mt.* appear in gospel harmonies and books of hours in the thirteenth through fifteenth centuries. A few examples are especially noteworthy. Milan, Biblioteca Ambrosiana, SP II 64 (ca. 1400, Lombardy) includes both a Latin *Evangelica historia* about Jesus' life and 158 pen-and-ink drawings to illustrate the text, several of which accompany scenes from Jesus' childhood.[88] Another notable witness for images is the *Klosterneuburger Evangelienwerk* in Schaffhausen, Stadtbibliothek, Gen. 8 (ca. 1340, Austria), the oldest copy of a German synthesis of biblical and apocryphal stories about Jesus and the apostles, with over 400 pencil drawings illustrating the text in the margins. Included in this codex is a retelling of events in Jesus' childhood based on *Ps.-Mt.*, the *pars altera*, and additional episodes, accompanied by marginal illustrations (fols. 20^r–29^r).[89] Several images may also be found in the Holkham Bible Picture Book in London, British Library, Add. 47682 (ca. 1327–ca. 1335, Southeast England), which contains a biblical picture book with some explanatory text, mainly in Anglo-Norman French but with parts in English. Among the images is a series of miniatures depicting Jesus' childhood miracles based on *Ps.-Mt.*, the *pars altera*, and additional episodes, with explanations in Anglo-Norman (fols. 14^v–15^v). While these are only a handful of notable examples, many more exist from the later medieval period, testifying to the major influence that *Ps.-Mt.* had on visual imagination.

---

85. For analysis, see Sheingorn, "Reshapings of the Childhood Miracles of Jesus."

86. For some examples, see Dzon, *Quest for the Christ Child*, 265 n. 80.

87. See photographs and description at "Tring Tiles" (web site address provided in the bibliography below); and for an image and discussion of one of these tiles, see Dzon, *Quest for the Christ Child*, 158–59.

88. For analysis, see Sheingorn, "Reshapings of the Childhood Miracles of Jesus."

89. Facsimile online at http://www.e-codices.unifr.ch/en/searchresult/list/one/sbs/0008.

Translation

This volume presents a new translation of *Ps.-Mt.* accompanied by the first full commentary of the text in English. Since Gijsel's critical edition, only two complete English translations have appeared. The first is found in Bart D. Ehrman and Zlatko Plese's *The Apocryphal Gospels*, which includes the Latin A-text, with select variants noted, and a translation.[90] Ehrman and Plese preface the text with a brief introduction and add cross-references to biblical sources and parallels. The second translation appears in *A Synopsis of the Apocryphal Nativity and Infancy Narratives* by J. K. Elliott.[91] His text is a sort of hybrid translation; while Elliott states in his introduction that he translates the A-text, his translation also reflects certain textual divergences in the P recension. Elliott's translation is not presented together in full, but printed in sections, synoptically, alongside parallel narratives.

The present translation is based on Gijsel's critical edition, with a selection of other related materials. For *Ps.-Mt.* proper, I have used the A-text, since it generally represents the earliest surviving version. In the notes, I have singled out variations in minority witnesses to the A-text and some significant readings from the P-text. Cross-references to biblical allusions and quotations, textual notes, and commentary are indebted to Gijsel's own extensive notes, as well as his and Beyer's introductory material to the critical edition, supplemented by subsequent scholarship and my own research. At times, however, I have not included Gijsel's references to biblical parallels when they seem rather vague or do not offer distinct equivalents. Even where my own interpretations differ, I am grateful for the meticulous work of Gijsel and Beyers.

In addition to the A-text of *Ps.-Mt.*, I also include translations of a number of works demonstrating significant developments for the medieval transmission and reception of this apocryphon. These include the pseudepigraphal letters attributed to Chromatius, Heliodorus, and Jerome that often preface the A-text; the "Ego Iacobus" prologue found in manuscripts with the P-text; twelfth-century additions known as the *pars altera*; other additions found in Paris 11867; and the *Trinubium Annae* appended to *Ps.-Mt.* in many manuscripts. My translations of the prefatory letters and the "Ego Iacobus" prologue follow Gijsel's critical edition. For the *pars altera*, I have translated Tischendorf's text from his *Evangelia*

90. Erhman and Plese, *Apocryphal Gospels*, 73–113.
91. Elliott, *Synopsis*.

Apocrypha, which is, so far, the only edition of this material.[92] For the additions in Paris 11867, I rely on Dimier-Paupert's transcription.[93] Finally, for the *Trinubium Annae*, I have used Hall's transcription of the earliest version, from St. John's College 35.[94] All of these texts are meant to represent the outgrowths attached to *Ps.-Mt.* during the medieval period, although each addition characterizes a particular type of example within a generally fluid and dynamic tradition.

A special note about the translation of the *pars altera* is warranted. Tischendorf's edition remains problematic in a number of ways, since it is a constructed, composite text based on only two late (and not especially reliable) manuscripts, and further research has revealed much still to be studied concerning the Latin translations of *Inf. Gos. Thom.*[95] Nonetheless, Tischendorf's edition does generally represent a version of the textual tradition as found in some of the late medieval versions of the expanded *Ps.-Mt.* In addition to the two manuscripts on which he relied, other witnesses also generally align with his text (aside from expected variants). For example, in the order of episodes and in many particular readings, the *pars altera* is similar to the text found in Paris 11867. But Tischendorf's text should not be taken to represent all of the witnesses to the earlier Latin translation of the *Inf. Gos. Thom.* (Lm), as demonstrated by its divergence from manuscripts that include other additions or differ in the ordering of materials. The present translation of the *pars altera*, therefore, is only preliminary—and representative of only part of the medieval tradition—until a more comprehensive critical edition of this material is published.

For all translations, I have used a new versification system to facilitate more specific references to shorter passages, although verse divisions from Gijsel's and Tischendorf's editions are indicated in parentheses.

Biblical quotations pose a special case for translation. While the Bible is more often alluded to via parallels, there are a number of places where the Bible is quoted (and sometimes even cited) as a direct source. In biblical references, I use chapter and verse numbers according to the Latin Vulgate—the predominant version of the Bible used in the medieval

---

92. Tischendorf, *Evangelia Apocrypha*, 93–112.

93. Dimier-Paupert, *Livre de l'Enfance du Sauveur*.

94. Hall, "Earliest Anglo-Latin Text," 115.

95. See descriptions of the Q and R manuscripts, in Gijsel, *Libri de nativitate Mariae*, 151–86; Voicu, "Verso"; Voicu, "La tadition latine des *Paidika*"; and Burke, *De infantia Iesu euangelium Thomae graece*, 144–60.

West—which sometimes differs from the Hebrew Bible or modern translations (especially for the Psalms). In some cases, I have noted Old Latin parallels following the Septuagint (LXX) when they are especially relevant for comparison with the Vulgate. I have generally followed the Douay-Rheims translation of the Vulgate (with some modernizations), except where it does not accurately reflect an Old Latin reading; in these cases, I have rendered the phrasing to follow the older translation. For references to *Prot. Jas.*, I use the chapter and verse numbers as in Hock's edition and translation. For references to *Inf. Gos. Thom.*, I use the chapter and verse numbers as in Burke's editions of Greek A (for the *pars altera*) and Greek D (for the additional supplements from LT in Paris 11867).

Prefatory Letters

(From manuscripts of the A-text)

1 ¹*To the most beloved brother Jerome the Priest, Bishops Chromatius and Heliodorus*ᴬ *greet you in the Lord.*

²In apocryphal books we have found the birth of Mary, Queen of Virgins, together with the birth and childhood of our Lord Jesus Christ. ³Considering that many things in them are contrary to our faith, we believed that the writings should be completely rejected, lest, with Christ as pretext, we give joy to Antichrist. ⁴Then, while we were considering this, the men of God Armeniusᴮ and Virinusᶜ came, who were saying that your holiness found a volume in Hebrew written by the hand of the most

---

A. *Bishops Chromatius and Heliodorus:* Chromatius (died ca. 406/407), likely born in Aquileia, was bishop of this city from 387/388 until his death. Heliodorus (ca. 330–ca. 390), born in Dalmatia, was the first bishop of Altinum (date uncertain). The two bishops are appropriate choices for this pseudepigraphic correspondence: Jerome (ca. 347–420) addressed his *Epist.* 7 and the preface to his translation of Chronicles to Chromatius, *Epist.* 14 and 60 to Heliodorus, and the prefaces to his translations of Tobit and the Books of Solomon (Proverbs, Ecclesiastes, and Song of Songs) to the two bishops together. Both men were later canonized as saints.

B. *Armenius:* a number of manuscripts in the Q family give this name as *Parmenius*. A priest named Armenius contemporary with Jerome, Chromatius, and Heliodorus was executed with Priscillian (the famous bishop of Avila) and others condemned for heresy at a trial at Trier in 385.

C. *Virinus:* manuscript witnesses present a discrepancy concerning this name: in A, *Virinus* and *Verinus*; and in Q, *Ierinus*, *Vrinus*, and *Vltimus*. The identity of this figure is unknown.

blessed Matthew the Evangelist, in which was written about the Virgin Mother and the childhood of our Savior.[A] [5]For that reason, seeking your charity through our Lord Jesus Christ himself, we request that you translate it out of Hebrew for Latin ears, not so much for perceiving which things are signs of Christ, as for rejecting the craft of heretics, who, in order to teach evil doctrine, have mingled their lies with the good birth of Christ, so that they might hide the bitterness of death through the sweetness of life. [6]Therefore, it will be the purest charity should you obey us, asking as your brothers, or if you prefer, you could pay us as bishops demanding a debt of charity that you believe is fit for us to receive. [7]Be strong in the Lord and pray for us.

A. *in Hebrew . . . Savior:* the Latin phrasing used here to indicate the apocryphon's contents is parallel to titles of the apocryphon found in manuscripts (see the introduction). However, in this instance, the grammar does not seem to fit the context, since *uirginis matris* ("the Virgin Mother") is in the genitive case. It is possible (and would explain the problematic Latin) that the author of this spurious letter relied on a titular ascription for this phrasing but did not alter the grammar to fit the sentence.

2 [1]*To the holy and most blessed lords Bishops Chromatius and Heliodorus, Jerome, a humble servant of Christ, greets you in the Lord.*

[2]Whoever digs in ground known for gold[A] does not immediately seize whatever the torn trench might pour out, but first holds the sifting shovel, lifting up the shining stone from the bottom,[B] pausing to turn and overturn the dirt, and maintains hope for profits not yet increased. [3]Arduous work is put upon me, since this was commanded me by your blessedness—something not even Saint Matthew the Apostle and Evangelist wanted to be published openly. [4]For, indeed, if this were not more secret, certainly he would have added it to the Gospel that he did publish. [5]But he made this little book in Hebrew letters as a sealed document, which he never published, so that today the book—written in Hebrew letters by his own hand—is possessed by the most religious men, who have received it from their predecessors over successive ages. [6]They never handed over this book to anyone to translate, but they have told its story one way and another. [7]Thus it came to pass that this book was published by a disciple of Manichaeus named Leucius[C] (who also wrote the false acts of the apostles),

A. *Whoever digs in ground known for gold:* the image of digging in the mud for gold in relation to apocrypha is found in Jerome's *Epist.* 107, written to a noblewoman named Laeta about the education of her daughter, Paula. There, Jerome writes, "Let her take care with all apocrypha and, if ever she wishes to read them, not for the truth of their doctrines but for respect for miracles, let her know that they are not by those to whom they are ascribed, that many faults are interspersed in them, and that it demands great discretion to seek out gold in the mud." Jerome makes a similar statement in his *Epist.* 54, to a widow named Furia about the best way to preserve her chastity in widowhood. The author of this letter seems to take Jerome's imagery as inspiration for the extended, more digressive, and more complicated metaphor that follows.

B. *shining stone from the bottom:* this phrase (*fulgidos fundos pondus*) is problematic. Although Gijsel notes that the sense seems clear, the questionable reading in the manuscripts (which likely represents textual corruption) presents an uncertain philological crux. Unfortunately, the Latin in this passage is also more generally problematic, as the vocabulary, grammar, and syntax reflect post-classical constructions—including convoluted phrasing and ambiguity that is difficult to translate.

C. *Leucius:* the tradition about a certain man named Leucius associated with the composition and dissemination of apocryphal acts of apostles developed during the patristic period. Augustine mentions him in this context in

presenting the material not for edification but for destruction; and so in a synod it was judged according to its merits that the ears of the church should not be open to it.

[8]Let the bites of those who bark cease, for we do not add this little book to the canonical Scriptures, but we translate the writings of an apostle and evangelist for exposing the falsehood of heresy; in this work, we obey the commands of pious bishops as much as we oppose impious heretics. [9]Therefore, it is the love of Christ that we satisfy, believing that those who gain knowledge about the holy childhood of our Savior through our obedience might assist us in their prayers.

Fel. 2.6, and another reference appears in the *Pseudo-Gelasian Decree* 5.4.4, but the fullest account of Leucius as author of apocryphal acts is found in Photius, *Bibliotheca* 141. See Junod and Kaestli, *L'histoire des actes apocryphes*, 137–43; and Schäferdiek, "Manichean Collection," 92–94.

Prologue

(From manuscripts of the P-text)

I, James,[A] son of Joseph the carpenter, having lived in the fear of God, wrote in full all that I saw with my own eyes that happened in the time of the Nativity of Saint Mary and the Savior, giving thanks to God, who gave me wisdom about the history of his advent, manifesting fulfillment through the twelve tribes of Israel.[B]   cf. *Prot. Jas.* 25:1

A. *James:* the pseudonym of James (as in *Prot. Jas.*) is in contrast to the prefatory letters, which claim that Matthew the Evangelist wrote it in Hebrew. While scholars have seen this prologue as taken from *Prot. Jas.* 25 (where it is an epilogue), the only verbal commonality between them is that both state "I, James . . . wrote." Otherwise, the details differ. Especially notable is the added detail that this James was "son of Joseph the carpenter," meant to clarify that he was both the brother of Jesus (as in Mark 6:3 and Gal 1:19) and one of Joseph's sons from a previous marriage (see *pars altera* 41 and 42). This detail runs counter to the medieval tradition of the *Trinubium Annae* often appended to *Ps.-Mt.* in later manuscripts, distinguishing James the Lesser as the son of Alphaeus and James the Greater as the son of Zebedee.

B. *fulfillment . . . Israel:* this concept is thematically developed throughout the text, especially in the following ways: 1) relationships between depictions of Anna and Joachim and Jewish law in the Hebrew Bible; 2) the depiction of Mary in relation to biblical women in the Hebrew Bible; and 3) narrative episodes about Jesus' birth and childhood miracles posed as fulfillments of Israelite prophecies in the Hebrew Bible. The latter are particularly pronounced in 14:1–4, 18:5–6, 19:6–9, 23:1–2, and 39:3–9 (in the *pars altera*). The Latin here is ambiguous about the nature of this fulfillment concerning the twelve tribes of Israel, though it does seem indebted to typological interpretation.

2

The Gospel of Pseudo-Matthew

1 (1) ¹In those days there was a man in Israel named Joachim from the tribe of Judah, and he was the shepherd of his sheep, fearing the Lord in simplicity.ᴬ ²He had no care for anything but the flock, from the harvest of which he nourished all who fear God; in fear of God he offered double the gifts to those laboring in doctrine and offered simple gifts to those ministering to them. ³So he arranged into three parts all of his lambs, his kids, his wool, and all of his possessions. One part he gave to widows, orphans,

cf. 1 Tim 5:17;
Tob 1:6

A. This description of Joachim (1:1–3) is adapted from the brief passage in *Prot. Jas.* The author omits the reference in *Prot. Jas.* 1:1 to an ambiguous source about Joachim in the "Histories of the Twelve Tribes of Israel" (mentioned again in *Prot. Jas.* 1:3, also omitted in *Ps.-Mt.*), but otherwise the description of Joachim is amplified. In his exemplary status as a man of God, an outstanding member of Israel, and his blessings because of God's favor, Joachim is depicted in the same terms as the patriarchs of the Hebrew Bible. It is significant that he is from the tribe of Judah, as this aligns Joachim with the southern Kingdom of Judah that supported the Davidic line when the Israelite nation was split (ca. 930 BCE). By establishing these connections with the Hebrew Bible, the author centers the narrative on Jerusalem, the temple, and the biblical concept of the Kingdom of Judah as inheritors of special status. This is also one of the first indications that *Ps.-Mt.* establishes its narrative as a typological fulfillment of the Hebrew Bible (especially notable in its references to the Prophets). Gijsel notes that the portrayal of Joachim is similar to what was expected of a Merovingian nobleman, which he uses to date *Ps.-Mt.* to the early seventh century, within the reign of King Dagobert I (629–639); but he does not substantiate this claim with further evidence.

pilgrims, and the poor; another part to those who worship God; a third part to himself and everyone in his home.[A]

cf. Tob 1:7–8; Deut 26:12; *Prot. Jas.* 1:1–2

(2) [4]Now,[B] since he did these things, God multiplied the flock, so that there was no man like him among the people of Israel. He began, moreover, to do this at the age of fifteen years old. [5]When he was twenty years old he took as his wife Anna the daughter of Issachar, from the tribe and family of David,[C] with whom he lived[D] for twenty years but had no children.[E]

2 (1) [1]And it came to pass that at the time of the feast,[F] Joachim stood among those who offered incense to the Lord, preparing

A. Cf. RM 91.48–52 concerning "*Quomodo suscipi debeat filius nobilis in monasterio*" ("How the son of a noble is to be accepted into the monastery"), in which the tripartite division is generally parallel to that of Joachim's possessions. In *Prot. Jas.*, Joachim offers a "double portion of his gifts to the Lord," so that the extra may be distributed to the needy. In *Ps.-Mt.*, the description is further divided into three, as is prescribed for nobles who enter the monastery in the RM.

B. *now*: throughout *Ps.-Mt.*, the author follows the classical and biblical style of including conjunctions and particles to relate connections between ideas from one sentence (or sense unit) to the next, although in a much more exaggerative and repetitive style than usual. Despite the exaggeration and repetition, this practice seems to be indebted to the style of the New Testament, especially the Gospel of Matthew. This is particularly true of the many uses of *autem*. One might compare, for example, RB, in which the word seems to be one of Benedict's favorites (see de Vogüé and Neufville, *La Règle de Saint Benoît*, 1:245–314). The present translation seeks to render such instances in order to relay something of the style.

C. *David*: as in Matthew (1:1–17) and Luke (3:23–38), *Ps.-Mt.* is explicit about linking the genealogy of Anna—and therefore Mary and Jesus—with David, another effort by the author to establish typological associations between *Ps.-Mt.* and the Hebrew Bible. This association with the line of David is made all the more pronounced in *Nat. Mary*.

D. *lived*: the word *moratus* used here evokes a sense of waiting, delay, and expectation. This is emphasized by the following clause about their lack of children.

E. *no children*: the lives of Joachim and Anna are parallel to a number of biblical stories, such as those about Abraham and Sarah, the prophet Samuel, Susanna, Tobit and Anna, and Elizabeth and Zechariah; for further discussion, see the section of the introduction about the Bible as a source.

F. *feast*: the feast is not specified in the text (it is also ambiguous in *Prot. Jas.*), but it is likely a reference to either Passover or Shavuot, both Jewish pilgrimage festivals ordained in the Torah in which sacrifices were made: the Paschal Lamb for Passover and the First Fruits for Shavuot.

cf. Luke 1:9   his gifts in the sight of the Lord. [2]And, approaching him, a scribe of the temple of the Lord[A] named Ruben said to him, "You are not permitted to stand among the sacrifices of God, because God did cf. Isa 61:9; *Prot. Jas.* 1:4–5; 1 Sam 5–6   not bless you by giving you offspring in Israel." [3]Thus, enduring shame in the sight of the people, Joachim departed from the temple of God lamenting and did not return to his home, but went to his flocks and led shepherds with him into the distant mountains, cf. *Prot. Jas.* 1:9   so that for five months his wife heard nothing from him.[B]

(2) [4]Meanwhile, Anna wept in her prayers and said, "Lord, since you have already given me no children, why have you taken my husband from me? For behold, five months have passed and I have not seen my husband, and I do not know where he cf. *Prot. Jas.* 2:1   might be dead, or where I might make his tomb."[C] [5]While she

A. *scribe of the temple of the Lord*: the terminology used for Israelite religious officials is complex and varied in *Ps.-Mt.* and in the additions (as in the *pars altera* and Paris 11867). For example, the term used here is *scriba templi domini* (*scriba* is also used in 16:3), but elsewhere the author uses *pontifex* ("high priest," in 3:12; 7:1, 3; 8:3, 5, 12, 16, 17, 20, 21, 26, 30, 32; 12:2, 6), *pontifices templi* ("high priests of the temple," in 4:5; 6:18), *summus pontifex* ("highest priest," 8:26), *sacerdos* ("priest," in 7:1; 8:5, 9, 17, 24; 12:2, 8, 11, 23), and *sacerdotes dei* ("priests of God," 10:9). It is especially odd that the author sometimes uses the plural form of *pontifex* when indicating multiple priests (*pontifices*), since the status of High Priest in post-Exilic Israel was reserved for only one man. Chap. 8 is particularly illustrative of the complexity of terminology, as it contains the most focus on the priests and the author juxtaposes the different types in appositive phrases like *sacerdotum et pontificum* (8:5) as well as additional details in phrases like *sacerdotibus super duodecim tribus* ("priests over the twelve tribes," in 8:9) and *summus pontifex* for the figure Abiathar (8:26). Aside from titles for Israelite religious officials, the term *pontifex* is used for the priests of the Egyptian temple in 24:2. In the *pars altera* and additions in Paris 11867, this array of titles is similarly diverse, with terms such as *sacerdos* (39:2) *sacerdos templi* (28:1), and *scriba* (54:1), as well as the added terms *princeps sacerdos* ("chief priest," in 27:9), the Greek loanword in the phrase *presbyteros totius ecclesiae Israel* ("priests of the entire church of Israel," in 30:4), *magistratus synagogue* ("magistrates of the synagogue," in 54:1), and the Greek loanword *archisynagogus* ("chief priest of the synagogue," in 54:7). To these titles we might also add several references to Pharisees (*Pharisaeus/Pharisaei*) in 8:1; 16:3; 27:9; 30:13, 15; and 54:1. The present translation seeks to capture this variance in the terminology.

B. *five months*: in *Prot. Jas.*, Joachim goes into the wilderness to fast and pray for 40 days and 40 nights, whereas here, he leaves his life behind to become a shepherd. While the text says that he was away for five months, there is a sense that he imposes his self-exile indefinitely.

C. Anna's prayer is amplified from the one in *Prot. Jas.*

wept exceedingly in the garden of her home, lifting her eyes in prayer to the Lord, she saw a nest of sparrows[a] in a laurel tree and sent her voice to the Lord with lamentation and said, [6]"Lord, God almighty, who has given children to all your creatures, beasts, and draught animals,[b] and reptiles, and fish, and birds—they all rejoice over children. Do you exclude me alone from the gift of your kindness? [7]You knew, Lord, from the beginning of my marriage I vowed that if you would give a son or daughter to me, I would bring it to your holy temple."[c]

cf. Gen 2:24–25

cf. 1 Sam 1:11; *Prot. Jas.* 3:1–8

(3) [8]While she said these things, an angel of the Lord appeared before her saying, "Do not be afraid, Anna, for your sprout is in God's design, and that which will have been born from you will be given admiration in all ages to the end." [9]When he said these things, he disappeared from her sight. [10]But she, trembling at having seen such power and having heard such words, entered her room and threw herself onto her bed and, as if dead, she remained in prayer all day and all night.[D]

cf. Prov 8:22; *Prot. Jas.* 4:1

(4) [11]After these things she called to her servant girl and said to her, "You see me as a widow in anguish, but you do not want to come to me?"

[12]Then, murmuring, she responded, "If God closed your womb and took your husband away from you, what might I do for you?" [13]Hearing these things, Anna began to weep greatly.[E]

cf. Gen 16:2, 20:18

cf. *Prot. Jas.* 2:2–7

A. *sparrows*: evoking Luke 12:7//Matt 10:31, which also discusses the significance of humans relative to sparrows.

B. *draught animals*: the terminology used for various pack animals and wild beasts is rather diverse in *Ps.-Mt.* and the *pars altera*. Here, in addition to *creatura* and *bestia*, the author uses *iumentum*, which is often used for an animal like a mule or ass, but can mean any type of draught animal or beast of burden. The same term is used in 13:4, 8; 18:1; 20:2, 11; *bestia* ("beast") is used here and in the *pars altera* at 35:11 and 12; *fera* ("wild animal") is used in 18:9 and 19:3; and *sagmarius* ("beast of burden") is used in 19:10.

C. Anna's vow to dedicate her child to God appears in *Prot. Jas.* after she has received news of her pregnancy (not before). The vow conforms with the command in Exod 22:29, further emphasizing how Joachim and Anna follow the Hebrew laws.

D. Anna's prayer after the angel's visit is new to *Ps.-Mt.* In *Prot. Jas.* she is visited immediately after by two angels, who tell her about Joachim's return home.

E. *Ps.-Mt.* reorders this passage, as it appears before the angel's visitation in *Prot. Jas.* In this change, the passage seems to imply there is still tension

3 (1) ¹Now, at that same moment, a certain youth appeared in the mountains where Joachim fed his flocks and said to him, "Why do you not return to your wife?"ᴬ

²And Joachim said, "I have had her for twenty years. But now, since God does not want to give me children from her, I left the temple of God with shame from reproach. ³So why should I return to her after I was cast out? For now, I will be here with my sheep, for as long as God wants me to live. ⁴But by the hands of my servants I will give the proper parts to the poor and widows and orphans and those who serve God."

(2) ⁵When he had said these things, the youth responded to him, saying, "I am an angel of God, who appeared to your wife today as she wept and prayed, as a comfort to her; you should know that she conceived a daughter from your seed.ᴮ ⁶This (daughter) will be the temple of Godᶜ and the Holy Spirit will rest in her,ᴰ and she will be a blessedness above all holy women, so that no one might say that there was ever such a one before her, but also that after her no other will be like her. ⁷Therefore, descend from

cf. 1 Cor 6:19
cf. Luke 1:42

---

between the message given to Anna by the angel and the possibility of her pregnancy.

A. In *Prot. Jas.* Joachim's encounter with the angel is only a brief command for him to return home (as in *Ps.-Mt.* 3:7), after which he commands his companions to gather ten lambs for an offering and then heads out on his journey. *Ps.-Mt.* expands this episode to include further dialogue and a second visit after Joachim hesitates to return home. In this adaptation, Joachim makes his sacrifice even before he has decided to go back to Jerusalem, rather than at the temple after he has returned.

B. *daughter*: in *Prot. Jas.* the gender of the child is not revealed until after her birth (5:2). Here, the extended angelic prophecy to Joachim creates a closer parallel with those made to Zachariah in Luke 1:13–17 and to Mary in Luke 1:28–33. The angel's revelation also establishes more pronounced veneration of Mary and foreshadows her role later in the narrative.

C. *this (daughter) will be the temple of God*: the majority reading in witnesses of the A-text reads *Haec templum dei erit* (which this translation follows), but j reads *Haec in templo dei erit* ("She will be in the temple of God"), as do later recensions as in witnesses to the P, Q, and R texts.

D. *temple . . . rest in her*: in his *Epist.* 22.23 (to Eustochium), Jerome refers to holy virgins as "vessels of the temple" (*uasa templi*), and further remarks, "and no gold or silver vessel was ever so dear to God as is the temple of a virgin's body" (*neque enim aureum uas et argenteum tam carum deo fuit, quam templum corporis uirginalis*). Jerome's imagery is indebted to 1 Cor 6:19, and *Ps.-Mt.* uses similar language to describe Mary.

the mountains and return to your wife and you will find her pregnant. For God brought forth a seed in her and made her the mother of eternal blessing." cf. *Prot. Jas.* 4:3–4

(3) [8]And Joachim, worshipping him, said to him, "If I have found favor before you, sit a little while in my tent and bless your servant." cf. Gen 33:10; Judg 6:17

[9]And the angel said to him, "Do not call yourself my servant but a fellow servant with me. Truly we are servants of the one Lord.[A] [10]For my food is invisible, and my drink cannot be seen by mortal humans. [11]For that reason, refrain from asking me to enter your tent, but present what you would give to me as a burnt offering to God." cf. Rev 19:10, 22:9 cf. Tob 12:19

[12]Then Joachim took a spotless lamb and said to the angel, "I would not have dared to offer a burnt offering to God unless your command had given me the right to a high priest's offering."

[13]And the angel said to him, "Nor would I have urged you to the offering unless I had known the will of the Lord." [14]And it came to pass that when Joachim offered the sacrifice, the angel ascended to heaven together with the odor of the sacrifice as if with the smoke. cf. Judg 13:20

(4) [15]Then Joachim fell on his face from the sixth hour of the day until evening. [16]But his servants and hired men came and, not knowing what the cause was, were afraid; and thinking that he might want to kill himself, they picked him up with difficulty. [17]When they heard his story, they were struck with so much wonder and admiration that they urged him to carry out the command of the angel without delay and to return to his wife quickly. [18]When Joachim wavered and debated in his mind if he should return, it happened that he was gripped by a deep sleep. cf. Tob 12:16, 22

[19]And behold, the angel who appeared to him while awake appeared to him in sleep saying, "I am the angel who was given to you by God as a guardian.[B] [20]Descend untroubled and return to

---

A. Cf. RB 61.10.

B. *I am . . . guardian:* the idea that each person has a guardian angel (or two, representing good and evil) was widespread in early Jewish and Christian literature. This view may rest behind Matt 18:10; it is also found, for example, in patristic works such as Clement of Alexandria, *Strom.* 7.16, and Justin Martyr, *Dial.* 5; and in apocrypha such as Herm. *Vis.* 5; 6:2; *Apoc. Paul* 14; and *Hist. Jos. Carp.* 13. See Ginzberg, *Legends of the Jews,* 5:76–78.

Anna, because the works of compassion that you and your wife have done have been recited in the presence of the Most High. ²¹Such offspring is given to you that never have prophets nor saints possessed from the beginning, nor will they ever."

²²And it came to pass that when Joachim awoke, he called all of his servants to him and told his dream to them. ²³Then they worshipped God and said, "See that you do not further disregard the angel of God. But get up—let us depart and walk slowly, shepherding the flocks."

(5) ²⁴After walking for 30 days, they arrived and the angel of the Lord appeared to Anna standing in prayer saying to her, ²⁵"Go to the gate that is called 'golden'ᴬ and run to meet your husband, since he will come to you today." ²⁶She went with haste with her servant girls and she began, standing in that gate, to pray and to wait all day. ²⁷When she was disheartened from waiting for so long, she lifted her eyes and saw Joachim coming with his flocks.

²⁸And Anna ran to meet him and hung onto his neck, giving thanks to God saying, "I was a widow and behold, now I am not; I was sterile and behold, I have conceived." ²⁹And it came to pass that there was joy among all their friends and family, so that all the land and people rejoiced about this news.

4 (1) ¹Now, after these things, when her nine months were fulfilled, Anna gave birth to a daughter and named her Mary. ²Indeed, when she had nursedᴮ her for three years, Joachim and his wife Anna went together to the temple of the Lord.ᶜ ³And offering sacrifices to the Lord, they gave their baby girlᴰ Mary to the com-

cf. Matt 6:5

cf. Luke 15:20

cf. Judg 13:3; Rev
1:18; Prot. Jas. 4:8–9

cf. Luke 1:58

cf. Prot. Jas. 5:5

cf. Prot. Jas. 7:4–6

ᴀ. *the gate that is called 'golden'*: this reference, added in *Ps.-Mt.*, alludes to the eastern entrance into the old city of Jerusalem in premodern times. It is known as the Gate of Mercy in Hebrew and the Golden Gate in Christian literature, and has also been equated with the gate through which Jesus entered Jerusalem on Palm Sunday (Mark 11:1–11 par.; John 12:12–19) as well as the Beautiful Gate in Acts 3.

ʙ. *nursed*: the Latin word *perlactare* is a *hapax legomenon*, from *per* + *lactare*, signifying a continued action.

ᴄ. *Ps.-Mt.* omits *Prot. Jas.* 6:1–2, in which Mary is able to walk at six months old (6:1) and Mary is blessed by the priests at her first birthday (6:2). *Ps.-Mt.* also moves Anna's song (*Prot. Jas.* 6:3) to after Mary is left at the temple.

ᴅ. *baby girl*: the Latin diminutive term *infantula* (cf. *infantulus* for a baby boy, as in 20:6 below) is a post-classical construction, but here emphasizes

pany of virgins who continued in the praises of God night and day.^A ^4When she was placed before the temple, she ascended the fifteen steps of the temple^B so quickly that she did not look back at all, nor did she look for her parents as children are accustomed.^C ^5Everyone was struck by wonder at that deed, so that the priests of the temple themselves were astonished.

cf. *Prot. Jas.* 7:9–10

5 (1) ^1Then Anna, filled with the Holy Spirit, before everyone said,^D

cf. *Prot. Jas.* 6:11–13

Mary's status as a young child (a "baby girl" or "little girl").

A. *company of virgins:* the community of virgins in the temple that Mary joins largely resembles a female monastery, an anachronism projected onto the temple by the author. In *Prot. Jas.* 7:2, the "undefiled daughters of the Hebrews" greet Mary with blazing torches so that she will be captivated by love of the temple, but *Ps.-Mt.* makes the reference here more explicit. A number of early Jewish texts allude or refer to women who might be understood as virgins living in the temple, but they are by no means clear references. For example, both Exod 38:8 and 1 Sam 2:22 mention pious women waiting at the doors of the tabernacle, and 2 Macc 3:19–20 mentions "the virgins also that were shut up." More substantial references to virgins who lived in the temple and wove the veil are found in texts composed in the first few centuries CE, such as 2 Bar 10:19, *m. Sheqalim* 8.5–6, and *b. Ketubbot* 106a. In his description of the temple in *B.J.* 5.5.6 [227], Josephus mentions cloisters, but does not provide further details.

B. *fifteen steps:* Mary's ascent up the steps of the temple evokes the fifteen Gradual Psalms (119–33 LXX, or 120–34 in the Hebrew psalter), a group of psalms all containing the ascription *canticum graduum* ("Shir Hama'aloth," or "Song of the Ascents," in Hebrew). In Benedictine monasticism, these psalms were given their own special category and status. In some Jewish and Christian traditions, the fifteen Gradual Psalms are meant to be recited while ascending the steps of the temple; see, for example, *t. Sotah* 7.7 in the Mishnah. In the Middle Ages, this became a common belief about the origin and use of this group of psalms. In his *Tract. Ps.*, Jerome allegorizes the fifteen Gradual Psalms with the fifteen stages of a Christian seeking to attain perfection. The association between Mary's ascent and the Gradual Psalms is made all the more pronounced in *Nat. Mary*, where they are directly mentioned.

C. *Prot. Jas.* concludes this scene with the priest blessing Mary, then placing her on the third step of the altar where she dances in front of the people.

D. Anna's song (5:1–7) shares some general thematic parallels with the song in *Prot. Jas.* 6:11–13, but there is very little overlap in the details. Instead, the author of *Ps.-Mt.* seems to have composed a wholly new song for Anna, some of it echoing similar songs of praise in the Bible: cf. the prayer of Hannah in 1 Sam 2:1–10; the "Magnificat" of Mary in Luke 1:46–55; and the song of Zechariah in Luke 1:67–79. Many of the individual phrases also echo various passages in the Bible, as the cross-references demonstrate.

cf. Pss 8:5, 104:8

²"The Lord God of hosts is made mindful of his word,

cf. Luke 1:68

and God visited his people with his holy visitation

cf. Jdt 8:20; Pss 53:5,
85:14

³so that, as for the peoples who were rising up against us,

the humble ones, he might turn their hearts back to himself.

cf. Wis
48:10; Mal
4:6; Luke
1:17

cf. Ps 9:38 LXX; 1 Pet
3:12

⁴He uncovered his ears to our prayers

cf. Tob 8:18

and kept the insults of our enemies away from us.

cf. 1 Sam 2:5

⁵The sterile woman was made a mother

and she brought forth exultation and joy in Israel.

cf. Isa 54:1;
Wis 3:13;
Luke 1:14

⁶Behold, I will be able to offer gifts to the Lord,

and my enemies will not be able to prevent me.

cf. Zeph 3:15

⁷For the Lord turned them from me

cf. Ps 15:11; Isa 61:7

and gave me eternal joy."

6^E (1) ¹Then everyone was in admiration of Mary, who, at three years old, walked with such mature steps and spoke so perfectly and was so devoted to the praise of God that she was regarded as not a little girl but an adult.^F ²And as if she were already 30 years old, she persevered in prayer; and her countenance shone so brightly that it was scarcely possible for anyone to look upon her face. ³But she persisted in working with wool, and anything that the old women were not able to do, she was able to untangle,^G even at a tender age.

cf. Prot. Jas. 8:1

cf. Exod 33:20–23;
Matt 17:2, 28:3

E. Almost all of *Ps-Mt.* 6–7 is new, except for the mention of Mary being fed by an angel (*Prot. Jas.* 8:1). Much of the description of Mary's life in the temple is reliant on the ideals of early medieval monasticism. The depiction of her daily activities is especially indebted to RM and RB, with close parallels to both, and to earlier literature on which these rules rely (such as Cassian's *Institutes*). Beyers has demonstrated that this description is meant not as a depiction of actual monastic life but as a literary portrait, likely based on a model like Ambrose, *Virg.* 2.2.6–19. In all likelihood, the author (probably a monk) was knowledgeable of a number of texts about virginity and monasticism and synthesized them in this description in order to portray Mary as the model virgin.

F. *not a little girl but an adult*: this description of Mary is evocative of the episode about Jesus talking to the teachers in the temple at twelve years old (Luke 2:41–52). The difference in age, however, is telling, as Mary is still only a young child at age three.

G. *untangle*: the verb used here, *explico* (*explicabat*), with multiple possible meanings, is especially related to explaining or offering exegesis; that is, Mary was able to see the deeper spiritual meanings and untangle them when even those with experience of age could not. This detail also evokes the dual nature of work in a monastery as both physical and intellectual, as in the

(2) [4]Now, this was the rule she had set for herself:[A] [5]that from morning to the third hour she would persist in prayers; [6]indeed, from the third hour up to the ninth she occupied herself at work with weaving. [7]Indeed,[B] from the ninth hour again she did not retire from prayer until there appeared the angel of God, from whose hand she might receive food, [8]and so she progressed more and more in the fear of God.[C] [9]Then when she was taught by the older virgins to offer the praises of God, she was busying herself with such great zeal, that she was found first at vigils, more learned in the wisdom of the law of God, more modest in humility, more elegant in the songs of David, more gracious in charity, more pure in purity, more perfect in all virtue. [10]For she was constant, immovable, and in this manner more and more she advanced daily.

cf. 1 Kgs 19:5–7; Ps 77:25; Wis 16:20; Prot. Jas. 8:2

(3) [11]No one saw her angry; never did anyone hear her speak evil.[D] [12]All of her speech was so filled with grace that God could be recognized in her language. [13]She always persisted in prayer and the study of God's law.[E] [14]She was anxious about her companions, lest any of them should sin by a single word, lest any might raise her voice in laughter,[F] lest any should appear unjust or proud in the company of an equal.[G] [15]She blessed God without ceasing;[H] [16]and, not to be taken away from the praise of the Lord by chance or in greeting anyone, if anyone greeted her, she responded with the greeting,[I] "Thanks be to God."[J] [17]So it was originally from her

cf. Wis 21:20

cf. 1 Thess 5:17

cf. 1 Cor 15:57, 2:14

Benedictine dictum *ora et labora* ("pray and work").

A. *rule:* this term (*regula*) establishes a close connection with monastic precepts like those found in RM and RB, and a number of parallels with these texts appear in the following description.

B. *indeed:* the repetition of this word (*vero*) signals another feature of the author's style, likely based on biblical models but exaggerated in this text.

C. Cf. RB 48.10–14.

D. Cf. RM 3.24; and RB 4.22–23 and 28.

E. Cf. RM 3.61–62; and RB 4.55–56.

F. *raise her voice in laughter:* cf. RM 10.75–79; and RB 4.51–54; 6.8; and 7.56–59.

G. *unjust . . . equal:* cf. RM 3.39; and RB 4.34.

H. *she blessed God without ceasing:* cf. RM Theme Pater 71; and RB 4.75.

I. *not to be taken away . . . with the greeting:* cf. RM 3.27; and RB 4.25.

J. *Thanks be to God:* cf. RM 23.2 and 54.5; RB 66.3; and Augustine, *Enarrat. Ps.* 132:6. This phrase is also a common liturgical formula based on Paul's

that the saints, when they returned greetings to each other, would say, "Thanks be to God."

[18]Every day she was so refreshed by the food that she received from the hand of the angel that, indeed, that which she received from the priests of the temple she divided among the poor. [19]They would see angels speaking with her frequently, and they attended to her like one most beloved. [20]Moreover, if anyone among those with infirmities should touch her, that one was returned to health by her in that very hour.[A]

7 (1) [1]At that time the priest Abiathar[B] offered endless gifts to the high priests so that he might take her to be given to his son as a wife. [2]But Mary prevented them saying, "It cannot happen that I know a man nor that a man know me."

[3]And the high priests and all of her family said to her, "God is honored in children and worshipped in legacy, just as it has always been for the people of Israel."[C]

cf. Isa 31:9 LXX

[4]And, responding, Mary said to them,[D] "God is primarily esteemed and worshipped in chastity.[E] (2) [5]For before Abel

---

words in 1 Cor 15:57 and 2:14, but this detail attributes its origins to Mary instead of the apostle.

A. The comment about Mary's miraculous powers of healing echoes Jesus' healing of the woman with an issue of blood in Mark 5:25–34.

B. *Abiathar:* in 1 Sam 22–23, Abiathar is the son of Ahimilech, High Priest of Nob, who fled to David as the sole survivor when Saul had all of the priests killed. He is also mentioned in Mark 2:26. *Ps.-Mt.* seems to draw on this tradition in giving this name to the High Priest, another gesture that aligns the narrative with David and the Hebrew Bible. It is curious, however, that Abiathar is here called a "priest" (*sacerdos*), but later is called "high priest" (*pontifex*, 8:20, 830) and "highest priest" (*summus pontifex*, 8:26). See also notes about various terms for religious officials at 2:2 and on the name Issachar in 8:3.

C. In Old Latin (following the LXX), Isa 31:9 reads, "Blessed is he who has seed in Zion and a family in Jerusalem" (*beatus qui habet in Sion semen, et domesticos in Jerusalem*).

D. Mary's speech (7:4–9) is stylized, in many ways, like a sermon: an address to the people with a specific thematic focus, filled with allusions to the Bible, and highlighting noteworthy exempla.

E. *chastity:* the superiority of chastity is both deeply ingrained in monasticism and a common topic in discussions about and to women in early Christianity. The concept of holy chastity appears in the Pauline epistles (esp. 1 Cor 7:32–40), and other early Christian writers continued to develop the

no one was just among humans.[A] [6]Now that man pleased God through offering, but he was harshly struck down by the one who displeased. [7]Yet he received two crowns, for offering and for virginity, because he admitted no bodily defilement to his flesh.[B] [8]Thereafter also Elijah for the same reason was taken up while in the flesh, because he guarded his flesh as a virgin.[C] [9]These things, therefore, I have learned in the temple of God from my infancy: that a virgin may be very dear to God, and for that reason I

cf. Matt 23:35; Heb 11:4

Gen 4:1–16

2 Kgs 2:11–12

---

idea, especially regarding virginity. Indeed, old men telling women how to act as virgins became something of a cottage industry in late antiquity: see, for example, Tertullian, *Virg., Ux.,* and *Exh. cast.*; Gregory of Nyssa, *Virginit.*; Ambrose of Milan, *Virg.* and *Virginit.*; Jerome, *Helv.* (related to *Ps.-Mt.* in theme and some content) and *Epist.* 22 (to Eustochium); Augustine, *Contin., Bon. conj., Virginit.,* and *Vid.*; and, later, Aldhelm, *De virginitate.* Notions of chastity and virginity became part of the core tenets of monasticism as it developed, achieving codification in precepts like RM and RB.

A. *just among humans:* the tradition of ascribing the epithet *just (iustus)* to Abel developed in late antiquity, deriving ultimately from Jesus' words in Matt 23:35 and Heb 11:4. It became widespread in patristic writings; see, for example, Cyprian of Carthage, *Epist.* 6.2.1; Ambrose of Milan, *Parad.* 19.2 and 22.3, and preface to *Enarrat. Ps.* 7.2; Augustine, *Epist.* 157.21 and *Nat. grat.* 45; and Jerome, *Epist.* 22.39.

B. The imagery of dual crowns and associations with Abel as a righteous man and virgin evoke some intersecting ideas from late antiquity and the early medieval period. The image of a virgin being rewarded a crown originated in late antiquity and became widespread in the medieval period: for example, Ambrose of Milan discusses the dual crown of martyrdom and virginity (*aut martyr, aut virgo . . . corona*) in *Virg.* 2.4.24; and Jerome similarly discusses the crown of virginity throughout *Epist.* 22, with his most explicit reference (*virginitatis coronam*) in chap. 15; later, Gregory the Great uses the imagery of the dual crown of martyrdom and virginity (*virginitatis coronam et martyrii*) in the preface to his *Liber sacramentorum.* More generally, the belief that Abel died as a virgin was widespread, though not universally accepted. The Hiberno-Latin *De mirabilibus sacrae Scripturae libri tres* (written around 655 and attributed to an "Irish Augustine") suggests that if Abel had followed God's injunction to reproduce (Gen 1:28), he would have left heirs—about which the Bible is silent—and regards him as a virgin, priest, and martyr. Gijsel also cites the anonymous Hiberno-Latin *Oratio Sancti Brendani*, which names Abel as the first martyr, priest, and virgin; but the date of this text is uncertain, and it survives only in manuscripts from the eleventh or twelfth century onward.

C. As with Abel, the tradition that Elijah was a virgin when he was assumed into heaven was widespread in late antiquity; see, for example, Tertullian, *Mon.* 8; and Jerome, *Epist.* 22.21.

decided in my heart that I will not know a man in my innermost part."

8 (1) [1]And it came to pass that Mary reached the age of fourteen years old[D] and on this occasion the Pharisees said that now, on account of her womanly experience,[E] it was not possible for her to remain in the temple of God. [2]And a plan of this sort was invented: that a herald would be sent through all the tribes of Israel, so that everyone would assemble at the temple of the Lord in three days.[F] [3]When, indeed, the entire people had assembled, the high priest Issachar[G] arose and ascended to a higher step so that he might be seen and heard by all the people.

cf. *Prot. Jas.* 8:3–4

[4]And when there was a great silence, he said,[H] "Hear me, sons of Israel, and receive my words with your ears. [5]Since this temple was built by Solomon, there have been in it daughters of kings and prophets and high priests and pontiffs,[I] and they were great and wonderful. [6]Yet when they came to the lawful age they took men in marriage, and followed the course of those before them and pleased the Lord. [7]A new course of living was found

---

D. *fourteen*: in *Prot. Jas.* Mary is twelve years old when the priests decide she must leave the temple.

E. *womanly experience*: the language obscures references to Mary reaching puberty and the age of menstruation, seen as an issue of ritual purity in Hebrew law (cf. Lev 15:19–20). Being ritually impure during menstruation, she would not be allowed to live in the temple after this age. This issue is made more explicit in *Prot. Jas.*

F. In *Prot. Jas.* an angel visits the high priest (named Zechariah) and tells him the plan. In what follows, the author of *Ps.-Mt.* expands the narrative from *Prot. Jas.* to extend the action and suspense.

G. *Issachar*: manuscript witnesses present a discrepancy concerning the name of the high priest: the A-text gives the name as Issachar here, although Abiathar is later called high priest (8:17, 20, 26; 12:6); the P-text has Abiathar, although one branch influenced by A (P^3) has *Abiathar uel Ysachar*. See also notes about various terms for religious officials at 2:2 and on the name Abiathar at 7:1.

H. This speech (8:4–8) is not found in *Prot. Jas.*

I. *high priests and pontiffs*: here the terminology of religious officials is further made ambiguous, in the appositive phrase *summorum sacerdotum et pontifium*—both terms used for "high priest" elsewhere.

by Mary alone,[A] who promises God to keep herself a virgin.[B] [8]Wherefore it seems to me that by our questioning and God's answer, we should take pains to identify to whom she should be entrusted for her care."

(2) [9]Then this speech pleased the entire synagogue, and the lot was cast by the priests over the twelve tribes, [10]and the lot fell to the tribe of Judah, and they all addressed the tribe of Judah,[C] saying that the following day whoever was without a wife should come and bring a branch in his hand.[D] [11]So it came to pass that Joseph, an old man in the company of youths, brought a branch.   cf. *Prot. Jas.* 9:1

[12]When they had handed over their branches to the high priest, he presented a sacrifice to God and questioned the Lord, and the Lord said to him,[E] [13]"Send the branches of all into the Holy of Holies and let every branch remain there, and command them that they come in the morning to receive their branches from you. [14]From the point of one branch will come a dove and

A. *new course of living . . . alone:* here the various witnesses diverge, which Gijsel attributes to some amount of corruption in the hyparchetype of the A-text. For the main edition of the A-text, Gijsel gives *A sola Maria nouus ordo tacendi inuentus est* ("A new course of silence was found by Mary alone"); yet the kL branches omit *tacendi,* while some manuscripts of the A[1]e and A[3]b branches replace this word with *uiuendi* ("of living"). The P-text has *Nunc uero a sola Maria nouus ordo placendi domino inuentus est* ("Now, truly, a new course pleasing to the Lord was found by Mary alone"). The present translation follows the witnesses that include the variant *uiuendi,* since this detail coherently aligns this comment with the description of Mary's rule (*ordo*) in chap. 6.

B. *keep herself a virgin:* this passage emphasizes that Mary is the first biblical woman to choose celibacy and asceticism parallel to the same ideals as contemporary monasticism. This text, then, presents Mary as the progenitor of female monastic life as a choice.

C. *tribe of Judah:* references to the tribe of Judah reaffirm the interest of the author in linking Jesus' ancestry to the line of David and the Israelite monarchy.

D. *bring a branch in his hand:* the means of choosing Mary's husband resembles that used in Num 17:1–9, in which Aaron is chosen as the leader of the Israelites. God instructs Moses to inscribe twelve rods with the names of the leaders of the tribes of Israel and leave them in the tabernacle. The next day, Moses redistributes the rods and everyone witnesses Aaron's rod fully blossomed, with leaves spread and almonds growing on it—a sign of God's choosing Aaron.

E. This speech (8:13–14) is new to *Ps.-Mt.,* but the details echo the plan given to the high priest by an angel in *Prot. Jas.* 9.

it will fly to the heavens. To the man in whose hand the returned branch will have given this sign, entrust Mary to him as her guardian."

cf. Num 17:1–9

(3) [15]And it came to pass that early the next day everyone came;[A] [16]and when the offering of incense had been made, the high priest, having entered the Holy of Holies, carried out the branches. [17]And when he had distributed them to each man and from no branch did a dove go forth, Abiathar the high priest put on priestly robes with twelve bells, and having entered the Holy

cf. Exod 28:33–35

of Holies, burned a sacrifice, and there poured forth a prayer. [18]Then an angel appeared and said to him, "This is the shortest branch: the one that you counted as nothing and did not carry out with the others. When you bring it out and give it away, it will show the sign that I declared to you."

[19]Now this was Joseph's branch that was held for worthless, since he was an old man and not able to receive Mary, nor did he want to inquire after his branch. [20]And since he stood farthest away and humbly, Abiathar the high priest called out to him with a great voice saying, "Come and receive your branch, since we are waiting for you." [21]And Joseph went forth terrified, since the high priest had called to him with so great a shout. [22]But as soon as he stretched out his hand and received the branch, immediately

cf. Matt 3:16 par; John 1:32; Matt 4:5; Luke 4:9

a dove came out of the point of the branch, brighter than snow, exceedingly beautiful;[B] and flying for a while along the top of the temple,[C] it made for the heavens.

cf. Prot. Jas. 9:6–7

(4) [23]Then all of the people congratulated the old man saying, "You are blessed in old age that God showed you to be suitable to take Mary."

[24]But when the priests said to him, "Take her, because from all of your tribe you alone are chosen by God," [25]Joseph began to

---

A. This episode (8:15–22) is expanded; in *Prot. Jas.* the high priest distributes all of the rods and there is no confrontation by an angel correcting his actions.

B. *dove*: this detail evokes the descending of the Holy Spirit in the form of the dove at Jesus' baptism (Matt 3:13–17 par.; John 1:29–34).

C. *top of the temple*: this phrase (*per temple fastigium*) is reminiscent of Jesus' temptation on top of the temple in Matt 4:5 (*supra pinnaculum templi*) and Luke 4:9 (*supra pinnam templi*). Significantly, in both Gospels this episode follows Jesus' baptism and the appearance of the Holy Spirit as a dove (Matt 3:13–17//Luke 3:21–23).

implore and ask them, and, indeed with shame, to say, "I am an old man and I have children. Why would you consign to me this little girl—the age of my granddaughter, and who is younger than my grandsons?"

²⁶Then Abiathar the highest priest said, "Remember, Joseph, how Dathan and Korah and Abiram perished, because they despised the will of the Lord. ²⁷So it will happen to you, if you despise what is firmly imposed upon you by God."ᴬ

Num 26:9

cf. *Prot. Jas.* 9:8–10

²⁸And Joseph said to him, "Indeed, I do not despise the will of God, but I will be her guardian until the time when it is also possible to know this from the will of God: which of my sons should have her as a wife. ²⁹Let some virgins from among her companions be given, with whom she might pass the interim."

³⁰And Abiathar the high priest responded, saying, "Indeed, virgins will be given as her help,ᴮ until the set day comes on which you will take her. For she cannot be joined in marriage to another."

(5) ³¹Then Joseph received Mary with the other five virgins who would be with her in Joseph's home.ᶜ ³²Now, these were Rebecca, Sephora, Susanna, Abigea, and Zahel,ᴰ to whom were

cf. *Prot. Jas.* 9:11–12

A. While Joseph shows the same reluctance in *Prot. Jas.*, the high priest does not berate him for despising God's will as harshly as he does in this speech. Joseph's response (vv. 28–29) and Abiathar's following speech (v. 30) are also new to *Ps.-Mt.*

B. *help:* in medieval Latin, *solatium* has the meanings of "comfort," "consolation," and "help" in the sense of domestic or military meanings that signify companionship.

C. In *Prot. Jas.* the priests gather the "undefiled virgins," including Mary, back in the temple to make the curtain for the Holy of Holies. The rest of this episode about the work of the virgins is greatly expanded in *Ps.-Mt.*, especially the names of the companions and additions about Mary being called "Queen of the Virgins."

D. *Rebecca . . . Zahel:* the list of Mary's companions is unique to *Ps.-Mt.*, though their names vary in the manuscripts: *Rebecca, Repecca, Reuca uel Rebecca,* and *Ronca; Sephora, Seffora, Symphira,* and (oddly) *Tasepiphoras; Susanna* and *Sunna; Abigea, Abigael, Abiegna, Abigena, Abiegia, Abiea, Abieia* and the outliers *Abgazabel* and *Abgazabes; Zahel, Zabel, Zael, Zeel, Pahel,* and *Iabel.* The names recall various biblical figures: Rebecca, the wife of Isaac and mother of Jacob and Esau; Sephora or Zipporah, the wife of Moses; Susanna, the chaste heroine of the additions to the book of Daniel; *Abigea* or *Abigail,* the wife of Nabal and third wife of David; while a parallel to Zahel is not easily identifiable, it is possibly meant to evoke the name of Rachel, the wife of

cf. Exod 26:31–36, 35:25, 37:6

given by the high priest silk, and hyacinth, and scarlet, and flax, and purple, and linen.[A] [33]Now, they cast lots between themselves about what each virgin should do. [34]And thus it came to pass that it fell to Mary to take the purple to be woven for the curtain of the temple of the Lord.[B]

cf. Prot. Jas. 10:1–10

[35]And when she had taken it, the virgins said, "Since you are the last and humblest, how are you worthy to receive the purple?" [36]Saying these things mockingly, they began to call her "Queen of the Virgins."[C]

[37]And as they were acting in this way amongst themselves, an angel appeared in their midst and said, "These words will not be spoken in vain;[D] rather, you have anticipated the truest prophecy."[E] [38]And so they were terrified by the appearance of the angel and by his words, and they began to ask Mary that she might forgive them and pray for them.

9 (1) [1]Now, on the second day, while Mary stood in front of the fountain to fill up her pitcher, an angel appeared to her and said to her, [2]"You are blessed, Mary,[F] because you prepared a dwelling-place in your soul[G] for God. Behold, a light from heaven will

---

Jacob, or the name of the midwife later in the narrative (chap. 13).

A. *silk . . . linen*: these materials are mentioned in Exodus as the fabrics used for the veil of the temple.

B. Details about Mary and the other virgins weaving the temple veil (8:32–34) conform to late antique traditions cited previously about the community of virgins living in the temple (see commentary on 4:3).

C. *"Queen of the Virgins"*: Ps.-Mt. is likely the first (or one of the first) texts to use this Marian epithet (*regina uirginum*), since it appears in other texts only around 800, especially in liturgical invocations; see Canal, "Antiguas Versiones Latinas," 448–49 n. 12.

D. *in vain*: as Beyers observes, the word translated here as "in vain," *inemissus*, "seems to be a hapax [legomenon], at least before the ninth century, but it is clear that the word must be understood as 'not sent, not issued, unspoken', hence 'spoken in vain'" ("Transmission of Marian Apocrypha," 130–31).

E. *prophecy*: this word (*praeuaticinatione*) is an uncommon compound, combining *prae-* and *uaticinatio*, a "foretelling" or "prophecy."

F. *you are blessed, Mary*: the phrase used here is the same as the formula *Beata es Maria*, common in Western liturgy from the early medieval period onward.

G. *in your soul*: the Latin phrase (*in mente tua*) literally means "in your mind," but it can be translated with a range of meanings, all evocative of one's

come to live in you, and, through you, to shine throughout all the world." ³Likewise, on the third day, while she worked the purple with her fingers, a young man of indescribable beauty came to her. ⁴When Mary saw him, she was terrified and trembled. ⁵He said to her, "Do not be afraid, Mary, for you have found favor with God. ⁶Behold, you will conceive and bring forth a king who will rule not only on earth but also in heaven, and he will reign forever and ever."ᴬ

cf. Acts 22:6; *Prot. Jas.* 11:1–2

cf. Judg 13:3–7; Ps 9:37 LXX; Tob 9:11; Heb 1:8; Luke 1:28–33; *Prot. Jas.* 11:5–8

10 (1) ¹While these things were going on, Joseph was in Capernaum by the sea—occupied by his work, for he was a carpenter—where he stayed for nine months. ²So when he returned to his home, he found Mary pregnant and he trembled all over. ³Prostrated in anguish, he exclaimed and said, "Lord, Lord, take my spirit, because it is better for me to die than to live."ᴮ

cf. Tob 3:6; Jonah 4:3; *Prot. Jas.* 13:1–5

⁴To which those virgins who were with Mary said, "We know that no man has ever touched her. We know that purity and virginityᶜ have been persistently guarded as immaculate in her. ⁵She persevered always in God, always in prayer. Daily an angel of the Lord speaks with her, daily she receives food from the hand of an angel. ⁶How should it be that there is any sin in her? ⁷For if you want us to relate our suspicion to you, no one has made her pregnant but an angel of God."

(2) ⁸Joseph said, "Why do you mislead me so that I should believe you, that an angel of God impregnated her? It is possible that someone disguised himself as an angel and deceived her." ⁹And saying these things, he wept and said, "How can I show

---

inner spiritual state: in your mind, heart, and soul.

A. *Prot. Jas.* includes a speech by Mary, following the Annunciation, in which she doubts herself as being worthy to be the mother of the Messiah, and a response by the angel reassuring her. *Prot. Jas.* 12:2–3 also relates Mary's visit to her cousin, Elizabeth, as in Luke 1:39–56.

B. Joseph's speech asking for death and the testimony of Mary's companions (10:3–9) are added. In *Prot. Jas.* 13, Joseph offers a wholly different lament, and the following confrontation is between only Joseph and Mary, who denies her relationship with any man. *Ps.-Mt.* omits Mary's response to Joseph from *Prot. Jas.* 13:3.

C. *purity and virginity*: this pair of terms (*integritas et uirginitas*) emphasizes Mary's moral purity, although the first word could be translated in many ways, including *integrity, purity, chastity, virginity, moral uprightness, wholeness*, and *perfection*.

my face before the temple of God? How can I face the priests of God?[A] What will I do?"[B] ¹⁰And saying these things, he began to contemplate hiding himself and sending her away.

cf. Matt 1:19; Prot. Jas. 14:4

cf. Prot. Jas. 13:6–7

11 (1) ¹When he had arranged to rise up and flee from there at night, behold, that night an angel of the Lord appeared to him in his sleep, saying, ²"Joseph, son of David, do not be afraid to take Mary as your wife, because what is in her womb is from the Holy Spirit. ³She will bring forth a son who will be called Jesus; for he will save his people from their sins."

Matt 1:20–21

⁴So rising up from his sleep, Joseph gave thanks to his God and spoke to Mary and the virgins who were with her, and he told them his vision. ⁵And he was comforted concerning Mary, saying, "I have sinned, because I had any suspicion about you."[C]

cf. Prot. Jas. 14:5–8

12 (1) ¹Now it came to pass that a rumor went forth that Mary was pregnant,[D] ²and she and Joseph, having been arrested by the ministers of the temple, were led to the high priest, who together with the priests began to reproach him (Joseph), ³"For what reason did you defile such a great and upright virgin, whom an angel of God nourished like a dove in the temple of the Lord, who never wanted to see any man, who had the best instruction in the law of the Lord? ⁴If you had done no violence to her, she would have persisted in her virginity to this day."

cf. Prot. Jas. 15:1–9

⁵But Joseph placed himself under oath, swearing that he had never ever touched her, even in his mind.[E] ⁶To which Abiathar the high priest said, "As the Lord lives,[F] now as a test I will make

cf. Prot. Jas. 15:14–15

A. *show my face . . . face the priests:* the Latin presents parallel phrasing with synonyms (*qua fronte . . . qua facie*), in an example of wordplay known as paronomasia.

B. *Ps.-Mt.* omits Mary's response to Joseph from *Prot. Jas.* 13:3

C. Joseph's apology is new to *Ps.-Mt.*

D. In *Prot. Jas.* Annas the scribe visits Joseph and sees that Mary is pregnant and then reports this to the priests.

E. In *Prot. Jas.* the priests first address Mary, who denies having sex with any man, and then Joseph, who denies having sex with Mary. Here (12:2–5), the address to Mary and her response are omitted.

F. *as the Lord lives:* a common phrase to introduce affirmations and oaths in the Hebrew Bible (e.g., Judg 8:19; 1 Sam 14:39, 45; etc.).

you drink the water of the Lord's drinking and immediately your sin will become apparent."[A]

cf. *Prot. Jas.* 16:3

(2) [7]At that point, the entire multitude—too great to be counted—was gathered, and again Mary was brought to the temple of the Lord. [8]And, weeping, the priests, her parents, and her family were saying to Mary, "Confess your sin to the priests, for you were like a dove in the temple of God and received food from the hand of an angel."

[9]But Joseph was summoned to the high altar and the water of drinking was given to him; if a liar tastes it and circles the altar seven times, God makes a certain sign on his face. [10]Therefore, when Joseph drank it fearlessly and went around seven times, no sign of sin appeared in him. [11]Then all the priests and the ministers and people declared him to be holy, saying, "You are blessed, because no guilt was found in you."

(3) [12]And summoning Mary, they said to her, "What excuse are you able to offer, or what greater sign will appear in you than that which betrays you: the pregnancy in your womb? [13]We ask of you only that since Joseph is free of sin in your regard, you confess who has deceived you. [14]For it is better that your own declaration betray you than that the anger of the Lord, with a sign on your face and in front of the people, exposes you."

[15]Then Mary, resolutely unshaken, said, "If any impurity or any sin or any lust is within me, let the Lord expose me in front of all the people so that I might be admonished by all as an example of admonishment." [16]And she went up to the altar of the Lord and took the water of drinking and tasted it and circled seven times, and no sign nor mark of any sin was found in her.[B]

cf. *Prot. Jas.* 16:4-5

(4) [17]When all the people were amazed at seeing her pregnant belly, they began to be agitated with each other, all chattering

---

A. A similar ritual concerning a test for adultery is related in Num 5:11–31, although the details are different and *Ps.-Mt.'s* version is somewhat confused about the full procedure.

B. The testing of both Joseph and Mary (12:9–16) is much more brief in *Prot. Jas.*: both are given the drink and sent into the wilderness, and when they return without incident, the high priest absolves them of any guilt. *Ps.-Mt.* expands the account, adding many details and individually focusing first on Joseph's trial and then on Mary's with added speeches. Further expansion occurs in *Ps.-Mt.* 12:4–5 with the doubt and veneration of Mary by the people.

different things. [18]One was saying she was holy, while another was still accusing her of having an evil conscience. [19]Then Mary, seeing the suspicion of the people that she had not been entirely exculpated, said with a clear voice to all who were listening, [20]"As the Lord of all hosts lives, before whose face I stand, I have never known any man; to the contrary, I decided never to know one when I was in my childhood. [21]And I made this vow to God from my infancy so that I would persist in the purity[A] of the one who created me, by which I am confident that I live for him alone and serve him alone and abide in him alone without any impurity for as long as I should live."

(5) [22]Then they all began to kiss her knees, asking her that she grant indulgence for their wicked suspicions. [23]And all the people and the priests and all the virgins led her away with exultation and joy all the way to her home, calling out and saying to her, [24]"Blessed be the name of the Lord,[B] who has revealed your holiness to the whole people of Israel."

cf. Tob 3:23;
Matt 21:9

13 (1) [1]Now, it came to pass that after some time a proclamation was made by an edict of Caesar Augustus that everyone should hasten to their native land.[C] [2]This proclamation was first made by Cyrinus, the governor of Syria, and made it necessary that Joseph go to Bethlehem with Mary, because Joseph and Mary were from the tribe of Judah and from the house and family of David. [3]When, therefore, Joseph and Mary were going along the road that leads to Bethlehem, Mary said to Joseph, "I see two peoples before me, one weeping and the other rejoicing."

cf. Prot. Jas. 17:1;
Luke 2:1–4

cf. Prot. Jas. 17:9

cf. Gen 25:23

[4]To which Joseph responded, saying, "Sit and hold onto your mule[D] and do not speak unnecessary words to me."

[5]Then a beautiful boy appeared before them dressed in gleaming clothing and said to Joseph, "Why did you say that the words you heard about the two peoples were unnecessary?

A. *purity*: as in 10:4, *integritas* is used here.

B. *blessed be the name of the Lord*: a biblical blessing. See Ps 112:2, Job 1:21, and Dan 2:20; cf. also similar phrasing in Tob 3:23 and Ps 71:17.

C. In *Prot. Jas.* 17:1, Joseph expresses his anxieties about how to enroll Mary's child in the census.

D. *mule*: the author uses the word *iumentum*; see note on 2:6 and cf. 13:8; 18:1; 20:2, and 11.

⁶For she saw the Jewish people weeping because they have with-
drawn from God, and the gentile people rejoicing because they
have drawn near to the Lord, which he promised to your fathers^A
Abraham and Isaac and Jacob. ⁷For the time has come that by the
seed of Abraham a blessing shall be given to all nations."^B

(2) ⁸And when he had said these things, he ordered the mule
to stand still, and instructed Mary to get down from the mule^C
and go into a cave^D in which there was always darkness because,
in its innermost parts, it did not have the light of day.^E ⁹But when
Mary went in, the whole cave began to fill with great brightness;
and as if the sun were in it, so did the whole (cave) begin to ex-
hibit the gleaming of light; and as if it were the sixth hour of the
day, so did the divine light illuminate that same cave.^F ¹⁰This light

cf. Prot. Jas. 18:1; Isa
33:16

cf. Prot. Jas. 19:15

A. *your fathers:* some manuscripts read "our (*nostris*) fathers."

B. *To which Joseph responded . . . shall be given to all nations* (13:4–7): In
Prot. Jas. 17:2, Joseph does not respond, nor does a boy (an angel) appear to
substantiate and explain Mary's vision. With her vision and confirmation by
the angel in *Ps.-Mt.*, Mary becomes a prophet, following in the line of the Israelite prophets, especially Isaiah, who is most often quoted or echoed in this
apocryphon. The adaptation of this scene further allegorizes Mary's vision,
adding an element of exegesis that associates the narrative with typological
fulfillment of promises in the Hebrew Bible.

C. *mule:* the author uses the word *iumentum;* see note on 2:6 and cf. 13:4;
18:1; 20:2; and 20:11.

D. *cave:* for the cave as Jesus' birthplace, *Ps.-Mt.* depends upon *Prot. Jas.,*
but the detail is also attested in Justin Martyr, *Dial.* 78 and Origen, *Cel.* 1.51.
Origen conflates the traditions of the cave and the manger (as in Luke 2:7),
saying that the manger may be found inside of the cave, also relating that
visitors may still visit this cave in Bethlehem. Justin equates the cave with the
prophecy in Isa 33:16, which in the Greek LXX uses the image of the Messiah
living in a high cave of a strong rock. The resonance is somewhat lost when
comparing *Ps.-Mt.* with Jerome's Latin Vulgate, but Old Latin witnesses (on
which the author of *Ps.-Mt.* relied) follow the Greek: *Iste habitabit in excelsa
spelunca petrae . . .* ("He shall dwell in a high cave of rocks . . ."). Although
the author followed the source in this detail, nonetheless, the echo of Isaiah's
prophecy as a proof-text for Jesus' birth as Christ is significant in this passage,
extending the fulfillment of messianic prophecy from Luke's gospel into this
account.

E. In *Prot. Jas.* 18:1, Joseph leaves Mary with his sons and goes in search
of a midwife. In *Prot. Jas.* 18:2–19:1, Joseph experiences an extended vision
of all of nature pausing around him, and then he finds a midwife, an event
alluded to in *Ps.-Mt.* 13:13 only at his return.

F. Cf. Pseudo-Ambrose, *Life of Saint Agnes* 2 (*PL* 17.816): "When she

did not withdraw, neither day nor night, until Mary gave birth to a male, whom angels surrounded at birth;^A ^11and when he had been born on his feet,^B immediately^C they worshipped him, saying, "Glory to God in the highest, and on earth peace to men of good will."

Luke 2:14

(3) ^12And Joseph, finding Mary with the child to whom she had given birth,^D said to her, ^13"I have brought Zahel, a midwife, to you; behold, she is standing right outside of the cave, but is unable to enter because of the great brightness." ^14Hearing this, Mary smiled. ^15Then Joseph said to her, "Do not smile, but take

cf. Gen 18:12

---

went into the place of wickedness, she found an angel of the Lord ready there, surrounding her with immense light, so that none might approach her nor see her. For it illuminated the entire cell, like the light of the sun in its strength" (*Ingressa autem turpitudinis locum, Angelum Domini illic praeparatum inuenit, vt circumdaret eam immenso lumine, ita vt nullus posset eam prae splendore nec contingere nec videre. Fulgebat enim tota cella illa, quasi radians sol in virtute sua*). See Berthold, "Zur Datierung des Pseudo-Matthäus-Evangeliums."

A. In *Prot. Jas.* 19:15, a cloud overshadows the cave and a light illuminates it, but no angels appear.

B. *born on his feet:* this detail is new to *Ps.-Mt.* The author follows a long and widespread tradition of depicting great heroes as being born able to stand, including figures such as Moses, Hercules, Buddha, and Alexander the Great. Compare the Latin Pseudo-Linus *Martyrdom of Blessed Peter the Apostle* 13–14, in which the notions of being born head-first and feet-first (breach) are juxtaposed and allegorized in relation to Christ's dual nature (divine and human) and associated with Peter's request to be crucified upside-down.

C. *immediately:* the Latin grammar and syntax for this sentence (*et natum super pedes suos statim adorauerunt eum*) leaves it unclear whether this adverb modifies the clause about Jesus being born on his feet or the angels worshipping him. This translation opts for the latter since it offers a more conventional meaning overall, though the grammar of the whole sentence is generally ambiguous.

D. *she had given birth:* here the P-text diverges substantially from the A-text, with an additional passage focused on the midwives. This section begins with a clarification about Joseph's whereabouts during Jesus' birth that adds some cohesion to the narrative: "Now when the time had come, Joseph went seeking a midwife. When he had found her (or them), Joseph returned to the cave and found Mary with the child to whom she had given birth" (*Iam enim dudum perrexerat Ioseph ad quaerendam obstetricem. Quam cum inuenisset, reuersus est Ioseph ad spluncam et inuenit cum Maria infantem quem genuerat*). Although the noun "midwife" is in the singular in the transition sentence, in the P-text Joseph brings two midwives, named Zelomi and Salome.

care that she inspect you,[A] in case you need her medicine." [16]And Mary commanded her to enter.[B]

[17]When Mary allowed herself to be scrutinized, the midwife called out in a loud voice and said, "Great Lord, have mercy! [18]Never before has it been either heard or suspected that the breasts might be full of milk, and yet this newborn makes manifest that his mother is a virgin. [19]No stain of blood is on the child, and no pain was evident in the birth. [20]A virgin has given birth and after giving birth she has continued to be a virgin."[C]

cf. Prot. Jas. 19:18

(4) [21]Hearing this cry, another midwife named Salome said, "Certainly I will not believe this unless indeed I verify it." [22]And Salome went in to Mary and said to her, "Let me examine you so that I should know if the words that Zahel declared to me are true."

cf. Prot. Jas. 19:19

[23]Now when Mary allowed her examination,[D] as soon as Zahel drew away her right hand from the inspection,[E] the hand

A. *inspect:* several words are used for the midwives' inspections: Joseph says, *cauta esto ut inspicio te* (v. 15); about Zahel's examination, *Cumque permisisset se Maria scrutari* (v. 17); Salome requests, *Patere tu conspici a me* (v. 22); about Salome's examination, *Cumque permisisset Maria conspectum suum* (v. 23, though see the note on this phrasing as a textual crux); and when Salome draws back her hand, it is *ab aspectione*. The present translation seeks to capture this variance in the terminology.

B. *And Joseph . . . Mary commanded her to enter* (13:12–16): this dialogue between Joseph and Mary about the midwife is new to *Ps.-Mt.*

c. In *Prot. Jas.* the inspection (13:17–20) is much less explicit, and the midwife's exclamation is brief, not mentioning Mary's virginity directly until she meets Salome and tells her about the incident. Zahel's declaration of Mary's virginity is parallel with similar formulas in many other texts, especially those written after the Lateran Council of 649, when Mary's perpetual virginity was defined. For an earlier example of such a declaration, cf. Augustine, *Serm.* 51.11; and, for a later example, cf. Paschasius Radbertus, *De partu Virginis* 1.

D. *Now when Mary allowed her examination:* here the manuscript witnesses present a textual crux. Gijsel's edition follows two manuscripts of the A-text (A^{4}a4 and A^{4}a8) for the reading on which this translation is based (*Cumque permisisset Maria conspectum suum*), but other variants exist: the majority of A manuscripts have *Cumque permisisset se Maria in conspectu suo* ("Now when Mary allowed herself to be examined"); the A^4 branch has *Cumque permisisset Maria inspectum suum* ("Now when Mary allowed her inspection"); and the A^{2}b branch reads, *Cumque permisisset Maria inconspectum suum* ("Now when Mary allowed her inspection").

E. *as soon as . . . inspection:* the A-text does not include the second

cf. *Prot. Jas.* 20:1-2
withered and [24]she began to be most violently stricken by the pain and to cry out, weeping and saying, "Lord, you know that I have always feared you and have taken care of all the poor without the worry of payment.[A] I have taken nothing from the widow and the orphan and I have never sent the destitute away from me empty-handed. [25]And behold, I am made wretched because of my unbelief, because I have dared to test your virgin, who gave birth
cf. *Prot. Jas.* 20:3-4
to the Light and after this birth remained a virgin."

(5) [26]And while she was saying these things, a brilliant young man appeared beside her saying, "Go to the child and worship him, and touch him with your hand, and he will heal you, because this is the Savior of all who hope in him." [27]And quickly
Matt 9:20//Luke 8:44; Mark 6:56// Matt 14:36
Salome went to him and worshipped the child and touched the hems of the cloths in which the child was swaddled, and her hand was immediately healed.[B] [28]Then she went out and began to cry out and to speak about the great deeds of power that she had seen,[c] and what she had endured, and how she had been cured,
cf. *Prot. Jas.* 20:8-12
so that many believed because of her proclamation.

(6) [29]So also shepherds were claiming that they had seen angels in the middle of the night singing a hymn to God, and

---

midwife's name in this passage (*ut manum suam dexteram ab aspectione eius abstraxit*), although the identity is implied given the context. The P-text, however, includes a more direct reference to Salome: *Cumque permisisset Maria ut palparet eam, misit manum suam Salome. Cumque misisset manum suam dexteram et ab inspectione eam abstraxit . . .* ("Now when Mary allowed her (Salome) to touch her, Salome advanced her hand. And when she had advanced her right hand and drew it away from the inspection. . .").

A. *without worry of payment*: the Latin phrase (*sine tribulatione acceptionis*) leaves it unclear whether the worry is on the part of the midwife or of the patients. Given the issues of healthcare and payment raised here, with resonances for both ancient and modern cultures, this is a rather striking comment from the midwife.

B. *Hearing this cry . . . her hand was immediately healed* (13:21-27): this episode generally echoes the story of the apostle Thomas doubting Jesus' resurrection (John 20:24-29), the woman with an issue of blood who is healed by touching the hem of Jesus' garment (Matt 9:20//Luke 8:44), and the general comment in Mark 6:56//Matt 14:36 that many were healed who touched only the hem of Jesus' garment. More generally, Salome's withering hand also echoes the withering fig tree in Mark 11:20-21//Matt 21:18-20, and the withering plants from seeds sown on rocks in Luke 8:6.

C. In *Prot. Jas.* an angel addresses Salome again after the miracle, urging her not to tell anyone what she has seen until the child arrives in Jerusalem.

from them they heard that the Savior of humans had been born, who is Christ the Lord, in whom the salvation of Israel would be restored.^A ^30Also, an enormous star shone from evening until morning. This star made known the birth of Christ, who would restore not only Israel but also all peoples as he had promised.

cf. Luke 2:8–20

cf. Matt 2:1–10

14 (1) ^1Now, on the third day after the birth of the Lord, Mary went out of the cave and into a stable, and she placed the boy in a manger, and an ox and an ass bent their knees and worshipped him. ^2Then was fulfilled what was spoken by the prophet Isaiah, who said, "The ox knows his owner and the ass the manger of his Lord." ^3And these animals, staying by his side, were constantly worshipping him. ^4Then was fulfilled what was spoken by the prophet Habakkuk, who said, "Between the two animals you will make yourself known."^B ^5And so Joseph and Mary remained in the same place with the child for three days.

cf. Luke 2:7

Isa 1:3

Hab 3:2 LXX

15 (1) ^1Now, on the sixth day, (Joseph) entered Bethlehem, where he stayed for seven days. ^2And on the eighth day^c he led

A. From here onward, *Ps.-Mt.* diverges from *Prot. Jas.*, not relating chaps. 22–24 but expanding the narrative with other episodes from Luke 2 and Matt 2 and adding most of chap. 14. Episodes in chaps. 16–17 (the visit of the magi, their encounter with Herod, and the slaughter of the innocents) are generally parallel to *Prot. Jas.*, but details in *Ps.-Mt.* are closer to the canonical Gospel accounts, with many passages taken verbatim from Luke and Matthew.

B. The image of the two animals is attested in the Greek LXX and Old Latin versions of Hab 3:2, but not in the Hebrew nor Jerome's Latin Vulgate. This chapter represents the first two instances of several in *Ps.-Mt.* in which the narrative depicts direct fulfillments of prophecies in the Hebrew Bible. As in the canonical Gospels, these prophecies are used as proof-texts to lend authority to belief in Jesus as the Messiah as found in the Hebrew Bible. This is especially true in Matthew, which poses one connection between the canonical Gospel and the attribution of this apocryphon to the same author. In each instance in *Ps.-Mt.*, the author interjects to note the fulfillment ("Then was fulfilled. . ." [*Tunc adimpletum est. . .*]) and to quote the related prophecy. None of the fulfillments in *Ps.-Mt.* occurs in the canonical Gospels, nor are any of the prophecies from the Hebrew Bible used in this gospel quoted in the New Testament—demonstrating *Ps.-Mt.* as a unique witness to traditions about these fulfillments. The image of the ox and ass in particular was a significant addition to this tradition, as it influenced many depictions of the Nativity in medieval art and literature.

C. *and on the eighth day*: here some manuscripts of the A-text (A²b1, k, and A⁴c1) include an additional passage: "On the eighth day they had the

the child into the temple of the Lord. ³And when the child had received circumcision,ᴬ they offered for him a pair of turtledoves

cf. Luke 2:21–24 and two young doves.

(2) ⁴Now, in the temple there was a man of God, a prophet and righteous man named Simeon, who was 112 years old.ᴮ ⁵He had received this response from God: that he would not taste death until he should see Christ, the Son of God, in the flesh. ⁶When he saw the child, he exclaimed in a loud voice, saying, "God has visited his people, God has fulfilled his promise." ⁷And immediately he worshipped the child. ⁸After these things, taking him up in his robe, he worshipped him and was kissing the soles of his feet, saying, ⁹"Now dismiss your servant, Lord, in peace, because my eyes have seen your salvation, which you have prepared in the sight of all peoples, a light to the revelation of the gentiles

cf. Luke 2:25–35 and the glory of your people Israel."

(3) ¹⁰Now, also in the temple of the Lord was Anna, daughter of Phanuel, who had lived with her husband seven years from

---

boy circumcised and he was called Jesus by name, which is what he was called by the angel before, when he had been conceived in the womb. After they had fulfilled the purification of Mary, according to the Law of Moses, they brought him to Jerusalem to the temple of the Lord" (*Octauo autem die circumcidentes puerum uocatum est nomen eius Iesus* [omitted in A⁴c1], *quod uocatum est ab angelo antequam in utero conciperetur. Postquam autem impleti sunt dies purgationis Mariae secundum legem Moysi, detulerunt eum in Hierusalem ad templum domini*).

A. *And when the child had received circumcision:* many of the witnesses to P omit this clause, but a branch of P influenced by the A-text (group P³) reads, "they had the boy circumcised and he was called Jesus by name" (*circumcidentes puerum et uocatum est nomen eius Iesus*). For "circumcision," the text uses *perithomen*, a rough transliteration of Greek περιτομή, and an anomaly given the widespread use of *circumcisio* in Latin texts from the patristic period onward. The divergence is made all the more pronounced since three manuscripts of the A-text (and the P³ branch influenced by A) add a passage using the phrase *circumcidentes puerum*, more common in the Latin West. *Prot. Jas.* has no mention of Jesus' circumcision. In Luke 2:21, the verb περιτέμνω is found in the Greek, while the verb *circumcido* is found in both the Old Latin and Vulgate versions. All of this presents evidence for an interest in Greek behind the creation of *Ps.-Mt.*

B. *112 years old:* the age of Simeon varies across manuscript families: in the majority and most reliable of the A manuscripts, his age is given as 112, although some witnesses have 122 and others 92; in P, his age is given as 113. This variation is also representative of a wider trend in apocryphal literature that includes references to Simeon.

her virginity. ¹¹And she was a widow for 84 years, who had never departed from the temple of the Lord, being free to devote herself to fastings and prayers. ¹²She, too, coming forth, worshipped the child, saying that in him would be the redemption of the generation.

cf. Luke 2:36–38

16 (1) ¹Now, when two years had passed, magi from the East came to Jerusalem carrying great gifts, and they earnestly questioned the Jews, saying, "Where is the king who is born to us?ᴬ ²For we saw his star in the East and come to worship him."

³This report reached King Herod and so terrified him that he sent word to the scribes and Pharisees and doctors of the people, and he inquired of them where the prophets foretold the Christ would be born. ⁴But they told him, "In Bethlehem. ⁵For so it is written: 'And you, Bethlehem, in the land of Judah, are not the least among the princes of Judah. For out of you will come forth the leader who will rule my people Israel.'"

Mic 5:2

⁶Then King Herod called the magi to himself and diligently questioned them about how the star had appeared to them, and he dispatched them to Bethlehem, saying, "Go, and as soon as you find him, bring word back to me, so that I also might come and adore him."

cf. Prot. Jas. 21:1–9; Matt 2:2–9

(2) ⁷Now, as the magi were travelling along the road, the star appeared and, as if providing guidance to them, it went before them until they arrived at where the child was. ⁸So, seeing the star, the magi rejoiced with great joy, and going in they found the child Jesus sitting in Mary's lap. ⁹Then they revealed their treasures and presented Mary and Joseph with remarkable gifts, but to the child himself they each offered a single gold coin.ᴮ ¹⁰One offered gold, another incense, the third, indeed, myrrh. ¹¹But when they wanted to return to King Herod, they were warned in a dream what Herod had planned. ¹²And so they worshipped the child againᶜ and with all joy they returned to their own land by another road.

cf. Prot. Jas. 21:10–11

cf. Prot. Jas. 21:12; Matt 2:10–12

A. *to us*: some manuscripts read "to you" (*uobis*).

B. *single gold coin*: the meaning of this passage (*singuli singulos aureos*) is obscure, as is the significance of this detail, which does not appear in Matt 2 nor in *Prot. Jas.* 21.

C. *they worshipped the child again*: this phrase is translated as in A

17 (1) ¹Now, when King Herod saw that he had been deceived by the magi, his heart was inflamed, and he sent (soldiers) along all the roads, as he grew determined to capture them. ²But when he was utterly unable to find them, he sent (soldiers) to Bethlehem and killed every child two years old and under,ᴬ in accord with the timing that he had learned by questioning the magi.

cf. *Prot. Jas.* 22:1–2;
Matt 2:16

(2) ³But indeed, one day before (Herod) had done this, Joseph was warned by an angel of the Lord: "Take Mary and the child and go by the desertᴮ road to Egypt."ᶜ

cf. Matt 2:13

18ᴰ (1) ¹And when they arrived at a certain cave, so that they might cool off in it, Mary climbed down from the muleᴱ and sat and was holding Jesus in her lap. ²Now, there were three male servants making the journey with them, and one maidservant with Mary. ³And behold, suddenly many dragons came out of the cave, and when the servants saw them they cried out. ⁴Then the

---

(*readorauerunt infantem*) but it is simplified in P to *adorauerunt infantem*. Beyers ("Transmission of Marian Apocrypha," 131) notes that "*readorare* is a hapax, but it is a rather obvious compound."

A. *every child two years old and under:* like *Prot. Jas.*, this text differs from the biblical version in that Herod kills all children under the age of two, not only the males.

B. *desert:* the word *heremus* is a loanword from Greek ἔρημος that does not appear in Classical Latin, nor in the parallel verse in Matt 2:13. As in 15:3 (with *perithomen*), this is striking evidence for interest in Greek behind the creation of *Ps.-Mt.*

C. *to Egypt:* following this verse, A²b1, k, and A⁴c1 add: "'For King Herod will seek to kill the child (or: seek the child to kill him). Then Joseph arose from sleep, took Mary and the child, and made haste to Egypt" (*Rex enim Herodes quaerit occidere infantem* [L adds: *eum*]. *Surgens autem a somno Ioseph accepit Mariam et puerum et pergebat in Aegyptum*); cf. Matt 2:13–14.

D. Between chaps. 17 and 18, A¹e4 includes a new title: *Narratio Elysiodorii de factis Iesu Christi* ("Narrative of Elysiodorus on the Acts of Jesus Christ"). For chaps. 18–24, the compiler used an unidentified source (or multiple unidentified sources). It is possible that such a source was also used for earlier parts of the narrative, since there is no clear evidence that *Prot. Jas.* was used after 13:28. This unidentified source is also reflected in parallel episodes in the Irish *Leabhar Breac* (126–29 and 133–36), and it must have been related to other infancy narratives with similar parallels (as identified in the following notes).

E. *mule:* the author uses the word *iumentum*; see note on 2:6 and cf. 13:4, 8; 20:2, 11.

Lord, although he was not yet two years old,[A] roused himself and, standing on his feet, stood before them.[B] [5]Those dragons, indeed, worshipped him, and when they had finished worshipping him, they went away. [6]Then was fulfilled what was said by the prophet who wrote the Psalms, saying, "Praise the Lord from the earth, dragons and all the depths."

Ps 148:7

(2) [7]Now, he himself—the Lord Jesus Christ, still a small child—began walking along with them so that he not weigh them down. [8]But Mary and Joseph were saying to each other, "It would be better if those dragons were to kill us than to hurt the child."

[9]But Jesus said to them, "Do not consider me to be a small child; for I always was and am the perfect man,[C] and it is necessary that I make tame every kind of wild beast."[D]

19[E] (1) [1]Likewise, both lions and panthers[F] worshipped and accompanied him in the desert[G] wherever Mary went with Joseph;

A. *two years old:* this indication of Jesus' age contradicts the earlier statement, in 16:1, that two years had passed since his birth. Gijsel explains this discrepancy due to the difference in sources used.

B. *standing . . . before them:* cf. the comment about Jesus being "born on his feet" in 13:11.

C. *I always was and am the perfect man:* Jesus' assertion (*ego enim semper uir perfectus fui et sum*) poses substantial Christological and Trinitarian ideas. Some of these ideas are further explored in later medieval additions to the text, such as the episodes translated below.

D. *wild beast:* the author uses the word *fera*; see note on 2:6 and cf. 18:9 and 19:3.

E. This chapter (and the dragons in the preceding chapter) is evocative of the late antique and medieval tradition of the *Physiologus*, an encyclopedic collection in which animals are depicted, described, and moralized through Christian allegory. The *Physiologus* became the basis for later medieval bestiaries. Particularly noteworthy are the lion (usually the first animal discussed in this tradition), which is allegorized as representing the nature of Christ (fully human and fully divine), as well as his Crucifixion and Resurrection; the panther, which is allegorized as representing Christ; and the panther's enemy, the dragon, which is allegorized as the devil. Many other creatures (mythological and actual) are included in the *Physiologus* and the myriad medieval texts and images influenced by it.

F. *lions and panthers:* A²b1 and A⁴c1 add: "and various types of wild beasts came from everywhere" (*et uaria ferarum genera undique uenientes*).

G. *desert:* in contrast to the previous use of the Greek loanword *heremus* (17:2; cf. 20:1), here the author uses the more common Classical Latin *desertus*.

75

[cf. Tob 11:9]

[2]and they would go before them, showing the road and displaying their obedience: bowing their enormous heads with reverence, they displayed their servitude by wagging their tails. [3]But the first day that Mary saw lions and panthers and various monstrous wild beasts[A] coming around them, she was exceedingly terrified. [4]But at the sight of her face, the child Jesus smiled, and, speaking to her in a comforting voice, said, "Do not be afraid, mother; truly, they hasten to come not to injure you but to serve you." [5]And with these words, he removed the fear from their hearts.

[cf. Isa 11:6]

(2) [6]Therefore, lions and asses and oxen and the pack-horses that carried their provisions walked together, and wherever they made a stop, they would go together to pasture. [7]There were also tame rams who had come out of Judea together and followed them, and who walked among wolves without fear. [8]None feared another and none was hurt by another in any way. [9]Then was fulfilled what Isaiah said: "The wolves will feed with lambs, and

[Isa 65:25]

the lion and the ox will feed on straw together." [10]Indeed, there were two oxen on their journey as beasts of burden,[B] whom lions guided on the journey of our Lord Jesus Christ, whose provisions they carried.

20[C] (1) [1]Now, it came to pass after these things, on the third day from their departure, that Mary became fatigued by too much sun in the desert,[D] and seeing a palm tree she wanted to rest in its shade for a little while. [2]And hastening, Joseph led her to the

---

A. *various monstrous wild beasts*: in the Latin phrase used here (*uaria ferarum monstra*), the word *monstra* can be translated with a range of meanings, especially since its use was in flux from late antiquity through the medieval period. Possible meanings include *monstrous* (as here), *wondrous*, and *supernatural*; cf. *uariarum monstra ferarum* in Virgil, *Aen.* 6.285, during Aeneas's trip to the underworld. See note on 2:6; and cf. 18:9 and 19:3.

B. *beasts of burden*: the author uses the word *sagmarius*; see note on 2:6.

C. Close parallels with the incident of the palm tree in chaps. 20–21 appear in the *Liber requiei* (Ethiopic *Dorm. Vir.*) 5–9 and the fragmentary Georgian *Dorm. Vir.* 1–11, which both comprise a speech by Jesus to Mary about this miracle, including Jesus' blessing of the tree and its ascent into Paradise after it has provided its fruit. There are also general parallels in the Qur'an 19:23–26, in which Mary seeks solitude before Jesus' birth and is nourished with both water and dates from a palm tree.

D. *desert*: here the author again uses the Greek loanword *heremus*.

palm and took her down from the mule.[A] [3]And when Mary had sat down, looking at the foliage of the palm, she saw that it was full of fruit, and said, "Oh, if only it were possible that I might gather some of those fruits of the palm."

[4]And Joseph said to her, "I am amazed that you say this, when you see the great height of this palm. Indeed, you think about the fruits of the palm. [5]But I think about water that we now lack in the water bags and how we have nowhere to refill them or to revive ourselves."

(2) [6]Then the baby boy[B] Jesus, sitting in the lap of his mother, the virgin,[C] called out to the palm tree and said, "Bend down, tree, and refresh my mother with your fruit." [7]Immediately, then, at his voice, the palm bent its top down to Mary's feet, and gathering the fruit from it, all were refreshed. [8]But even after all its fruit was collected, it remained bent down, expecting that it should arise at the command of the one by whose command it had bent down. [9]Then Jesus said to it, "Raise yourself, palm, be both strengthened and be a companion to my trees, which are in my Father's Paradise. Uncover, then, secret springs from your roots, and may water flow from them in abundance." [10]And immediately the palm rose, and springs of water began to flow through its roots, clear and cold and most sweet. [11]Seeing, then, the springs of water flowing, they rejoiced with great joy and they drank together as beasts[D] and humans, giving thanks to God.

21 (1) [1]Now, on the next day, they departed. But when they began to go, Jesus turned to the palm and said, [2]"I give this inheritance[E] to you, palm: that one of your branches be transplanted by

A. *mule:* the author uses the word *iumentum*; see note on 2:6 and cf. 13:4, 8; 18:1; and 20:11.

B. *baby boy:* here the author again uses *infantulus*, as for Mary in 4:3.

C. *called out:* A²b1 and A⁴c1 have: "and hearing and knowing what she had said, called out" (*et audiens et intelligens quae dicebantur exclamauit*).

D. *beasts:* the author uses the word *iumentum*; see note on 2:6 and cf. 13:4, 8; 18:1; and 20:2.

E. *inheritance:* the word *exagilium* (or variants) occurs in a handful of texts composed between the fifth and seventh centuries, including the *Confessions* of Saint Patrick (d. 461), *Life of Epiphanius* of Ennodius (d. 521), *Virtutes Iohannis* (sixth century), and RM (sixth century); see Bieler, "Exagellia." The parallel in RM (91.48–52) is especially intriguing, since the word occurs

my angels and established in my Father's Paradise. [3]I will confer, moreover, this blessing upon you: that to everyone who is victorious in any sort of contest it will be said, 'You have achieved the palm.'" [4]As he was saying these things, behold, an angel of the Lord appeared standing above the palm tree, and taking one of its branches went flying away. [5]And seeing this, they all fell down on their faces and made like they were dead.

cf. Matt 28:4

[6]Then, speaking to them, Jesus said, "Why has terror seized your hearts? Or do you not know that this palm that I have had transplanted will be made ready for all the saints in the Place of Delights,^A just as it was made ready for you in this desert?"

22^B (1) [1]Joseph said to him,^C "Lord, because the excessive heat is boiling us away, if you wish, let us hold to the road to the sea so that we might be able to pass by the cities of the sea to rest."

[2]Jesus says to him, "Do not be afraid, Joseph, I will shorten the stages for you,^D so that, whereas it should have been thirty days of hurrying for you, in this one day you arrive at your chambers.

---

in the passage about the tripartite division of a noble's possessions, which is parallel with Joachim's tripartite division of his possessions (see the note on this parallel in 1:3 and discussion in the introduction).

A. *Place of Delights*: for the term used here (*loco deliciarum*), cf. Gen 2:10 (*loco voluptatis*). An Old Latin reading is perhaps reflected in Augustine, *Gen. imp.* 2:10: "Therefore, a river went out from Eden, that is, from the Place of Delights" (*exibat ergo flumen de Eden, id est de loco deliciarum*).

B. Other accounts of the Flight into Egypt also mention that it took only a day; see, for example, *Arab. Gos. Inf.* 10.

C. In contrast to much of *Ps.-Mt.*, the style of this section (22:1–3) is marked by asyndeton, in which the author's characteristic use of conjunctions and particles are notably lacking (see note on 1:4). Certain witnesses do include such particles (*autem* and *et*), or instances of expanded phrasing to convey more connective coherence; witnesses to the P-text include similar instances. The verbs in this section also switch to present tense: *Dicit ei Ioseph* . . . ; *Dicit ei Iesus* . . . ; and *Adhuc eo loquente* . . . —all of which have been translated here in the present tense to mark the shift in style. In addition to these stylistic details, the chapter notably has no transition or exposition to establish the narrative context for this episode; thus, there is no coherent connection between chaps. 21 and 22.

D. *stages for you*: the second-person pronoun used throughout the verse is plural (*uobis*).

³As he is still speaking, behold, looking into the distance, they saw the mountains of Egypt and its plains.ᴬ

(2) ⁴Both rejoicing and exulting,ᴮ they went into one of the cities, which was called Sohennen.ᶜ ⁵And because they knew no one in that place who would put them up as guests, they went into the temple, which is called the Capitoline of this same city of Egypt.ᴰ ⁶In this temple were placed 365 idols, to whom divine honors were offered, each on its own day, by the sacrilegious.

23ᴱ (1) ¹Now, it came to pass that when Mary entered the temple with the little child, all together the images fell, and all of

A. *plains:* the word used here is *aequitates.* Beyers observes, "That is what should have been the original reading, but most A manuscripts have *equitatus,* the cavalry, and P has changed the wording into 'they started to see the mountains of Egypt and its cities'" (*uidere coeperunt montes Aegyptii et ciuitates eius*). She also notes the rarity of this use, since, "In the present state of our knowledge, this meaning is not otherwise attested" ("Transmission of Marian Apocrypha," 132–33).

B. *rejoicing and exulting:* A²b₁ and A⁴c₁ add: "they arrived in the end at Hermopolis and" (*deuenerunt in finibus Hermopolis et*). Gijsel suggests that the toponym *Hermopolis* might come from Pseudo-Rufinus, *Hist. mon.* 7; or Cassiodorus, *Historia tripartita* 6.42.6; 10.7.5; and 10.14.6; the name also appears in Pliny, *Nat.* 5.49; Ammianus, *Rerum gestarum* 22.16.2; and Augustine, *Civ.* 8.26.6. A reference to this story in the eighth-century Hiberno-Latin *De enigmatibus* (possibly derived from a common source) includes the city name *Helipolem.*

C. *Sohennen:* manuscript witnesses present a discrepancy concerning this toponym: in A, *Sohenen, Sohennem, Sihenen, Syenem, Syene, Semen, Senan, Shohen, Sochen, Soennen,* and *Serasenim;* in P, *Sotinen, Sothinen, Sotyne, Socinen,* and *Sorhem;* in Q, *Sotine, Socinem, Sotien, Siene,* and *Sonne;* and in R, *Sotriana, Sotriena, Sotriona, Socrina, Sodonia,* and *Socitia.* Beyers notes that the author possibly meant to refer to the ancient city of Syene (now Assuan) or the city of Tanis (Hebrew Soan, now San el-Hagar); see "Transmission of Marian Apocrypha," 127 n. 41; and Canal, "En torno al Evangelio del Pseudo-Mateo," 208. The eighth-century Hiberno-Latin *De enigmatibus* includes the city name *Sothinent.*

D. *called the Capitoline:* the author seems to be equating the Egyptian temple in Sohennen with the Capitoline Hill (here called *capitolium*) in Rome—that is, this temple is the equivalent of the Capitoline for being the cultural center of the area.

E. Similar stories about pagan idols falling down because of Jesus appear in the *Arab. Gos. Inf.* 10 (translated from the East Syriac *History of the Virgin*); *Arm. Gos. Inf.* 15:13–16 and 16:4; and *Vis. Theo.* pp. 19–21. None of these apocrypha, however, includes a similar comment about the fulfillment of prophecy. An association between Isa 19:1 and idols falling at Jesus'

the idols of their own accord, cast down on their faces, revealed themselves quite clearly to be nothing. ²Then was fulfilled what the prophet said: "Behold, the Lord will come upon a swift cloud and all of the graven images of Egypt will be shaken by his presence."

Isa 19:1; cf. Exod 12:12; Num 33:4

24 (1) ¹Then, when this was announced to Afrodisius,ᴬ he went to the temple with all of his army and with all of his friends and companions. ²But all of the high priests of the temple hoped that he would say nothing to those for whose sake they had fallen. ³Nevertheless, having entered the temple and seeing that what he had heard was true, he immediately went to Mary and began to worship the child whom Mary held in her lap as Lord. ⁴And when he had worshipped him, he addressed his entire army and all his friends and said, "If this were not the Lord of these our gods, they would not prostrate themselves before him, and indeed, lying prostrate in his presence, they testify publicly that he is their Lord.ᴮ ⁵Therefore, if we do not carefully do what we see our gods doing, we will all rather run the risk of incurring

---

arrival in Egypt appears in Pseudo-Rufinus, *Hist. mon.* 7, where the city of Hermopolis is also mentioned. The eighth-century Hiberno-Latin *De enigmatibus* includes a reference to Jesus causing idols to fall in an Egyptian temple and also indicates this miracle as a fulfillment of Isa 19:1, which it quotes. Another intriguing parallel, and possibly the closest, appears in the *Legend of Aphroditianus* (or the "Narrative of Events Happening in Persia on the Birth of Christ" falsely attributed to Julius Africanus), a pseudo-pagan text that describes events at Jesus' birth and explains the journey of the magi. Chap. 3 of this *Legend* relates that, at Jesus' birth, a star descended above the head of a certain statue of Pege (Mary) in the Temple of Hera, and all of the other pagan idols fell down upon their faces in adoration. Beyond plot parallels, it is also not easy to dismiss the similarity between the names *Afrodisius* and *Aphroditianus*, which appears in ascriptions of authorship for the text in Greek and Slavonic manuscripts (see Heyden "Legend of Aphroditianus," 9 n. a.).

A. *Afrodisius*: A²b1, k, and A⁴c1 add: "the governor of this city" (*principi eiusdem ciuitatis*), which adds context oddly lacking in the other witnesses.

B. *not prostrate . . . publicly*: this sentence presents a case of paronomasia (an act of punning wordplay) on the terms *se prosternerent* ("prostrate themselves"), *prostrati* ("prostrate"), and *protestarentur* ("testify publicly")—the last two terms playing on the idea that, by prostrating themselves, the idols protest.

his displeasure and will all together come to destruction, just as happened to Pharaoh, the king of the Egyptians,[A]

A. Here the endings of *Ps.-Mt.* diverge considerably, as the parallel translations show. I have given the manuscript groupings in which the conclusions occur according to Gijsel's sigla. Gisjel observes that "The diversity of the conclusions poses a problem" ("La diversité des conclusions pose un problème"). He hypothesizes that the archetype of the A-text "presented a gap, an obscurity or an awkwardness, which prompted the revisers/copyists to intervene" ("présentait une lacune, une obscurité ou une maladresse, qui a incite les réviseurs-copistes à intervenir"). For the main text, Gijsel retains the conclusion from A^1a2, b, A^1c1, and e, because the manuscripts represented often give the more primitive (oldest) variants, and the brevity and abrupt ending seem to beg for the kinds of revisions found in the other witnesses. Yet his reasons for dismissing the other conclusions are shaky: the second for its explicit last statement; the third because it is difficult to explain why the other witnesses would not retain the echo of Matt 2:20; and the last because the doxology "is clearly secondary" ("est clairement secondaire"). He does not offer any further justification for any of these assertions, which seem to be value judgments rather than measured assessments of the evidence. In P, the conclusion is largely the same as in A^3a1 and j, but lacking in the final sentence referring to the "holy gospel." In Q, the conclusion is the same as in A^2b1, k, and A^4c1, with the doxology. It is also worth providing the conclusion in R: "'who by his unbelief pursued the children of Israel and with all of his army was drowned in the Red Sea. And for the children of Israel the waters were opened like a wall to the right and to the left.' (cf. Exod 14:8, 15:4, and 14:22) Then all the people of that city worshipped Jesus Christ, saying: 'Let us bless the God of heaven, who has given to us a great prophet in Israel.'" See Gijsel, *Libri de nativitate*, 478–80 n. 1. The statement in A^3a1 and j about *everything . . . the evangelist attested eloquently in the truthful holy gospel* is puzzling, since both the noun "evangelist" (*euangelistae*) and the verb "attested" (*protestati*) are given in the plural nominative case, but the phrase "truthful holy gospel" (*sacro euangelio ueridico*) is given in the singular case. Given the lack of any specific name(s) for the author(s) or gospel(s) being referred to, this is a rather ambiguous reference to one or more of the canonical Gospels.

A¹a2, b, A¹c1, and e

⁶who lived in those days when God performed great wonders ᴬ in Egypt and brought his people out by his mighty hand."ᴮ

g

⁶who was hardened in his heartᶜ from believing in all the wonders of God that were performed by Moses and Aaron in those days." ⁷Here ends the word.

A³a1 and j

⁶who disdained to listen to God."ᴰ Not much later, an angel said to Joseph, "Return to the land of Judah, for those who sought the life of the child are dead."ᴱ ⁷Then was fulfilled everything about Jesus that the evangelist attested eloquently in the truthful holy gospel.

A²b1, k, and A⁴c1

⁶who did not believe the many wonders and was drowned in the sea with all of his army."ᶠ ⁷Then all the people of that city believed in God and our Lord Jesus Christ and the Holy Spirit, to whom is honor and glory together with the Father and Holy Spirit forever and ever. Amen.

A. Cf. Ps 135:4
B. Cf. Exod 13:3

C. Cf. Exod 7:22

D. Cf. Num 15:31
E. Cf. Matt 2:20

F. Cf. Exod 14:28; Wis 10:19

3

The Pars altera

(From manuscripts of the Q-text)

25 (1) ¹Not much later, an angel said to Joseph, "Return to the land of Judah; those who sought the life of the child are dead."ᴬ

cf. Matt 2:20

26 (1) ¹And it came to pass that after the return of Jesus from Egypt, when he was in Galilee,ᴮ as he was just beginning his fourth year of age, one Sabbath day he began playing with other children along the bank of the Jordan.ᶜ ²Now then, when he had sat down, Jesus made for himself seven pools in the mud, to each of which he made trenches, by which, at his command, he brought water

---

A. Cf. the conclusion of *Ps.-Mt.* in A^3a1 and j.

B. *from Egypt . . . Galilee*: references to the return from Egypt and the holy family's residence in Galilee (not found in *Inf. Gos. Thom.*) are likely intended to bring this chapter into line with the preceding one, creating coherence between these episodes and *Ps.-Mt.* proper. The reference to Galilee is one of many place names added in the *pars altera* and extra episodes in Paris11867. Biblical geography, it seems, is of special interest to the translator of the Latin version of *Inf. Gos. Thom.* represented by the *pars altera*. A number of these geographical references indicate movements of the holy family to different locations during Jesus' childhood, which pose particular problems of chronology. For other instances, see chaps. 32, 36, 40, 41; and Paris 11867, chaps. 57 and 59.

C. *fourth year of age . . . Jordan*: in *Inf. Gos. Thom.*, Jesus' age is given as five years old, reference to the day being a Sabbath is not revealed until later, and the location is a rushing stream, not the River Jordan.

cf. *Inf. Gos. Thom.*
2:1
from the river into the pool and brought it back again.ᴬ ³Then one of those children,ᴮ a child of the devil, in the spirit of envy, closed the passage that supplied water to the pools and ruined the work that Jesus had done. ⁴Then Jesus said to him, "Woe to you, child of death, child of Satan! Do you destroy the works that I have done?"ᶜ ⁵And immediately he who had done it was dead.

cf. *Inf. Gos. Thom.*
3:1–3

(2) ⁶Then, with discordant voices the parents of the dead child called out against Mary and Joseph, saying to them, "Your child cursed our child, and he is dead." ⁷When Joseph and Mary had heard, immediately they went to Jesus because of the discord of the boy's parents and the gathering of the Jews.ᴰ ⁸But Joseph said to Mary in secret, "I do not dare to speak to him; but you admonish him and say, 'Why have you aroused the hatred of the people against us, so that we must endure the grievous hatred of the people?'"

⁹And when his mother had come to him, she solicited him, saying, "My Lord, what did he do to be killed?"

¹⁰He said, "He was worthy of death, because he destroyed the works that I had done."

A. While 26:1–2 derives from *Inf. Gos. Thom.* 2, this episode is also the basis of chaps. 27–28, which are closer to the source in parallels.

B. *one of those children:* in *Inf. Gos. Thom.* 3, the child is the son of the priest (sometimes called a scribe) Annas (as in chap. 28); the epithets used here to demonize the child are added, as is the detail of him being "in the spirit of envy" (*animo invido*).

C. *the works that I have done:* this question (*Opera quae operatus sum tu dissipas?*) and the reference to the these "works" in v. 3 are added, emphasizing a theological point about Jesus' divinity. With these additions, the implication is that the child not only destroys Jesus' pools but also rejects God's work.

D. *the gathering of the Jews:* this is the first reference of many to Jews and the Jewish people set in opposition to Jesus throughout the *pars altera* and the additions in Paris 11867. Many of these references are added, but some witnesses to the Greek *Inf. Gos. Thom.* include similar details (Greek S 2:3 and 6:2b; Greek A 2:1, 3; 5:1, 2; 6:2c; 8:1; and Greek D Prol:4; 4:1; 6:2c; and 8:1). Added references in the *pars altera* bring an uncomfortable anti-Judaism to the text, as it situates the Jewish people against Jesus, Mary, and Joseph. Sheingorn has discussed this issue in relation to illustrations of certain episodes from the *pars altera* in some medieval manuscripts ("Reshapings of the Childhood Miracles of Jesus"); and Dzon has discussed anti-Judaism in late medieval texts related to *Ps.-Mt.* (*Quest for the Christ Child, passim,* esp. 174–81).

(3) [11]Therefore, his mother questioned him, saying, "Do not, my Lord, because everyone will rise up against us."

[12]And so, not wanting to sadden his mother, with his right foot he kicked the dead child's rump[A] and said to him, "Arise, child of iniquity, for you are not worthy to enter the rest of my Father, because you destroyed the works that I had done." [13]Then he who had been dead arose and went away. [14]Jesus, truly, by his command, brought water through the aqueduct into the pools.[B]

27 (1) [1]And it came to pass after these things that, in the sight of everyone, Jesus took mud from the pools that he had made and from it he made twelve sparrows. [2]Now, it was the Sabbath when Jesus did this, and many children were with him. [3]Therefore, when a certain one of the Jews had seen him do this, he said to Joseph, "Joseph, do you not see the child Jesus working on the Sabbath, which is not lawful for him to do? For he has made twelve sparrows from the mud."

[4]When Joseph heard this, he scolded him, saying, "Why would you do this on the Sabbath—something that is not lawful to do?"

[5]But when Jesus heard Joseph, he clapped his hands and said to his sparrows, "Fly." [6]And at the sound of his command, they began to fly. [7]And there in front of all who stood by and saw and heard, he said to the birds, "Go and fly throughout the earth and throughout all the world and live." [8]Truly, when those who were present saw such signs, they were filled with great astonishment. [9]Some praised and admired him; others, indeed, disparaged him. And certain ones went to the chief priests[c] and to the leaders

cf. *Inf. Gos. Thom.* 2:2–5

A. *rump*: the word used is *nates*, commonly found (as it is here) in the plural form, from *natis*, meaning "rump" or "buttocks." In his *Etymologiae* 11.1.101, Isidore of Seville claims, "The *nates* are so called because we support ourselves (*inniti*) with them when we are seated."

B. *Then, with discordant voices . . . through the aqueduct into the pools* (26:6–14): in *Inf. Gos. Thom.*, the parents of the dead child confront Joseph (Mary is not included), but there is no extended dialogue between Joseph and Mary, nor is there an exchange between Mary and Jesus. The additions emphasize the relationship between Jesus and his parents, especially Mary. In some ways, this extends the Marian devotion already established in *Ps.-Mt.* proper.

C. *chief priests*: see the note about various terms for religious officials at *Ps.-Mt.* 2:2.

of the Pharisees and announced to them that Jesus, the son of Joseph, had performed great signs and wonders in the sight of all the people of Israel. ¹⁰And this was announced to the twelve tribes of Israel.ᴬ

28ᴮ (1) ¹Soon, again,ᶜ the son of Annas, a priest of the temple, who had come with Joseph, was holding a branch in his hand in the sight of all, and with great rage destroyed the pools that Jesus had made with his hands, and poured out the water from them that he had collected from the river. ²For indeed, he closed the very aqueduct through which the water had entered and afterward ruined it.

³Now when Jesus had seen these things, he said to that boy who had destroyed his pools, "O most evil seed of iniquity, O child of death, workshop of Satan,ᴰ truly the fruit of your seed will be without vigor, and your roots without moisture, and your branches dry, bearing no fruit."ᴱ ⁴And soon, in the sight of all, the boy withered up and was dead.

cf. *Inf. Gos. Thom.* 3

29 (1) ¹Then Joseph trembled and seized Jesus, and he went with him to his home and his mother came too. ²And behold, suddenly from the opposite direction a certain boy, himself also a worker of iniquity, threw himself into Jesus' shoulder at a run,

A. These last sentences (27:9–10) are unique to the *pars altera*. In *Inf. Gos. Thom.* 2, only children and a Pharisee witness the miracle. These additions both emphasize the public nature of Jesus' miracle (parallel with his public miracles in the canonical Gospels) and highlight Jesus' reputation throughout the whole land and peoples of Israel.

B. Cf. the episode in which Jesus curses a fig tree in Matt 21:18–20//Mark 11:12–14. The imagery of a tree and fruit also brings to mind the episode of the palm tree in *Ps.-Mt.* 20–21, in which Jesus blesses the tree rather than cursing it.

C. *again*: the use of this word (*iterum*) indicates that the compiler was aware of the repetition of episodes between chaps. 26 and 28.

D. As in chap. 26, the epithets used here to demonize the child—"most evil seed of iniquity" (*semen iniquitatis pessimum*), "child of death" (*fili mortis*), and "workshop of Satan" (*officina satanae*) are unique to the *pars altera*.

E. Throughout this speech, Jesus uses distinctly agricultural imagery: "fruit of your seed" (*fructus seminis*), "vigor" (*vigore*), "roots" (*radices*), "moisture" (*humore*), "branches" (*rami*), and "fruit" (*fructum*). Paired with the imagery of the water and aqueducts, this vocabulary is all the more striking.

wanting to mock him or to harm him if it were possible. ³But Jesus said to him, "You may not return whole from the way that you come." ⁴And suddenly he fell and was dead.

⁵And the parents of the dead child, who had seen what had happened, exclaimed, saying, "Where is this child from? It is apparent that every word that he speaks is true, and often it is fulfilled before he speaks."

⁶And the parents of the dead child came to Joseph and said to him, "Take that Jesus from this place; for he cannot live with us in this town. Or surely teach him to bless and not to curse."

cf. *Inf. Gos. Thom.* 4

⁷And so Joseph came to Jesus and began to admonish him, saying, "Why do you do such things? Already many, suffering, are against you and hate us because of you, and we endure the distress of the people because of you."

⁸Responding, Jesus said to Joseph, "No one is a wise son except he whom his father instructs according to the knowledge of his time, and the curse of one's own father hurts no one except evil-doers."ᴬ ⁹Then they were gathered against Jesus and were accusing him to Joseph. When Joseph saw this, he was greatly terrified, being afraid of the violence and discord of the people of Israel. ¹⁰In the same hour, Jesus seized the dead child by the ear and lifted him from the earth in the sight of everyone and they saw Jesus speaking with him just as a father with his son. And his spirit returned to him and he revived.ᴮ And all were amazed.

cf. *Inf. Gos. Thom.* 5:1

A. *No one is a wise son . . . except evil-doers:* this proverbial statement is not particularly close to the surviving Greek versions of *Inf. Gos. Thom.* 5:1, but Burke notes that "The wide variation in the sources and the unintelligible words in [the manuscripts] render the original reading uncertain" (*De Infantia Iesu,* 309 n. 1).

B. *he revived:* Jesus does not revive the boy in *Inf. Gos. Thom.* Instead, after Jesus rebukes Joseph, he causes the crowd gathered against him to become blind, and Joseph takes him by the ear, only earning further rebuke from Jesus. *Ps.-Mt.* thus emphasizes Jesus' mercy rather than anger and rebuke toward Joseph. This is one change among several in the *pars altera* and other additions to *Ps.-Mt.* that shift negativity away from Joseph, often redirecting it toward the Jewish people. See also the episode in Paris 11867, chap. 61.

30 (1) ¹Now, a certain Jewish master[A] named Zacchaeus[B] heard Jesus speaking such words, and seeing that there was insurmountable knowledge of power in him, he was suffering, and he began to speak against Joseph without discipline and foolishly and without fear.[C] ²And he said,[D] "Do you not want to give your son to me so that he might be instructed in human knowledge and fear? ³But I see that you and Mary want to value your son more than the traditions of the elders of the people. ⁴For it is proper that you honor the priests of the entire church of Israel more,[E] both so that he might have mutual love for the children and so that he might be taught Jewish doctrine among them."

(2) ⁵To this, Joseph said, on the contrary, "And who is it who would be able to keep and to instruct this child? But if you are able to keep and to instruct him, we in no way prohibit him from being instructed by you in the things that are learned by all."

A. *Jewish master:* like the terminology used for Israelite religious officials (see the note at *Ps.-Mt.* 2:2), the terminology used for teachers in the *pars altera* and Paris 11867 is complex and varied. The term used here (*magister*) translates the Greek καθηγητής ("teacher" or "guide"), and is probably meant to evoke the idea of a rabbi, as in the New Testament. The detail about him being Jewish is added. In *Ps.-Mt.*, the term *doctores populi* is used ("doctors of the people," 16:3; cf. *scribas populi* in Matt 2:4). In the *pars altera* and Paris 11867, the most frequently used term is *magister* (30:1; 31:1, 3, 20; 38:3, 5; 39:8; 60:1–2, 5–8; and 63:4)—sometimes even used for Jesus (31:20 and 63:4)—which appears once as *magister legis* ("master of the law," in 31:11); other terms include *legis doctor* ("doctor of the Law," 31:1) or *doctor* (60:4), *praeceptor* ("instructor," 31:5) or *praeceptor legis* ("instructor of the Law," in 30:6, twice), and the medieval *didascalus* ("teacher," 31:6; 39:3; and 39:7). The present translation seeks to capture this variance in the terminology.

B. *Zacchaeus:* manuscript witnesses present a discrepancy concerning the name of this teacher: in Q^4a2, *Zachyas*; in P^3a2, *Zachias*; and in R^2b1, *Zachemeus, Zacheus,* and *Zachaeus.*

C. *seeing . . . without fear: Inf. Gos. Thom.* says only that Zacchaeus "was greatly amazed" (ἐθαύμασεν σφόδρα) when he heard Jesus speaking.

D. This speech (30:2–4) is greatly expanded from the version in *Inf. Gos. Thom.* with details, including mentions of Mary, traditions of the elders, "the priests of the entire church of Israel" (*presbyteros totius ecclesiae Israel*), and "Jewish doctrine" (*iudaica . . . doctrina*).

E. *priests of the entire church of Israel:* the term *presbyteros* transliterates the Greek term πρεσβύτερος ("elder" or "old man"), which took on the ecclesiastical meaning of priest in late antiquity. The extended phrase seems to create a typological link between the community of Israelite priests and the later establishment of the Christian Church.

[6]When Jesus heard what Zacchaeus said, he responded to him and said, "Teacher of the Law: what you spoke about just now and all that you have named, are properly preserved by those who are instructed according to human institutions; but I am outside of your gates, because I have no fleshly parent.[A] [7]You who read the Law and are instructed in it, you abide in the Law; I, however, was before the Law. [8]But since you think you have no equal in teaching,[B] you will be instructed by me, since no one else is able to teach beyond those things that you have named. [9]For the one who is worthy, truly he is the one who is able. [10]For when I am exalted on the earth, I will make an end to every mention of your genealogy. [11]You are ignorant about when you were born,[C] but I alone know when you were born and for how long your life on earth will last."[D]

cf. Ps 45:11

(3) [12]Then all who heard these words disclosed were astonished and called out saying, "Oh, oh, oh, this great wonder and wonderful mystery! Never have we heard anything like it. [13]Never has it been heard by anyone else, nor has it been said or heard at any time by prophets, nor by Pharisees, nor by grammarians.[E] [14]We know where he was born and he is barely five years old; so from where does he speak these words?"

A. *parent*: the term used here for "parent" (*parens*) may refer to any parent generally, although the sense here, Christologically, does seem to imply a reference to God as Father.

B. *teaching*: the Latin word used here (*doctrina*) means teaching in a general sense, but from late antiquity onward, it also gained a more theological meaning, as in "doctrine." Notably, Christian doctrine was a hot topic of late antiquity and the Middle Ages, and this episode addresses some of the same issues of Christology debated at the time.

C. The numbers of nouns and verbs in Jesus' comments on the teachers' births and deaths shift throughout this sentence: in the first clause, they are second-person singular (*natus es*); in the second, they are plural (*nati estis*); and, in the last, second-person singular again (*vita vestra est*)—although *vestra* could be singular or plural.

D. In *Inf. Gos. Thom.* 6:2b, the latter part of this speech ("But since . . . how long your life on earth will last" 30:8–11) is directed at Joseph, not Zacchaeus.

E. *grammarians*: the use of the word *grammatica* is particularly interesting: in Classical Latin, this word is mainly used to denote the discipline of grammar, one of the seven liberal arts; in medieval Latin, it also becomes used as a word for a teacher of grammar, with the earliest attestations appearing around the seventh and eighth centuries (for example, in the works of Aldhelm and Alcuin).

[15]The Pharisees responded, "We have never heard such words spoken by a child so young."[A]

(4) [16]And responding, Jesus said to them,[B] "You wonder that such things are said by a child? Then why do you not believe me in what I have said to you? [17]Just because I said to you that I know when you were born, you all wonder. [18]I will say greater things to you, so that you really wonder. [19]I have seen Abraham, whom you call your father, and I have spoken with him, and he has seen me." [20]And hearing this, they were struck silent, and no one dared to speak. [21]And Jesus said to them,[C] "I have been among you with children, and you did not know me. [22]I have spoken to you as with wise men, but you did not understand my voice, because you are less than I am[D] and of little faith."

John 8:56-58

cf. Inf. Gos. Thom.
6:1-2e

31 (1) [1]Again, Master Zacchaeus, a doctor of the Law, spoke to Joseph and Mary,[E] "Give the boy to me, and I will hand him over to Master Levi,[F] who will teach him letters and instruct him." [2]Then Joseph and Mary, soothing Jesus, led him to school, so that he might be taught letters by old Levi. [3]When he had entered, he was silent. And Master Levi said one letter to Jesus, and beginning with the first letter *aleph* he said to him, "Repeat." [4]But Jesus was silent and responded with nothing. [5]At that the instructor Levi was angry, and seizing a storax-tree branch,[G] struck him on the head.

A. This statement by the Pharisees is unique to the *pars altera*.

B. This speech (30:16–19) is different in the other early versions of *Inf. Gos. Thom.* (Syriac, Georgian, and Ethiopic), but they all emphasize unbelief and a Trinitarian theology implied by Jesus aligning himself with God's knowledge. In distinction from the others, in this version Jesus claims to have spoken with Abraham.

C. *And Jesus said to them . . . of little faith:* in the other early versions of *Inf. Gos. Thom.* Jesus claims to have been playing or joking with the crowd and indicates their ignorance; in this version, he disparages the crowd's lack of knowledge, understanding, and faith at his words.

D. *because you are less than I am:* this phrase may be taken in a number of ways, as thematically established in the preceding scene: regarding Jesus' intellect, age, or general significance.

E. *Mary:* Mary does not appear here in other versions of *Inf. Gos. Thom.*

F. *Master Levi:* in *Inf. Gos. Thom.*, Zacchaeus remains the teacher through all of chaps. 6–8.

G. *storax-tree branch:* this reference to a specific branch of a tree is unique

(2) [6]Now, Jesus said to the teacher Levi, "Why do you strike me? [7]In truth you should know that the one who is struck teaches the one striking him more than he learns from him. For I am able to teach you what you are saying. [8]But all these who speak and hear are blind, like a resounding gong or a clanging cymbal, in which there is no sense of the things that are understood in their sound."

cf. 1 Cor 13:1

[9]And furthermore, Jesus said to Zacchaeus,[A] "Every letter from *aleph* up to *tau*[B] is discerned by arrangement. Therefore, say first what *tau* is, and I will say to you what *aleph* is." [10]And again Jesus said to them, "Whoever does not know *aleph*, how are they able to say *tau*? Hypocrites! Say first what is *aleph*, and then I will believe you when you say *beth*." [11]And Jesus began to ask the names of each letter and said, "Let the master of the Law say what the first letter is, or why it has many *triangles, gradations, subacutes, mediates, obducts, products, erects, strata, curvistrates*."[C] [12]Now, when Levi heard this, he was astonished at such an arrangement of the names of the letters.

cf. Inf. Gos. Thom. 6:2f–4

---

to the *pars altera*. The word used, *storatinam*, is a variant of later Latin *styracinus* or *storacinus*. A large number of tall shrubs or short trees belong to the genus *storax* (or *styrax*), indigenous to warm, temperate, and tropical regions in the Northern Hemisphere. They are often known for their odor, and have been used for making perfumes, incense, and medicine since antiquity. Storax plants continue to grow in the Near East. See the Old Latin and Vulgate versions of Gen 43:11 and Eccl 24:21 (24:15 in other versions). The addition of this detail seems consistent with other late antique references about the Near East, such as place names. Pliny the Elder, who describes the properties of the plant at some length, claims that the best variety of storax comes from "the region of Syria closest to Judaea" (*proxima Iudaeae Syria*) (*Nat.* 12.124–25).

A. *Zacchaeus:* here the text reintroduces Zacchaeus, although Jesus was seemingly alone with Levi before. This may represent some confusion about the masters (either by the translator or later scribes), due to the unique change of Jesus' master from Zacchaeus to Levi at the beginning of this chapter.

B. *tau:* Q[4]a2 has *thet*.

C. Tischendorf argues that this passage is corrupt, and it is clearly confused at the least. In comparison with the Greek *Inf. Gos. Thom.* 6:4, it is clear that the Latin translator attempted to understand the description of the form of the letter *aleph* through some knowledge of geometry. In a note to his translation, Walker claims that the passage refers to the pentalpha, pentangle, or Solomon's Seal, which appears in a variety of magical books from antiquity, especially those associated with the Pythagoreans (44 n. 3).

(3) [13]Then in the hearing of all he began to call out and to say, "Should this one live on the earth? Certainly he is worthy to be hanged on a great cross.[A] [14]For he is able to extinguish fire and mock other punishments. [15]I think that he lived before the flood and was born before the deluge.[B] [16]For what womb carried him? Or what mother birthed him? Or what breasts nursed him?[C] [17]I flee before him; for I am not able to endure the words from his mouth; no, my heart is astonished to hear such words. [18]Indeed I think that no man is able to follow his words unless God is with him. [19]Now I, miserable, have given myself up to be mocked by him. [20]For when I thought I had a student, I found my master, although I did not know him. [21]What may I say? I am not able to endure the words of this boy; soon I will flee from this town, because I am not able to understand these things. [22]I, an old man, am defeated by a child, because I am not able to find either beginning or end of what he asserts. For it is difficult to discover the beginning of him.[D] [23]Certainly I tell you—I am not lying—that before my eyes the working of this boy and the beginning of his speech and the conclusion of his intention appear to have nothing in common with humanity.[E] [24]Because of this, I do not know whether he is a magician[F] or a god, nor do I certainly know if an

A. *hanged on a great cross:* this reference to Jesus' crucifixion is not included the Greek *Inf. Gos. Thom.* 7:2, but the Ethiopic states, "truly a great cross is destined for whoever will be able to reveal this infant and teach him."

B. *I think . . . before the deluge:* this sentence diverges from the Greek *Inf. Gos. Thom.* 7:2, which has "Perhaps this child existed before the creation of the world"; but other early versions (Ethiopic, Georgian, and Syriac) also mention the flood.

C. *what breasts nursed him?:* this question is unique to the *pars altera.* In some ways it echoes Luke 11:27, as at 58:8 in Paris 11867.

D. *the beginning of him:* the reference to Jesus' "beginning" (*initium*) may call to mind the Arian controversy of the fourth century. The teacher's statement that he can find no "beginning of him" seems to be offered here as foreshadowing the orthodox position (which won the day at the first Council of Nicaea) over and against the Arian position, frequently summarized with the slogan "there was a time when he was not," signifying that Jesus did indeed have a "beginning."

E. *I am not able . . . with humanity:* this portion of the speech is unique to the *pars altera.* Other witnesses to *Inf. Gos. Thom.* vary greatly in this passage.

F. *magician:* mention of Jesus possibly being a magician is unique to the *pars altera.* Dzon suggests that this detail might have been added during in

angel of God speaks in him. [25]Whence he exists, or whence he came, or who he will be in the future, I do not know."[A]

cf. *Inf. Gos. Thom.* 7

(4) [26]Then Jesus, smiling at him with a joyful face, spoke with authority to all the children of Israel[B] standing by and listening, [27]"Let the unfruitful bear fruit, and let the blind see, and let the lame walk right, and let the poor enjoy the good things, and let the dead be revived, so that everyone might return to a renewed state and remain in him who is the root of life and perpetual sweetness."[C] [28]When the child Jesus had said this, immediately all were restored who had fallen under evil illness. [29]And they did not dare to say any more to him or to hear any more from him.

cf. Luke 7:22//Matt 11:5

cf. *Inf. Gos. Thom.* 8

32 (1) [1]After these things, Joseph and Mary went with Jesus from that place to the city of Nazareth;[D] and he lived there with his parents. [2]And there, when it was a Sabbath,[E] while Jesus was playing with the children on the roof of a certain home, it happened that one of the children pushed[F] another from the roof to the earth and he was dead. [3]And although they had not seen it, the parents of the dead child called out against Joseph and Mary, saying, "Your son threw our son to the earth, and he is dead." [4]But Jesus was silent and responded with nothing to them.[G]

---

the high Middle Ages because of anxieties about magic and related claims in contemporary literature about Jesus being a sorcerer (*Quest for the Christ Child*, 156–57).

A. *Whence he exists . . . I do not know:* the last sentence of this speech is unique to the *pars altera*.

B. *children of Israel:* reference to the crowd (*filiis Israel*) is unique to the *pars altera*.

C. *Let the unfruitful bear fruit . . . and perpetual sweetness* (31:27–28): this speech is different in all of the early versions of *Inf. Gos. Thom.* This version in the *pars altera* stands out for its references to the poor and dead, as well as the imagery of renewal linked with God as a root and his sweetness.

D. *Nazareth:* the move to Nazareth is new to the *pars altera*.

E. *Sabbath:* reference to the Sabbath is otherwise found only in the Syriac version of *Inf. Gos. Thom.*

F. *pushed:* in *Inf. Gos. Thom.* 9:1, the child is not pushed off but falls, after which the other children leave Jesus alone.

G. In *Inf. Gos. Thom.* 9:2, the parents directly confront Jesus, who denies pushing the child off the roof.

[5]Now, Joseph and Mary went to Jesus quickly, and his mother questioned him,[A] saying, "My Lord, tell me if you threw him to the earth."

[6]And immediately Jesus descended from the roof to the earth and spoke to the boy by his name, Zeno. [7]And he responded to him, "Lord."

[8]And Jesus said to him, "Did I cast you down to the earth from the roof?"

[9]And he said, "No, Lord."

[10]And the parents of the boy who was dead wondered, and honored Jesus for the miracle he had done. [11]And Joseph and Mary went with Jesus from that place to Jericho.[B]

cf. *Inf. Gos. Thom.* 9

33 (1) [1]Now Jesus was six years old,[C] and his mother sent him with a jug to the well to draw water with the children. [2]It happened, after he had drawn water, that a certain child struck him and dashed the jug down and shattered it.[D] [3]But Jesus stretched out the cloak that he was wearing, and in his cloak took up as much water as had been in the jug, and carried it to his mother. [4]When she saw it, she wondered, and contemplated, and kept all these things in her heart.

cf. Luke 2:19; *Inf. Gos. Thom.* 11

34[E] (1) [1]Again, on a certain day, he went out into a field and took a tiny bit of wheat from his mother's storehouse, and sowed it himself. [2]And it germinated, and grew, and multiplied excessively. [3]And, finally, it came to pass that he harvested it himself and collected three kors of fruit from it,[F] and he himself gave it to a great many of his own people.

cf. *Inf. Gos. Thom.* 12

A. *questioned him:* Joseph and Mary questioning Jesus is unique to the *pars altera*.

B. *Jericho:* the move to Jericho is unique to the *pars altera*.

C. *six years old:* in the Greek A, B, and D recensions of *Inf. Gos. Thom.* 11, Jesus also is six years old, but in Greek S (chap. 10 in this recension), he is seven years old.

D. *a certain child struck him:* in *Inf. Gos. Thom.* 11:1, Jesus is jostled because of the crowd, not struck deliberately.

E. This episode is generally parallel with *Inf. Gos. Thom.* 12, though in the Greek text Jesus sows with Joseph and there is no mention of Mary; cf. the episode in Paris 11867, chap. 55.

F. *three kors:* a *kor* was a unit of measuring volume, containing 6.25 bushels. It is mentioned throughout the Bible; for an example from the Vulgate,

35ᴬ (1) ¹There is a road that goes out of Jericho and extends to the River Jordan, to the place where the children of Israel crossed over; it is said that the Ark of the Covenant resided there.ᴮ ²Now Jesus was eight years old, and he went out of Jericho and went to the Jordan. ³And along the road there was a cave near the bank of the Jordan where a lioness nursed her cubs; and no one was able to walk on the road without fear. ⁴But Jesus, going from Jericho, knowing that the lioness had birthed her children in that cave, entered into it in the sight of all. ⁵Indeed when the lions saw Jesus, they ran together to him and worshipped him. ⁶And Jesus sat in the cave and the lion cubs ran about around his feet, fawning and playing with him. ⁷Indeed, the older lions, bowing their heads, stood at a distance and worshipped him, and wagged their tails before him.

⁸Then the people, who stood at a distance, not seeing Jesus, said, "Unless he or his parents had done grave sins, he would not offer himself to the lions." ⁹And when the people considered this among themselves and endured great mourning, behold, suddenly, in front of the people, Jesus exited the cave and the lions went before him and the lion cubs played among themselves before his feet. ¹⁰Indeed, Jesus' parents, bowing their heads, stood at a distance and observed; and likewise, the people stood at a distance because of the lions, for they did not dare to come near to them.

¹¹Then Jesus began to speak to the people, "How much better than you are the beasts,ᶜ who recognize and glorify their Lord, while you human beings, who are made in the image and likeness

cf. Josh 3:14–17

---

see Ezek 45:14.

A. This episode is not in *Inf. Gos. Thom.* and seems to be unique to the *pars altera*. In some ways, it is similar to the episode of the wild animals venerating Jesus and his family in *Ps.-Mt.* 19 and perhaps derives from the same tradition. Again, it evokes the medieval tradition of the *Physiologus* (see commentary on chap. 19).

B. References to Jericho and the River Jordan where the Israelites crossed attest to the compiler's interest in biblical geography. Like the more famous crossing of the Red Sea in Exodus, in Josh 3:14–17 the River Jordan is divided through the power of the Ark of the Covenant so that the Israelites cross over on dry land; cf. 36:1.

C. *beasts:* the author uses the word *bestia* here and in the next verse; see note on 2:6 and cf. 35:12.

of God, are ignorant. [12]The beasts recognize me and are tamed; humans see me and do not understand."[A]

36 (1) [1]After these things, Jesus crossed the Jordan with the lions in the sight of all, and the water of the Jordan was divided to the right and to the left. [2]Then he said to the lions, so that all might hear, "Go in peace, and may you hurt no one; but neither may a human harm you, while you return from where you came." [3]And bidding him farewell, not with voices but with their bodies, they went away to their places. [4]Jesus, indeed, returned to his mother.

37 (1) [1]And since Joseph was a carpenter,[B] and from wood he crafted nothing but oxen yokes and ploughs and tools for tilling the earth and cultivation, and also made wooden beds,[C] [2]it happened that a certain young man commissioned him to make a pallet six cubits long. [3]And Joseph ordered his servant[D] to cut wood with an iron saw according to the measurement he had sent. [4]But he did not keep to the defined measurements; rather, he made one piece of wood shorter than the other. [5]And Joseph began to consider with anger what was to be done about this.

(2) [6]And when Jesus saw him so disturbed in his thoughts, because this was an impossible task, he spoke to him with a comforting voice, saying, [7]"Come, let us hold onto the ends of each piece of wood, and put them together end to end, and level them, and pull them toward ourselves, for we will be able to make them equal."

[8]Then Joseph complied with the one giving orders; for he knew that (Jesus) was able to do whatever he wished.[E] [9]And Jo-

---

A. Cf. *Acts of John* 60–61 where, after bedbugs obey the apostle John's command and abandon the bed he is trying to sleep in, he proclaims: "This animal, having heard the voice of a human being, remained still in itself and did not transgress; we, hearing the voice of God, disobey the commandments and are slothful. For how long?" (trans. adapted from Spittler, *Animals in the Apocryphal Acts*, 97; see also Spittler's discussion at 96–110).

B. *Inf. Gos. Thom.* 13:1 begins by stating also that Jesus was eight years old.

C. References to the tools and beds are unique to the *pars altera*.

D. *servant*: no mention is made of a servant in *Inf. Gos. Thom.*; instead, Joseph is the one who cuts the wood incorrectly.

E. *For he knew . . . whatever he wished*: this second clause is unique to the *pars altera*.

seph seized the ends of the wood and pulled them toward the wall and in proportion to each other, and Jesus held the other end of the wood and pulled the shorter piece of wood toward himself and made it equal to the longer piece of wood. [10]And he said to Joseph, "Go to work, and do what you have promised to do."[A] [11]And Joseph did what he had promised.

cf. *Inf. Gos. Thom.* 13

38 (1) [1]It came to pass a second time that Joseph and Mary[B] were asked by the people that Jesus be taught his letters at school. [2]They did not refuse to do so, and according to the command of the elders they brought him to a master so that he might be taught in human knowledge. [3]And then the master began to teach him domineeringly, saying, "Say *alpha*."

[4]But Jesus said to him, "You tell me first what *beta* is, and I will tell you what *alpha* is."[C] [5]And at this, the enraged master hit Jesus, and soon after he hit him, he was dead.

(2) [6]And Jesus returned to his mother's home. [7]Now, being afraid, Joseph called Mary to him and said to her, "Truly you should know that my spirit is sad even to death because of this boy. For it is possible that at any moment somebody might strike this boy in malice and he might die."

[8]But Mary said in reply, "Man of God, do not believe that this is possible. With deep security believe that he who sent him to be born among humans will guard him from all malice himself and in his name will preserve him from evil."[D]

cf. *Inf. Gos. Thom.* 14:1–3

39 (1) [1]Again, a third time, the Jews asked Mary[E] and Joseph that they might bring him through flattery to another master for more learning. [2]And so, fearing the people and the insolence of the princes and the threats of the priests, they brought him again to the school, knowing that it was not possible for him, who had

---

A. *Go to work, and do what you have promised to do:* in *Inf. Gos. Thom.* Jesus says, "Do not be distressed but do what you wish."

B. *Mary:* Mary once again is added to the story. In *Inf. Gos. Thom.* 14:1, Joseph makes the decision to take Jesus to school again.

C. *alpha . . . what alpha is* (38:3–4): unlike the previous episode (chap. 31), the letters here are Greek, not Hebrew.

D. This dialogue between Joseph and Mary (38:7–8) is added.

E. *Mary:* Mary is not present in *Inf. Gos. Thom.*

perfect knowledge from God alone, to learn anything from a human being.[A]

(2) [3]Now when Jesus entered the school, led by the Holy Spirit,[B] he took the book from the hand of the teacher teaching the Law, [4]and in the sight and hearing of all the people, he began to read—indeed, not what was written in their book, but speaking in the Spirit of the living God,[C] just like a river of water might come from a living fountain, and the fountain would always remain filled.[D] [5]And thus with power he began to teach the people the mighty works of the living God, so that even the master himself fell to the ground and worshipped him. [6]For the heart of the people who sat together and heard him saying such things was turned in astonishment.

cf. 2 Cor 3:3

[7]But when Joseph heard, he went quickly to Jesus, fearing that the teacher himself was dead. [8]When the master saw him, he said to him, "You gave me not a student but a master; and who can restrain his words?" [9]Then was fulfilled what was said by the psalmist: "The river of God is filled with water. You have prepared their food, for so is its preparation."[E]

Ps 64:10; cf. Inf. Gos. Thom. 15

40 (1) [1]After these things, Joseph left with Mary and Jesus so that they might arrive at Capernaum by the sea,[F] because of the malice of his human adversaries.[G] [2]And when Jesus was living in Capernaum, there was in the city a certain person named Joseph, an exceedingly rich man. [3]But withering from infirmity, he died;

A. *the Jews asked Mary . . . from a human being*: in *Inf. Gos. Thom.* 15:1, the episode begins with a teacher approaching Joseph with a request to have Jesus taught by him, and Mary is not present.

B. *led by the Holy Spirit*: this is unique to the *pars altera*.

C. *Spirit of the living God*: the epithet *Deus vivens* is common throughout the Hebrew Bible (see, for example, Deut 5:26; Josh 3:10; and 1 Sam 17:26, 36), but the addition of the Spirit as here (*spiritu dei vivi*) is made in 2 Cor 3:3.

D. *just like a river . . . remain filled*: this is unique to the *pars altera*.

E. Reference to Ps 64:10 and emphasis on Jesus' fulfillment of this verse are unique to the *pars altera*.

F. *Capernaum by the sea*: another movement of location, especially significant since the source of this episode is unknown. For another reference to "Capernaum by the sea," see *Ps.-Mt.* 10:1.

G. *human adversaries*: this detail again emphasizes the adversarial relationship between the Jewish people and Jesus.

and having died, he was laid on a pallet. [4]Now when Jesus heard mourning and weeping and wailing in the city over his death, he said to Joseph, "Why don't you offer the benefit of your favor to this man, who is called by your name?"

[5]To which Joseph responded, "How is it in my power or ability to offer any benefit to him?"

[6]To which Jesus said, "Take the cloth that is over your head and go and place it over the face of the dead man and say to him, 'May Christ save you.' Immediately he will be saved and the dead man will rise from his pallet."

[7]When Joseph heard, immediately he went, running at Jesus' command, and entered the home of the dead man, and placed the cloth that he had over his head over the face of the one lying on the pallet, and said, "May Jesus save you."[A] [8]Immediately the dead man rose from the couch and began to ask who Jesus was.

41 (1) [1]And they went into the city of Capernaum from the city that is called Bethlehem,[B] and Joseph was with Mary in her home, and Jesus with them.[C] [2]And on a certain day Joseph called his firstborn son, James,[D] and sent him into the vegetable garden to collect vegetables for making a sauce.[E] [3]And Jesus followed his brother James into the garden, but Joseph and Mary did not know this.[F] [4]While James collected vegetables, suddenly a viper

A. *"May Jesus save you"*: the change in speech here is significant: Jesus tells Joseph to say *"Salvet te Christus,"* but Joseph instead says, *"Salvet te Iesus."*

B. *into the city . . . Bethlehem*: Tischendorf notes that this sentence is corrected in the manuscript, which originally read *in civitatem Capharnaum quae vocatur Bethleem* ("into the city of Capernaum, which is called Bethlehem"). In the context of this narrative among the other episodes, both readings are non sequiturs, since the holy family is already in Capernaum in the previous chapter.

C. *Joseph was with Mary . . . and Jesus with them*: direct mention of Joseph, Mary, and Jesus and their arrangement as a family is unique to the *pars altera*. This brings to light the subject of Joseph as Jesus' adoptive father and his other children.

D. *James*: the relationship of James to Jesus (stepbrothers) is a continuation of *Prot. Jas.* 9:8; 17:2, 5; 25:1 (seen also in *Ps.-Mt.* prol.; 8:11, 25) but is not made explicit in *Inf. Gos. Thom.*

E. *vegetables*: in *Inf. Gos. Thom.* 16:1 James goes out to the woods to collect sticks for the fire.

F. Explicit mention of James being Jesus' brother is unique to the *pars*

exited a hole and struck Jacob's hand, and because of the great pain he began to call out. [5]And failing quickly, he began to say with a bitter voice, "Alas, alas, an evil viper struck my hand."[A]

(2) [6]But Jesus, standing in the opposite direction, at the bitter voice ran to James and held his hand, and did nothing but blow on James' hand and cool it. [7]And immediately James was healthy and the serpent was dead. [8]And Joseph and Mary did not know what he had done; but at James' cry and Jesus' command, they ran to the garden, and found the serpent already dead and James well restored to health.[B]

cf. Inf. Gos. Thom. 16

42 (1) [1]Now, when Joseph went to a feast with his children— cf. Mark 6:3//Matt 13:55–56 James, Joseph, Juda, and Simeon, and his two daughters—Jesus went with them, along with his mother Mary and her sister, Mary Cleopas,[C] [2]whom the Lord God gave to her father Cleopas and her mother Anna, because they offered Mary the mother of Jesus to the Lord. [3]And this Mary was called by the same name, Mary, for her parents' consolation.[D]

(2) [4]And when they gathered together, Jesus sanctified and blessed them, and he first began to eat and to drink, for none of them dared to eat or to drink, nor to sit at the table or to break the bread, until he, sanctifying them, did so first.[E] [5]And if by chance he was absent, they waited until he did this. [6]And when he wanted to come to dinner, Joseph and Mary and his brothers, the children of Joseph, came. [7]Indeed, these brothers, having his life as a lamp before their eyes, observed and feared him. [8]And when Jesus slept, sometimes in the day and sometimes at night, the brightness of God shone upon him. [9]To whom be all praise and glory forever and ever. Amen. Amen.

---

altera, as is the ignorance of Mary (who is not mentioned at all in *Inf. Gos. Thom.*) and Joseph about Jesus' departure.

A. James' speech is unique to the *pars altera*.

B. This last passage about Joseph and Mary discovering the miracle is unique to the *pars altera*.

C. *Cleopas*: manuscripts give the name as *Cleophas* (cf. *Cleophas* in the *Trinubium Annae*), although the name is given as *Clopas* (Κλωπᾶ) in John 19:25.

D. Cf. the *Trinubium Annae* and the relationships explained there.

E. *sanctifying them*: in many ways, these details parallel the Last Supper in Mark 14:12–26 par. and John 13:1–17:26.

4

Later Additions

*(From Paris, Bibliothèque nationale de France,
lat. 11867)*[A]

53 [1]It happened at a certain time that many boys were following Jesus and playing together. [2]But a certain father of a family,[B] very angry because his son ran around with Jesus, so that his son might follow Jesus no more, imprisoned him in a tower most strong and most solid, [3]in which there was no door, window, opening, or any entrance or door to exit, and one little, narrow window just small enough to introduce light, and a secret, unmarked entrance. [4]The father went away; and it happened that one day Jesus returned

---

A. The Latin in Paris 11867 is particularly difficult because of its non-standard grammar, and, in many cases, the text of this manuscript is corrupt or problematic. Dimier-Paupert's text, in fact, is not a collated edition, but an uncorrected transcription of this single manuscript; the present translation thus reflects only readings in this witness and not a full collation of all manuscripts containing these same added episodes. Chapter numbers follow Dimier-Paupert's divisions, which differ from the numbering established by Tischendorf and Gijsel for *Ps.-Mt.* proper and the *pars altera*; verse numbers are added. References to the Latin *Inf. Gos. Thom.* used for these additions are based on the numbering of the Greek D recension in Burke, *De Infantia Iesu*, 391–451.

B. *father of a family*: this term (*pater familias*) is used for the head and leader of a Roman household—the oldest male of the family who was also a citizen. As such, he held a certain amount of status, legal privilege, and power both in the family specifically and the community more generally. The term *pater familias* is used here as well as in 53:4, 8; and 54:1.

to that place along with his playmates. [5]Hearing them, the imprisoned boy called through the window, saying, "Jesus, most beloved friend, I heard your voice and my spirit cheered and I am renewed. Why do you forsake me in prison?"

cf. Ps 21:2;
Matt 27:46

[6]Jesus said back to him, "Stretch out to me your hand or your finger through the window." [7]When he did it, Jesus seized his hand and drew the child who had followed him through the very narrow window. And Jesus said to him, "Recognize the power of God, and in your old age retell what God did for you in your childhood." [8]When the father saw him, first he went to the door and saw all was deserted and secure, and he stood there crying out that it was a phantom, and his eyes were closed so he might not recognize the divine power.

54 [1]The same father, Joseph, one of the most important men among the magistrates of the synagogue and Pharisees and scribes and doctors,[A] complained about Jesus, who performed novel miracles for the people, so much so that he was honored before God. [2]And he said excitedly, "Behold, our children, and my son among them, are following Jesus all the way to the field of Sichar." [3]Angry, he seized a club to beat Jesus and followed him all the way to a mountain that adjoins a plain growing beans. [4]Now,[B] Jesus escaped his anger by making a leap from the ridge of the mountains to a place that was as far from the mountain as a bow shoots an arrow. [5]When wanting to make a similar leap, the other children followed headlong, breaking their legs and arms and necks. [6]Because Mary and Joseph faced grave complaints about this, Jesus healed all of them and restored them even stronger. [7]When the chief priest of the synagogue[C] (who was also the father of the imprisoned boy) saw, together with all who were present at this sight, he worshipped God Adonai.[D] [8]So the place in which Jesus made his leap is called "Lord's Leap" still today.

A. *magistrates . . . doctors*: cf. the similar list of men that Herod consults in *Ps.-Mt.* 16:3.

B. Here (54:3–7), as elsewhere, Dimier-Paupert's text presents minimal punctuation, resulting in run-on sentences, often linked by conjunctions and particles. For sense, I have broken up these sentences.

C. *chief priest of the synagogue*: the term *archisynagogus* transliterates the Greek term ἀρχισυνάγωγος.

D. *God Adonai*: in the Hebrew Bible, Adonai is used as a proper name for

55 ¹Now it came to pass, when it was the time of sowing, that Joseph went out to sow wheat, and Jesus followed him. ²When Joseph began to sow, Jesus stretched out his hand and took as much wheat as he was able to hold in his fist, and he scattered it at the edge the field.ᴬ ³Joseph then went at harvest time to harvest his crops. Jesus went so that he might collect from him the grain that he had sown, and it made a hundred pecks of the best wheat. Three or four other fields did not yield such a quantity. ⁴And he said to Joseph, "Call to us the poor and widows and orphans and let the wheat of my sowing be distributed to them." And thus it was done. ⁵And again, in its distribution, it took on a very great and excellent increase, from which the poor were refreshed.ᴮ ⁶They were blessing the Lord with all their hearts, saying that the Lord God of Israel had visited his people.

cf. *Inf. Gos. Thom.* [LT] 12:1–2

56 ¹Now it came to pass again one day at the time of sowing, (that) when Jesus crossed a field of rye, he saw a certain farmer sowing a certain type of legume that is called a chickpea in a field, which is said to be the field adjacent to the Tomb of Rachel, between Jerusalem and Bethlehem. ²Jesus said to him, "Man, what do you sow?"

³But he, indignant and mocking that a boy of his age would think to question him, said, "Stones."

⁴Jesus said to him, "What you say is true, they are stones." ⁵And all the chickpea seeds were made into the hardest stones, in the form of chickpeas with respect to color and even the sprouts on their heads. ⁶They remain there today, and thus, by Jesus' word alone, while we sow all the grain we might, the seeds change into

---

God. The word itself is plural for Hebrew *Adon* ("lord" or "master"), often understood as a royal plural. Because Jews avoid pronouncing the Tetragrammaton as the name for God (YHWH) out loud, they substituted the name *Adonai* when reading Scripture.

A. *edge of the field:* mention of this detail (*in fine campi*) perhaps refers to Lev 19:9, which commands that the harvest should not be taken from the full field, but that some should be left at the edges. This echo emphasizes the idea that Jesus' seeds at the edge of the field yielded more than would be found in three or four other whole fields (in v. 3).

B. *the poor were refreshed:* Jesus distributing the harvest in this episode is parallel to his miracles of feeding the crowds in the Synoptic Gospels, as in Mark 6:30–44 par. and Mark 8:1–10//Matt 15:32–39.

stones; and even today in that field, those who carefully seek find only stones.

57 ¹On a certain day, early in the morning, when the dew still tempered the sun, Mary and Joseph went up[A] from the shores of Tyre and Sydon to Nazareth.[B] ²And as the sun was rising, Mary was oppressed; she sat on the ground fatigued and said to Joseph, "As it rises, so am I oppressed; what should I do? There is no shade in which I might be sheltered."

³And stretching out her hands to heaven, she prayed, saying, "O power of the Most High, according to the pleasant word that you sent me and I heard one day, overshadow me so my spirit might live, and give me your refreshment."

cf. Luke 1:35

⁴Now Jesus, hearing these things, was amused at the words. ⁵In his hand he held a dry branch as a walking–stick; he fixed it in the ground, and he commanded, "Immediately give a most agreeable shadow for my mother." ⁶And immediately that stick sprouted into a large and leafy tree that offered sweet rest for them while they rested.[C]

cf. Ps.-Mt. 20

58[D] ¹Now, one day in winter time, when the sun shone brightly in its strength, a sunbeam stretched itself, spanning from the window to the wall in Joseph's home. ²When other boys from the neighborhood were there playing with Jesus and running around the home, Jesus climbed onto the sunbeam and, with his garments spread out over it, sat down as if on a most solid beam. ³When the boys of the same age[E] playing with him saw, they thought that

A. *went up*: the manuscript reading is *ascenderum* (as in Dimier-Paupert), but likely should be emended to *ascenderunt*, as it is translated here.

B. *Tyre and Sydon to Nazareth*: mention of these toponyms presents another movement of location, especially significant since the source of this episode is unknown.

C. *offered sweet rest for them*: cf. the palm-tree episode in *Ps.-Mt.* 20–21. This miracle also calls to mind the miracles that Moses performed with his staff throughout Exodus, in front of Pharaoh and with the Israelites in the wilderness.

D. Parallels to this episode are found in *Arm. Gos. Inf.* 15:5, Ethiopic *Inf. Gos. Thom.*, and some Slavonic manuscripts. For some visual depictions, see Elliott, *Synopsis*, 219.

E. *same age*: the post-classical term *coaetaneus* (here *coetanei*) is used in the Vulgate (Gal 1:14) and medieval sources to mean "of the same age,"

they were able to do the same. ⁴They ascended so that they might sit with Jesus, playing by his example, but they were bruised.ᴬ ⁵So, Jesus, at the urging of Mary and Joseph, blew a light breath over all the hurt spots and healed all the wounds. ⁶And he said, "The Spirit breathes where he wills, and he heals and makes whole whom it wills. They have told all these things to our fathers."

cf. John 3:8

⁷It came to pass that these words were well known in Jerusalem and in the remote ends of Judea, and Jesus' fame was multiplied throughout the circuit of provinces. ⁸And they came to bless him and to be blessed by him, and they said to him, "Blessed is the womb that bore you and the breasts that have nursed you." ⁹Joseph and Mary rendered thanks to God for all that they had heard and seen.

cf. Luke 11:27

59 ¹When Jesus was three years old, he lived in Egyptᴮ in the home of a certain widow with his mother and Joseph. ²When he saw children playing, he began to play with them. ³Jesus took a very dry fish and let it go in the dirt and ordered it to wriggle. ⁴Again he said to the fish, "Reject the salt that you have within you, and go into the water." Thus it was done.ᶜ ⁵Now, seeing, the neighbors informed the widow in whose home he lived. ⁶As soon as she heard about this, she cast them out of her home with great haste.

cf. *Inf. Gos. Thom.* [LT] Prol. 3–4

60 ¹And while Jesus was walking with his mother Mary through the middle of the city square, looking around, he saw a master teaching his students. ²And behold, twelve sparrows fighting among themselves fell over the wall into the lap of this master

---

"contemporary," or "equal."

A. *bruised:* this sentence poses problems of sense, perhaps due to corruption. The likeliest explanation is that *conterimur* (the manuscript reading, as in Dimier-Paupert) should be emended to *conterentur* (*cos* + *tero*), translated here as "they were bruised."

B. *Egypt:* Like other references to different locations or movements of the holy family in the *pars altera*, this episode and the one following pose problems of chronology due to the use of a different source. The reference to Egypt situates this episode during the family's flight from Herod, although the other episodes in the *pars altera* and additions in Paris 11867 occur after their return.

C. *when he saw . . . thus it was done:* cf. *Acts of Peter* (i.e. *Actus Vercellenses*) 13, where the apostle revivifies a salted fish.

who taught the boys. [3]Now, when Jesus saw this, he began to laugh and stopped. [4]When the doctor saw him laughing, with great anger he said to his students, "Go, bring him to me." [5]When he had Jesus before him, the master seized him by his ear and said, "What did you see that made you laugh?"

[6]Jesus said to him, "Master, look: my hands (are) full of wheat. I showed it to them and scattered the wheat that they might risk collecting it;[A] because of this, they fight among themselves to divvy up the wheat."[B] [7]Jesus did not go from there until it was finished. [8]Because of this, the master undertook to cast him out of the city, along with Joseph and his mother Mary.

cf. *Inf. Gos. Thom.*
[LT] Prol. 5–7

61 [1]Another time, when Jesus was walking through the country, one of the children ran and struck Jesus on the elbow. [2]Now, Jesus said to him, "This is the end of your journey." [3]Immediately he fell to the earth and was dead. [4]At that, those who saw the wonder called out, saying, "Where does this child come from?" [5]They said to Joseph, "It is not proper for him to live with us, nor for us to have such a child." [6]At that, he (Joseph) went and took him, and they said to him, "Go away from this place, and if it is necessary for you to live with us, teach him to pray and not to blaspheme, for our children do not understand."

[7]Joseph called to Jesus and took him to teach him, "Why do you blaspheme and speak evil to others? The inhabitants in this place hate us."

[8]Now Jesus said, "Then I will be silent, father. But let them see their own folly."

[9]Immediately those who had spoken against Jesus were made blind. [10]Walking away, they said, "All the words that go out of his mouth are followed by weight and effect."

A. *risk*: the Latin phrase (*in periculo*) literally means "in danger," but both the Greek source and the context indicate that it is part of the verb phrase (as translated here) in Jesus' description of the birds collecting wheat.

B. *Jesus said to him . . . divvy up the wheat*: in *Inf. Gos. Thom.* (Greek D [LT]), Jesus gives a slightly different speech: "Teacher, look: a widow woman comes to you carrying grain which she brought with hard work. And here she must stumble and scatter the grain. Therefore, these birds fight over how many seeds each one ought to get." Voicu (following M. R. James) explains that the difference between "widow" and "hands" (here *manus*) likely derives from the translator confusing the Greek words χήρα ("widow") and χεῖρα ("hand"); see "Verso," 63.

¹¹And when Joseph saw what Jesus had done, with anger he seized him by the ear. ¹²In an uproar, Jesus said to Joseph, "It is sufficient for you to see me, but do not touch me, for you do not know who I am; and if you knew, you might not admonish me. ¹³Although I am with you presently, I was made before you."

cf. John 20:17

cf. Inf. Gos. Thom. [LT] 4:1–5:3

62 ¹Now, one day, when he had climbed to the top of a certain home, Jesus began to play with children. ²When one of the children fell headlong over the edge, the wretch was broken. ³When the parents of the dead child discovered this, lamenting, they called out and spoke against Jesus, "Truly he is the author of death;^A you made him rush over the edge. You plotted against him."

⁴Now, hearing this, Jesus said with a loud cry, "O slow of heart to believe, and unfaithful accusers with your words. Why do you fear the power of the Most High?" ⁵Then he stretched out his hands. And standing over the dead child, he summoned him, calling his name, "Child Synoe,^B child Synoe, arise and say if I made you fall."

⁶And when he had persisted in this several times, the child arose, healed, and said, "No, Lord. Even dead, I seek you with trepidation; and alive, I worship you." ⁷Prostrating himself at Jesus' feet, he worshipped him with tears. ⁸And seeing this, his parents increased the praises of his glory.

cf. Inf. Gos. Thom. [LT] 9:1–3

63 ¹After this (before a few days went by), in the same place,^C a certain child was cutting wood and struck his foot, making a terrible wound. ²When a great crowd came and saw him wailing, Jesus ran to him along with them, and they begged him to soothe his pain.^D ³Especially because the father and mother of

---

A. *Truly he is the author of death:* the close parallel "God is the author of death" (*deus auctor est mortis*) is used in the Pseudo-Augustinian *Hypomnesticon contra Pelagianos et Caelestianos* 1, composed ca. 430–435 (ed. Chisholm), 2:105, lines 27–28; on the date, see 1:24–30.

B. *Synoe:* the child is named Zeno in *Inf. Gos. Thom.*

C. *in the same place:* the text does not make clear what this place might be, especially considering the many references to different locations and movements of the holy family in the *pars altera* and these later additions.

D. *they begged him to soothe his pain:* the request for Jesus to heal the boy is unique to this version of the tale.

the wounded child could not handle his pain, Jesus had mercy on them and said, "Only believe and what you seek will be done."[A]

[4]After the master (Jesus) went to him, he breathed on his foot and caressed it, like a soothing physician, and said, "Arise whole; remember that you are healed by the power of God." [5]Completely healed, he began leaping and gave glory also in confession.[B]

cf. *Inf. Gos. Thom.*
[LT] 10:1–3 [6]When the crowd saw what had happened, they worshipped Jesus and said, "Truly we believe that you are God."[C]

64[D] [1]At yet another time, Mary said to her son, "Son, go to the spring of Gabriel and bring back some water drawn from it in a pitcher." [2]Obeying his mother, he took a vase and went. [3]And boys of the same age followed him playing, carrying their own similar pitchers. [4]Now, returning after filling the pitcher, Jesus forcefully struck it against a rock that was cast into the road, but it (the pitcher) was neither broken nor even cracked. [5]Seeing this, the others did likewise with their own and every one of them broke their pitchers. [6]The water for which they had gone poured out.

[7]Now, when an uproar and complaints arose about this, Jesus collected the fragments and, once all the vases were restored, refilled each vase with water. [8]And looking up at heaven, he said, "Father, in this way should the scattered humans who are lost be restored."

Ps 117:26 [9]All became speechless at the act and the word and spoke a blessing: "Blessed is he who comes in the name of the Lord." Amen.

A. *Only believe and what you seek will be done:* Jesus' words are unique to this version of the tale.

B. *he began leaping and gave glory:* the boy's celebration is unique to this version of the tale.

C. *Truly we believe that you are God:* in *Inf. Gos. Thom.* 10:3 (Greek D [LT] and Greek A), the people say, "Truly, perhaps God dwells in this child." This Latin version has added an emphasis on Christology and Trinitarian doctrine.

D. In some ways, this episode is parallel to that in *Inf. Gos. Thom.* 11:1–2 (see *pars altera* chap. 33), but many of the details diverge: in *Inf. Gos. Thom.*, Jesus is jostled by the crowd and his jug breaks, so he uses his cloak to gather up the water miraculously, the children do not follow suit, and there is no moralizing lesson from Jesus' miracle.

5

Trinubium Annae

(From Cambridge, St. John's College 35)

[1]Anna and Emeria were sisters. [2]From Emeria was born Elizabeth, the mother of John the Baptist. [3]Joachim took Anna as his wife, from whom was born Mary, the mother of the Lord Jesus. [4]When Joachim died, according to the Law of Moses, Anna married another man, called Cleopas,[A] from whom she had another child, to whom she gave the name of her first daughter. [5]She is called Mary Cleopas. [6]Later, Cleopas gave Mary, the mother of the Lord, who was also his step-daughter, to Joseph, his brother. [7]He also betrothed the other Mary, his own daughter, to Alphaeus, from whom were born James the Lesser and another Joseph; thus he is called James Alphaeus. [8]When Cleopas died, Anna married a third husband named Salome, according to the Law, from whom she had a third daughter, whom she likewise named Mary, in honor of the name of her first daughter, which was announced to her by an angel, and for love of her. [9]From her (Mary Salome), who married Zebedee, were born James the Greater and John the Evangelist. [10]Mary, the mother of James the Lesser, and Mary, the mother of James the Greater and John the Evangelist, and Mary Magdalene sought the Lord with spices in the tomb.

cf. John 19:25

cf. Mark 15:40//
Matt 27:56

cf. Mark 15:40//
Matt 27:56

cf. Mark 16:1

A. *Cleopas:* manuscripts give the name as *Cleophas* (cf. *Cleopas* in the *pars altera* 42:1–2), although the name is given as *Clopas* (Κλωπᾶ) in John 19:25.

The Nativity of Mary

Introduction

Among apocrypha categorized as infancy narratives, the *Nativity of Mary* (*Nat. Mary*) was one of the most popular works of the Western Middle Ages. This apocryphon is a condensed, adaptive retelling of the first 13 chapters of the *Gospel of Pseudo-Matthew* (*Ps.-Mt.*), which is, in turn, an expansive adaptation of the *Protevangelium of James* (*Prot. Jas.*). Soon after its composition, *Nat. Mary* became associated with the newly emerged Feast for the Nativity of Mary, enjoyed prevalence in Christian worship and private devotion, and influenced a wide range of medieval literature and art.

Summary

Nat. Mary is a synthesis of the canonical infancy narratives of Luke 1–2 and Matthew 1 with *Ps.-Mt.* 1–12, although it omits many details from the apocryphal source. The narrative begins by introducing Joachim and Anna, an Israelite couple living righteously according to the Law. Joachim goes to the temple to make a sacrifice for the Feast of Dedication, but the high priest Issachar rejects the offering because Joachim and Anna have remained infertile after twenty years of marriage. Because of his shame, Joachim goes into a sort of self-exile with shepherds in the countryside. An angel appears to Joachim, however, and proclaims a lengthy annunciation speech about the conception, birth, and life of Mary, to whom his wife Anna will give birth. The same angel also appears to Anna and proclaims another annunciation speech. According to the commands

111

of the angel, Joachim and Anna meet each other at the Golden Gate in Jerusalem, where they rejoice about the news of Anna's conception. The author briefly relates Mary's birth.

When Mary is three years old, Joachim and Anna take her to the temple, as they have dedicated her to the service of the Lord in a community of virgins. Mary amazes all of the people by climbing the steps of the temple mount by herself, and the author also relates her virtues as she grows older. When Mary is fourteen years old, the high priest announces that she will be given to a man as husband, although Mary protests. After the high priest consults with the Lord, the people hear a plan from God himself: all of the men of Israel will bring rods to the temple, and the one belonging to the man chosen to be betrothed to Mary will blossom before the people. This man turns out to be Joseph, an older widower with his own children. Despite his reluctance to marry someone younger than his grown children, he agrees to take Mary into his custody and, eventually, to marry her. Mary goes to live in Joseph's house with seven companion virgins.

The angel Gabriel visits Mary and announces that although she will remain a perpetual virgin, she will give birth; Gabriel also proclaims a lengthy annunciation about the Messiah who will be born. Mary accepts this responsibility and offers thanks to God. Joseph, however, discovers that Mary is pregnant and considers quietly divorcing her, until an angel appears to him and declares that Mary will give birth to God's Son, the Messiah, who will be named Jesus. According to the angel's command, Joseph takes Mary as his wife. The story ends with a brief mention of Jesus' birth nine months later, as related by the Evangelists of the canonical Gospels.

Transmission and Survival

Based on both material witnesses and influence, there is no doubt that *Nat. Mary* was one of the most popular apocrypha in Western Europe during the Middle Ages. In her 1997 critical edition for the Corpus Christianorum Series Apocryphorum, Rita Beyers identifies over 150 manuscripts of *Nat. Mary*, ranging in dates from the eleventh through the sixteenth centuries, surviving in libraries as widespread as France, Portugal, England, Belgium, Luxembourg, Germany, Austria, Switzerland, and Italy.[1]

1. See manuscript descriptions in Beyers, *Libri de nativitate Mariae*, 35–139, and

The manuscript witnesses are generally divided into two recensions: the A-text, closer to the original; and the B-text, a revision in style and grammar. Both A and B texts must have been composed by about the year 1000.[2] In addition, Beyers lists 19 manuscripts of "adaptations" to these basic text types, such as those including the narrative in larger compilations or those containing only extracts.[3]

Although the oldest manuscript witnesses represent the B-text, the A-text is more prevalent and represents the version closest to the original composition of *Nat. Mary*. This family is divided into nine sub-groups as well as a set of isolated witnesses. The oldest manuscripts of the A-text date from the middle of the eleventh century. Nine witnesses were created before the end of that century, and five of them represent the most prominent and reliable sub-group (A1a):

Chartres, Bibliothèque municipale 162 (second half of 11th cent.), now lost[4]

Paris, Bibliothèque nationale de France, lat. 3835 (11th cent., Vendôme)

Rouen, Bibliothèque municipale, U 36 (1390) (end of 11th cent., Saint-Aubin d'Angers)

Rouen, Bibliothèque municipale, A 271 (471) (11th cent., Holy Trinity Abbey, Fécamp)

Vendôme, Bibliothèque municipale, 42 (end of 11th cent., Trinity Abbey, Vendôme)

In addition, another four witnesses from the eleventh century represent the sub-groups A2, A3, A4, and Ax (listed in that order):

---

full "Listes des manuscrits du *Libellus de nativitate Sanctae Mariae*" in various groupings at 335–57.

2. For more details, see the section on "Date and Author" below.

3. On her classification of these types, see Beyers, *Libri de nativitate Mariae*, 127 n. 1.

4. Chartres 162 was destroyed (along with hundreds of other manuscripts) in a fire at the Chartres Bibliothèque municipale in 1944, but its contents are known and can be reconstructed based on earlier catalogues and notes on the manuscripts by Yves Delaporte. Amann published the prologue from this manuscript (fol. 56r) in *Le Protévangile de Jacques*, 340–64. See Beyers, *Libri de nativitate Mariae*, 42–43; Fassler, "Mary's Nativity," esp. 417–20; and Fassler, *Virgin of Chartres*, esp. 107–29 and 420–37.

Rouen, Bibliothèque municipale, Y 109 (end of the 11th cent., Jumièges)

Paris, Bibliothèque nationale de France, Nouv. acq. lat. 1455 (second half of 11th cent., Cluny)

Durham, Dean and Chapter Library, A.III.29 (end of 11th cent., Durham)

Vatican, Bibliotheca Apostolica Vaticana, Vat. lat. 9668 (middle of 11th cent., Mont-Saint-Michel)

The B-text family is divided into two major sub-groups: B1, which includes five branches; and B2, which includes two branches. The oldest manuscripts of the B-text date from the early eleventh century. Six witnesses to the B-text were created before the end of that century, and three of them represent the sub-group B1a:

Châlons-sur-Marne, Bibliothèque municipale, 73 (first half of 11th cent., Abbey of Saint-Pierre-aux-Monts, Châlons)

Maredsous, Bibliothèque de l'Abbaye, 51 (beginning of the second half of the 11th cent., Abbey of Tholey sur la Sarre)

Trèves, Stadtbibliothek, 1379/143 (early 11th cent., Abbey of Saint-Martin, Trèves)

In addition, another three witnesses from the eleventh century represent the sub-groups B1e (two witnesses) and B2a (listed in that order):

Cambrai, Bibliothèque municipale, 528 (11th cent., Abbey of Saint-Sépulcre, Cambrai)

Cambrai, Bibliothèque municipale, 530 (11th cent., Abbey of Saint-Sépulcre, Cambrai)

Douay, Bibliothèque municipale, 867 (11th cent., Marchiennes)

Based on these witnesses, Beyers suggests that the B-text derived from a version of the A-text, but not from any of the surviving sub-groups she identifies. The earliest surviving forms of the A-text and B-text, therefore, must have been established by about the year 1000 and circulated in different trajectories.

Aside from this material evidence, the earliest witnesses to the transmission of *Nat. Mary* are sermons by the preacher Fulbert of Chartres (ca. 960–1028). Born in the mid-tenth century to humble origins,

Fulbert moved to the important educational center of Rheims in the 980s; while there, he received his education and joined the cathedral school by the middle of the 990s. He was made a deacon in 1004, and in 1006 was appointed Bishop of Chartres, where he remained until his death. Fulbert is now seen as a major figure for the development of the Cult of Mary, especially the establishment of the Feast of the Nativity of Mary on September 8. Indeed, in overseeing the reconstruction of the Notre Dame Cathedral in Chartres after its destruction by fire in 1020, and through his many writings on the subject of the Nativity of Mary, Fulbert did much to propagate the cult of Mary in the eleventh century.[5] In his writings related to the feast, he refers to various texts containing traditions about Mary's birth and life, of which both *Ps.-Mt.* and *Nat. Mary* are a part.

Fulbert includes some key references to Marian apocrypha in three of his sermons: *Approbatae consuetudinis est* (his most famous sermon), *Mutuae dilectionis amore*, and *Fratres karissimi, in hac die*.[6] In all three, he considers traditions that inform our knowledge about the Nativity of Mary in the West. In both *Approbatae consuetudinis est* and *Mutuae dilectionis amore*, Fulbert mentions a book that he has read relating Mary's birth and life, a book that he says has been deemed apocryphal. His statement is vague enough for it to refer to a number of texts, including *Prot. Jas.*, *Ps.-Mt.*, and *Nat. Mary*; indeed, he even mentions that this book has been translated by Jerome, as stated in the prefatory material that often accompanies *Ps.-Mt.* and *Nat. Mary* in the manuscripts. More specifically, in *Approbatae consuetudinis est*, Fulbert mentions that Mary was the child of a father from Nazareth and a mother from Bethlehem—details that appear in *Nat. Mary* but not the earlier apocryphal texts. The most explicit evidence for Fulbert's knowledge of *Nat. Mary* appears in his *Fratres karissimi, in hac die*, in which he gives many more details about Mary's life, even to the extent that he quotes a passage that corresponds directly with *Nat. Mary* (1:3–6, 4:3, and 8:6). It is clear, then, that Fulbert was well aware of apocryphal traditions and specifically knew *Nat.*

---

5. See Fassler, *Virgin of Chartres*, esp. 79–130.

6. Fabricius, Thilo, Thischendorf, and Amann all discuss this topic (see Beyers, *Libri de nativitate Mariae*, 140 n. 3); Beyers examines the evidence at length in *Libri de nativitate Mariae*, 140–46, where she quotes the evidence from Fulbert's sermons, as does Fassler in "Mary's Nativity" and *Virgin of Chartres*, 79–130. For discussions and editions of Fulbert's sermons, see Canal, "Los sermones marianos" and "Texto crítico de algunos sermones marianos."

Mary.[7] Unfortunately, it is difficult to date Fulbert's sermons precisely, but he must have composed them between the 990s and 1028—and most likely after becoming bishop in 1006. Nonetheless, his comments remain valuable evidence for the circulation of *Nat. Mary* no later than the first few decades of the eleventh century.

In the modern period, *Nat. Mary* has enjoyed a long history as a printed text, mainly because of its associations with Jerome and his letters. In the fifteenth century alone, it was printed twelve times among the works of Jerome, and it later made its way into the major editions of Jerome's works in the sixteenth and seventeenth centuries.[8] In 1703, it was brought into the study of Christian apocrypha with its inclusion in the first major collection of apocrypha, Johann Albert Fabricius's *Codex apocryphus Novi Testamenti.*[9] At the same time, Fabricius also supplied a commentary running along the bottom of the page, which remained influential on printings of the text through the nineteenth century. This edition and commentary were published a number of times over the succeeding two centuries—among the works of Jerome in Dominic Vallarsi's edition and J.-P. Migne's *Patrologia Latina* (reprinted from Vallarsi's text),[10] as well as in Johann Karl Thilo's *Codex apocryphus Novi Testamenti.*[11] A new printed text appeared in 1853, when Constantin von Tischendorf edited the text in the first edition of his *Evangelia apocrypha.*[12] Tischendorf's edition remained the standard through the twentieth century. Finally, in 1998, Beyers provided the current critical edition of *Nat. Mary*, edited from all of the identified manuscripts to survive.[13]

---

7. It is also possible (as Beyers discusses) that Fulbert knew *Ps.-Mt.*, but this is less evident.

8. On the history of editions and studies, see Beyers, *Libri de nativitate Mariae*, 7–13, and on its inclusion among Jerome's letters specifically at 7–8. On the association with Jerome, see the section on "Title and Prefatory Matter," below.

9. Fabricius, *Codex apocryphus Novi Testamenti*, 1:19–38.

10. See Beyers, *Libri de nativitate Mariae*, 9.

11. Thilo, *Codex apocryphus Novi Testamenti*, 317–36.

12. Fabricius, *Codex apocryphus Novi Testamenti*, 1:19; and Tischendorf, *Evangelia Apocrypha*, 106–14.

13. Beyers, *Libri de nativitate Mariae.*

Title and Prefatory Matter

Five of the oldest and most important witnesses of the A-text bear the title *Libellus de natiuitate sanctae Mariae* ("Little book about the birth of Saint Mary"), which has become the standard Latin title of the work.[14] Beyers notes that other manuscripts have titles closer to (and even confused with) the one used for *Ps.-Mt.*, most usually given as *Natiuitas sanctae Mariae [uirginis] atque infantiam Iesu Christi* ("Nativity of Saint Mary the Virgin, and the infancy of Jesus Christ"). Some witnesses also include references to the figures named in the prefatory material: Jerome, Chromatius and Heliodorus, and Eustochium.

The prefatory material also provides a clue to how medieval scribes thought of the work and its title. This material includes two parts: a prologue written by the supposed compiler of *Nat. Mary*; and a letter forged in the name of Jerome to Bishops Chromatius and Heliodorus. Both of these pieces address the contents and transmission of the apocryphon, in some ways attempting to allay any doubts a reader might have about the work. Similar comments and themes are found in a set of letters appended to the A-family of *Ps.-Mt.* manuscripts, which are also spuriously attributed to Chromatius, Heliodorus, and Jerome.

The author of the prologue provides some sense of the content of *Nat. Mary* that relates to the title as found in the manuscripts. This anonymous compiler recounts finding information *de natiuitate sanctae ac beatissimae uirginis Mariae usque ad incomparabilem eius partum et prima Christi* ("about the birth of the holy and blessed Virgin Mary up to her incomparable birth and the beginnings of Christ") in a text described as *quodam libello* ("a certain little book"). This formulation indicates that the compiler relied on the A-text of *Ps.-Mt.*, since the prefatory material and the title echo the set of spurious letters ascribed to Chromatius, Heliodorus, and Jerome in witnesses to that recension of the source. The similarity of titles also accounts for the confusion of titles for *Ps.-Mt.* and *Nat. Mary* across late medieval manuscripts.

When Fabricius published his edition of *Nat. Mary*, he titled it *Evangelium de Nativitate Mariae*, and Tischendorf followed suit.[15] In

---

14. These manuscripts are Rouen U 36; Rouen A 271; Leiden, Bibl. Der Rijksuniversiteit, Voss. lat. F 11 (12th cent.); Vat. Lat. 9667; and London, British Library, Cotton Claudius A.i (12th cent.), all of which comprise the base manuscripts for Beyers's edition.

15. Tischendorf, *Evangelia Apocrypha*, 106.

her edition, Beyers gave the apocryphon its current title, based on the manuscript witnesses already discussed.[16]

Sources

The two main sources for *Nat. Mary* are the narratives found in the apocryphal *Ps.-Mt.* and the canonical Bible, especially the Gospels of Matthew and Luke. Although scholars previously believed *Nat. Mary* to be an older, earlier apocryphon based on *Prot. Jas.*, it is now clear that the author was working to adapt *Ps.-Mt.* The author generally follows the narrative of *Ps.-Mt.* chaps. 1–12, omitting everything about Jesus' birth and childhood, except for one brief reference (10:8). Although the author generally follows *Ps.-Mt.*, the details are condensed, at times left out completely, and at other times changed to suit the author's new audience. Specific verbal parallels between *Nat. Mary* and *Ps.-Mt.* are few.

On the other hand, the author of *Nat. Mary* also relies on many passages from the Bible, not only in general parallels but also in specific allusions and even verbal echoes. In most cases, the author uses the translation by Jerome, known as the Latin Vulgate, which was the prevalent version in the medieval West. Yet the author also draws on older Latin translations that predate Jerome's text. This is particularly true in a few of the author's uses of Psalms, since Old Latin translations rest on the Greek Septuagint (LXX) and are characteristically distinct, perhaps via exegetical traditions (see below) surrounding the Psalms that predate Jerome's Vulgate.

A few examples help to demonstrate the way that the author of *Nat. Mary* treats *Ps.-Mt.* and the Bible as sources together. In many of these cases, the author changes details from *Ps.-Mt.* to align more closely with details in or parallel to Matthew and Luke. One clear point of departure is a new emphasis on different geographical locations than those referred to in *Ps.-Mt.* The author makes clear that Joachim's family comes from Nazareth, while Anna's comes from Bethlehem (1:2), thus situating Mary's birth in same city as Jesus' own birth. Similarly, angelic announcements about Anna's conception of Mary to both Joachim and Anna (chaps. 3 and 4) echo the Annunciation account in Luke 1. Both of these speeches also draw on a range of other biblical passages, with allusions to other miraculous conceptions in Genesis, Judges 13 and 16, and 1 Samuel 1.

16. Beyers, *Libri de nativitate Mariae*, 268 n. 1.

These angelic speeches are representative of the whole text, which contains many examples of biblical allusions, parallels, and verbal echoes.

Such interweaving of the narrative plot from *Ps.-Mt.* with references and verbal details from the Bible demonstrate the author's deep knowledge of biblical and exegetical learning. Like the canonical Gospels and *Ps.-Mt.* before it, *Nat. Mary* often offers typological connections between its narrative and elements of the Hebrew Bible. This characteristic appears in citations of the prophets, particularly Isaiah. Beyond the author's reliance on notions of typology and prophetic fulfillment, the author also draws on a long tradition of commentaries on the Gospels of Matthew and Luke. Indeed, throughout chaps. 9 and 10, *Nat. Mary* resembles an exegetical gospel harmony, as it weaves together elements from Matthew, Luke, and *Ps.-Mt.* to bring them into agreement within this single narrative. In addition to using the Bible and *Ps.-Mt.* as sources, the author also incorporates details that must derive from patristic and early medieval commentaries and treatises on the Virgin Mary. Thus, the author draws on interpretive and even verbal parallels that evoke exegesis by major figures such as Ambrose (ca. 340–397), Jerome (ca. 347–420), Augustine (354–430), Bede (672/3–735), Hrabanus Maurus (ca. 780–856), Paschasius Radbertus (785–865), and Heiric of Auxerre (841–876).

Date and Authorship

The most solid information about the date of composition of *Nat. Mary* comes from manuscript evidence, which establishes a definite *terminus ante quem* for the text. As already indicated, the oldest surviving manuscripts were created in the early eleventh century. Although the A-text was composed earlier, a few manuscripts of the B-text represent the oldest surviving witnesses: Trèves, Stadtbibliothek, 1379/143, from the early eleventh century; and Châlons-sur-Marne, Bibliothèque municipale, 73, from the first half of the eleventh century. Given that these manuscripts rest on earlier exemplars—and that the B-text rests on an earlier version of *Nat. Mary*—the apocryphon must have been composed by about the year 1000.

In seeking a *terminus post quem*, however, we must rely on external evidence. Since *Nat. Mary* is a revision of *Ps.-Mt.*, it could not have been composed any earlier than that apocryphon. Based on its sources and manuscripts, we know that *Ps.-Mt.* was composed between about 550 and 800, and most likely in the seventh century.[17] In 1934, Cyrille Lambot suggested that *Nat. Mary* was composed by Paschasius Radbertus, a figure embroiled in Mariological controversies during the Carolingian period.[18] This argument was based on Lambot's discovery of a letter by Hincmar of Rheims (806–82), written to Odon, Bishop of Beauvais, in 868–69. In this letter, Hincmar discusses apocryphal works read publicly with three references that are pertinent: a text he calls the *historia de ortu sanctae Mariae* ("History of the birth of Saint Mary"); a series of fictional letters associated with the text that he says were written by Paschasius Radbertus and denounced by Ratramnus of Corbie (died ca. 870); and a work attributed to Jerome that he calls an *omelia de assumptione sanctae Mariae* ("Homily on the Assumption of Saint Mary"). Further work by Beyers, however, challenges Lambot's argument, since the manuscript traditions of *Ps.-Mt.* and *Nat. Mary* contradict his conclusions; furthermore, her stylistic analysis of *Nat. Mary* in comparison to Paschasius' works does not offer convincing parallels. Instead, it is likelier that Hincmar was referring to *Ps.-Mt.* and the prefatory letters that circulate in many manuscripts alongside it. Beyers concludes, then, that *Nat. Mary* probably was not known in Hincmar's time. Yet she also notes that some scholars still "prefer to see Paschasius as the author."[19] Nonetheless, if Hincmar did not know *Nat. Mary*, given his interests in such narratives, a logical *terminus post quem* for the work is 868–69. From the preceding evidence, the most likely date range for the composition of *Nat. Mary* may be set between about 900 and 1000.

In determining the date and author of *Nat. Mary*, other factors are also worth consideration. Fulbert's references to *Nat. Mary* are valuable witnesses to the circulation of this apocryphon, since they establish that it was in circulation by the first quarter of the eleventh century. Margot Fassler suggests that the bishop of Chartres might have even composed the apocryphon as part of his program of cultivating Marian devotion: "Indeed, it would be tempting to suggest the work is by Fulbert himself. Although there is no hard evidence for this, the interplay between the treatise [*Nat. Mary*], the letter that forms its preface, and the sermons

---

17. See details above pp. 24–26.

18. Lambot, "L'homélie du pseudo-Jérôme."

19. Beyers, "Transmission of Marian Apocrypha," 139.

attributed to Fulbert suggests powerful affinities."[20] For example, she discusses a complex of overlapping themes and imagery between *Nat. Mary* and Fulbert's sermon *Approbatae consuetudinis est*, concerning the use of Numbers 17, Isaiah 7 and 11, Mary's genealogy, Jerome's commentary on Isaiah, and the letter attributed to Jerome in the prefatory material. If Fulbert did not compose *Nat. Mary* himself, it is also possible that another member of the Chartres cathedral community did. Elsewhere, Fassler suggests that "one of the capable students from his school, Bernard of Angers or the cantor Sigo, are other possible authors."[21] Without further study, the question of authorship remains open.

In any case, there is a clear relationship between the eleventh-century development of Mary's feast at Chartres and *Nat. Mary*—either at its conception or its early transmission. This is borne out by the early manuscripts. As Fassler discusses, four of the five earliest manuscripts with the A-text (and some of the earliest, most important witnesses of the apocryphon in general) are associated with Chartres and Fulbert's work there: Chartres 162, Rouen U 36, Rouen A 271, and Vendôme 42 all contain *Nat. Mary* alongside sermons attributed to Fulbert.[22] Among the sermons in three of these collections (all but Rouen U 36) are Fulbert's *Approbatae consuetudinis est* and *Mutuae dilectionis amore*. These connections offer tantalizing gestures toward Fulbert's role in the origins and early transmission of *Nat. Mary* as part of his program to promote the Nativity of Mary as an emerging feast.

Theological and Thematic Content

Like *Prot. Jas.* and *Ps.-Mt.* before it, one of the key theological themes of *Nat. Mary* is Mary's purity. This is a pronounced concern from the very beginning of the text (1:1), which declares Mary to be a "perpetual virgin" (*semper uirgo*) at the same time as naming her other epithets, "blessed" (*beata*) and "most glorious" (*gloriosissima*). Immediately after, the author describes Anna and Joachim as "just before God, without blame and pious among the people." These qualities are further emphasized throughout by references to how they live their lives in accordance with Israelite laws in the Hebrew Bible. Mary's lineage, then, is established as

20. Fassler, "Mary's Nativity," 401; cf. *Virgin of Chartres*, 82.
21. Fassler, *Virgin of Chartres*, 82.
22. Fassler, *Virgin of Chartres*, 120–21.

related to Israelite law and piety. Mary's purity is also described in the angelic annunciations to Joachim and Anna, which foretell her life and her dedication to God, abstinence from any unclean food or drink, and, above all, virginity. As the angel tells Anna, "She will never know a man," and she will live "without stain, without corruption, without intercourse with a man, as a virgin" (4:3). This is, after all, her defining feature in medieval doctrine. Mary's purity and virginity play out through the rest of the narrative, but this speech contains the central point in relation to Mary's character as perpetual virgin and its theological implications for her as Mother of God.

Mary's purity and lineage in connection with Israelite law also intersect with another theme that becomes apparent early in *Nat. Mary*: her association with the Davidic line. In the same first verse emphasizing the three epithets of Mary's character, the author also asserts that she "was born from a royal line and of the family of David, born in the city of Nazareth"; and, shortly afterward, we learn that her father and mother come from Nazareth in Galilee and Bethlehem, respectively. Again, the angel's speech to Joachim and Anna emphasize this lineage all the more, as it alludes to Sarah and her son Isaac as well as Rachel, her husband Jacob, and her son Joseph. These same names and genealogy are those used in the first chapter of the Gospel of Matthew to emphasize Jesus' family line. All of this, of course, aligns with passages in the Psalms and the Prophets, which are used throughout *Nat. Mary* as proof-texts in relation to Jesus as Christ.

Nat. Mary—even more than *Ps.-Mt.*—demonstrates a concerted interest in angelology. This concern includes not only the various angelic appearances but also explanations for the interactions between angels and humans. For example, in 4:1, the angel announces to Anna, "I am the angel who has brought your prayers and offerings before the Lord," both echoing Tobit 12:12 and presenting the notion of angels as intercessors between humans and God. In another instance, when Gabriel visits Mary at the Annunciation, the author adds the explanation that Mary was not afraid of the angel, emphasizing her shock only at his message (9:3). The focus of this comment derives from the need to reconcile the Annunciation from Luke's Gospel with earlier details in *Nat. Mary* about Mary's fellowship with angels. In addition, the author extends the emphasis on angels and human interactions with them using a characteristic exegetical practice to gloss the synthesis of sources. In this instance, the focus on the theology of angels also becomes entangled with the author's theology of Mary and her character.

Later Influences

From the eleventh century onward, *Nat. Mary* became popular, widespread, and highly influential on medieval culture. In some ways, its transmission and use are tied up with the more general reception of apocryphal infancy narratives, especially *Ps.-Mt.*[23] Yet, in other ways, because this apocryphon focuses more specifically on Mary than Jesus (who is hardly mentioned)—and because it was written to align more consistently with the canonical Gospels—it enjoys an independent history and influence. Its popularity was especially due to association with the Feast of the Nativity of the Virgin. Fassler has demonstrated how *Nat. Mary* became associated with this feast, largely because of the efforts of Fulbert and liturgical developments at Chartres. Indeed, this apocryphon became a staple of the readings for the feast, and many manuscripts include it within collections of liturgical works. This is the case with some of the earliest witnesses, such as Chartres 162, Rouen U 36, Rouen A 271, and Vendôme 42.[24] This liturgical influence became all the more pronounced in the twelfth century and onward, as Marian devotion spread and the Feast of the Nativity became more widely practiced. Incidentally, the twelfth century was also the same period in which the most manuscripts of *Nat. Mary* were produced.[25]

Nat. Mary also found a prominent place within the landscape of medieval literature from the twelfth century onward. For example, Vincent of Beauvais used the narrative in his history of the world, the *Speculum historiale*. Similarly, Jacobus de Voragine heavily relied on it for his account of the Feast of the Nativity of the Virgin in the thirteenth-century *Golden Legend*. As bestsellers of the medieval period, these texts helped to disseminate the apocryphon even more widely than before, especially since many late medieval vernacular texts were based on the *Speculum historiale* and the *Golden Legend*.[26]

---

23. See Dzon, *Quest for the Christ Child*, esp. 109–85, and the introduction to *Ps.-Mt.*

24. Fassler, *Virgin of Chartres*, esp. 79–130.

25. See charts in Beyers, *Libri de nativitate Mariae*, 139.

26. Beyers, "La réception médiévale."

Some of the most renowned influences of *Nat. Mary* in medieval culture appear from visual arts, such as manuscript illuminations, wall paintings, and images on other material objects. In many cases, it is difficult to distinguish whether or not images are based directly on *Nat. Mary*, its source (*Ps.-Mt.*), or common iconographic traditions that grew out of these two narratives; in any case, Mary's life found resonance with artists and audiences.[27] The particular motif of Anna and Joachim at the Golden Gate is a popular image, as are images of Mary's birth and of Mary as a child playing with Anna and Joachim. These and other depictions of particular scenes are found in hundreds of manuscripts such as antiphonals, books of hours, breviaries, graduals, lectionaries, and psalters. In other cases, images accompany literary outgrowths related to *Nat. Mary*. One image of Joachim and Anna reunited appears in a copy of the *Golden Legend* from around 1402 (Geneva, Bibliothèque de Genève, Ms. fr. 57, fol. 400ʳ), accompanying the reading for the Feast of the Conception of Mary. Similarly, an illumination of Mary's birth is found in a fifteenth-century manuscript of the *Life of Our Lady* by the English poet John Lydgate (London, British Library, Harley 629, fol. 1ᵛ).

Manuscripts are not the only surviving artifacts of medieval art related to *Nat. Mary*. One major artistic program related to this narrative appears in Chartres Cathedral, probably from the twelfth century. A stained-glass window in the south side of the ambulatory (bay 28) depicts a cycle of images for the Life of the Virgin.[28] Among the scenes included are the high priest refusing Joachim's sacrifice; the annunciations to Joachim and Anna; Joachim and Anna reunited at the Golden Gate; the Nativity of the Virgin; the first bath of the Virgin; the presentation of the Virgin at the temple; the Virgin at school; and the betrothal and marriage of Mary and Joseph. As already mentioned, this series of images might be based on *Ps.-Mt.*, *Nat. Mary*, or common iconography rather than a specific source. Yet, given Fulbert's personal knowledge and promotion of *Nat. Mary*, and the central role of the Cathedral school in the early transmission of this work, it is likely that the stained-glass sequence is more closely related to this apocryphon. Further support comes in the sequence of angelic annunciations to Joachim and Anna, which coincides more closely with the interest in angels in *Nat. Mary*. This stained-glass

27. See Hawk, "Gospel of Pseudo-Matthew in Images."
28. See Whatling, "Life of the Virgin."

cycle remains a significant witness to the afterlife of this apocryphon in the medieval imagination.

Translation

This volume presents a new translation of *Nat. Mary* accompanied by the first full commentary of the text in English. Since Beyers' critical edition, only one complete English translation has appeared: in *A Synopsis of the Apocryphal Nativity and Infancy Narratives* by J. K. Elliott.[29] Two other English translations precede Beyer's work on the text: one by Jeremiah Jones (following Fabricius, reprinted by Hone) and the other by B. Harris Cowper (following Tischendorf).[30]

The present translation is based on Beyers' critical edition. Cross-references to biblical allusions and quotations, textual notes, and commentary are indebted to Beyers' own extensive notes, as well as her introductory material to the critical edition, supplemented by subsequent scholarship and my own research. I have followed the chapter and verse numbers adopted in the critical edition. At times, however, I have not included Beyers' references to biblical parallels when they seem rather vague or do not offer distinct equivalents. Even where my own interpretations differ, I am grateful for her meticulous work.

There are a number of places where the Bible is alluded to or quoted (and sometimes even cited) as a direct source. In biblical references, I use chapter and verse numbers according to the Latin Vulgate—the predominant version of the Bible used in the medieval West—which sometimes differs from the Hebrew Bible or modern translations (especially for the Psalms). In some cases, I have noted Old Latin parallels following the Septuagint (LXX) when they are especially relevant for comparison with the Vulgate. I have generally followed the Douay-Rheims translation of the Vulgate (with some modernizations), except where it does not accurately reflect an Old Latin reading; in these cases, I have rendered the phrasing to follow the older translation. For references to *Prot. Jas.*, I use the chapter and verse numbers as in Hock's edition and translation. For references to *Ps.-Mt.*, I use the chapter and verse numbers in my own translation.

29. Elliott, *Synopsis*.

30. Hone, *Apocryphal New Testament*, 17–24; and Cowper, *Apocryphal Gospels*, 84–98.

The Nativity of Mary

Prologue[A]

[1]YOU SEEK FROM ME a small favor,[B] seemingly light work but heavy because of wariness against falsehood. You ask that I write down everything that I have found by chance about the birth of the holy and blessed Virgin Mary up to her incomparable birth and the first beginnings of Christ.[C] This thing certainly is not difficult, but dangerous, as I said, for its dangerous presumption to truth. [2]For what you request of me, now that I have a white

A. This prologue and the following letter are similar in rhetoric and themes to the letter spuriously attributed to Jerome and addressed to Chromatius and Heliodorus, which is often found appended to Ps.-Mt. (and likely the source of the prologue and letter appended to this text). The brief letter is more confused about details than the prefatory material appended to Ps.-Mt.: for example, it mentions that Seleucus composed the book, but then also refers to the tradition that Matthew composed this apocryphon in Hebrew. Perhaps, as the author of the prologue says, this is due to poor memory of the letter's actual contents. Nonetheless, the prologue and letter contain a number of features characteristic of literary forgeries.

B. While this prologue seems addressed to a patron, no audience is named directly.

C. the birth . . . Christ: this phrasing (de natiuitate sanctae ac beatissimae uirginis Mariae usque ad incomparabilem eius partum et prima Christi) is parallel to elements found in titles of Ps.-Mt. (e.g., Natiuitas sanctae Mariae [uirginis] atque infantiam Iesu Christi, "Nativity of Saint Mary the Virgin, and the infancy of Jesus Christ") and phrasing used in the letter attributed to Chromatius and Heliodorus that often accompanies that apocryphon in the manuscripts (uirginis matris et saluatoris nostril infantia, "the Virgin Mother and the childhood of our Savior"); for further discussion, see the introduction to Ps.-Mt.

head,^A I learned about written in a certain little book that fell into my hands as a very young man; and certainly so much time has passed and other weighty things have intervened that some easy things might have slipped from my memory. ³Therefore, not unjustly, I may be accused, if I obey your request, of omitting or adding or changing some things. That it may be, I do not deny; but that it is done by my will, I do not concede. ⁴Thus, satisfying your wishes, and considering the curiosity of readers, I remind you and any reader of the little book I mentioned that, if I remember correctly, it likewise had a preface, with the sense like what follows.

Letter from Jerome to Bishops Chromatius and Heliodorus^B

¹You ask of me that I write back about a little book that some have on the nativity of Saint Mary. ²And therefore I want you to know that much in it is found to be false. For a certain Seleucus,^c who wrote the Passions of the Apostles, composed this little book. But just as he said what was true about their deeds and miracles, while lying much about doctrine, in this way too he fabricated many untruths from his heart. ³Therefore, I will be careful to translate

A. *white head*: this phrase (*cano capite*) as used to indicate old age is a particular favorite of Jerome, who uses it in *Epist.* 52.1; *Ruf.* 1.30; *Comm. Os.* 2.7.8/10; and *Comm. Am.* 2, prol. For other late antique examples and discussion, see Cain, *Jerome and the Monastic Clergy*, 73.

B. Chromatius (died ca. 406/407), likely born in Aquileia, was bishop of this city from 387/388 until his death. Heliodorus (ca. 330–ca. 390), born in Dalmatia, was the first bishop of Altinum (date uncertain). Jerome (ca. 347–420) addressed his *Epist.* 7 and the preface to his translation of Chronicles to Chromatius, *Epist.* 14 and 60 to Heliodorus, and the prefaces to his translations of Tobit and the Books of Solomon (Proverbs, Ecclesiastes, and Song of Songs) to the two bishops together. Both men were later canonized as saints.

C. *Seleucus*: although the name is different, the author refers to the tradition about a certain man named Leucius associated with the composition and dissemination of apocryphal acts of apostles developed during the patristic period. Augustine mentions him in this context in his *Fel.* 2.6, and another reference appears in the *Pseudo-Gelasian Decree* 5.4.4, but the fullest account of Leucius as author of apocryphal acts is found in Photius, *Bibliotheca* 141. See Junod and Kaestli, *L'histoire des actes apocryphes*, 137–43; and Schäferdiek, "Manichean Collection," 92–94.

word for word what it has in Hebrew, since it is said that the holy Evangelist Matthew composed the same little book sealed with Hebrew letters and placed it at the head of his gospel.

⁴Whether this is true I put to the author of the preface and the fidelity of the writer. I myself say this is doubtful, but I do not affirm it to be false. I say this freely, which none of the faithful will deny, that if this is true, or if this is false, great miracles preceded the holy birth of Saint Mary, and it was followed by the greatest (miracle); and for that reason those who believe by this that God is able to perform them are able to believe and to read without danger to their souls. ⁵Finally, as much as I am able to recall—following the sense and not the words of the writer, not by the same byway, nor proceeding by the same steps, by some digression but returning to the same path—in this way I will observe the style of the narrative, so that nothing is said other than either what is written there or what might reasonably be written.

1 ¹The blessed and most glorious Mary, perpetual virgin,ᴬ descended from a royal line and of the family of David, born in the city of Nazareth,ᴮ raised in the temple of the Lord in Jerusalem. ²Her father was called Joachim, her mother Anna. Her father's household was from Galilee and the city of Nazareth, her mother's family from Bethlehem.ᶜ ³Their life was simple and just
cf. Job 1:1 before God, without blame and pious among the people. ⁴They divided all of their belongings into three: keeping out one part

A. *blessed and most glorious Mary, perpetual virgin*: these three epithets—*beata*, *gloriosissima*, and *semper uirgo*—for Mary are widespread throughout the medieval period, especially associated with her cult. These phrases are especially linked to the Gelasian Sacramentary (ca. 750) and its prominent influence on liturgy (and, consequently, many other forms of medieval devotion) from the Carolingian period onward. The phrase *semper uirgo* for Mary appeared in the West at the beginning of the fifth century. The author makes the point to emphasize Mary's perpetual virginity at the very beginning of the narrative, which is in stark distinction to *Ps.-Mt.*

B. *Nazareth*: in both *Prot. Jas.* and *Ps.-Mt.*, Jerusalem is highlighted as the city in which Anna and Joachim live, and in which Mary is presumably born. In late antiquity, Mary's birthplace was disputed between the three cities of Jerusalem, Bethlehem, and Nazareth. Emphasis on Nazareth here seems to align the text more with details in Luke (esp. 1:26).

C. *Galilee . . . Bethlehem*: *Ps.-Mt.* does not specify the locations from which Anna and Joachim's families come, but does specify that Joachim is from the tribe of Judah and Anna is from the tribe and family of David.

for the temple and the temple's servants,[A] paying another part to pilgrims and the poor, reserving a third part for themselves and the needs of their little family.[B] [5]Righteous before God, pious to the people, they lived in chaste union[C] for about twenty years without having children. [6]However, they vowed that if by chance God gave them a child, they would dedicate it to the service of the Lord. For that reason, they were accustomed to visiting the temple of the Lord for every yearly feast.

cf. Luke 1:6

cf. 1 Sam 1:22

cf. Prot. Jas. 1:1–3;
Ps.-Mt. 1

2 [1]And it came to pass that the Feast of Dedication approached,[D] and Joachim went up to Jerusalem with some of his family. [2]At that time Issachar was the high priest there.[E] And when he saw Joachim standing among his other fellow citizens with his

cf. John 10:22

A. *temple's servants:* the term for servants here (*seruitor*) is related to monastic contexts, as used in RB 36.7 and 10, and 38.11.

B. *little family:* this diminutive (*familiola*) was used by patristic authors: for example, Jerome, *Epist.* 108.2 and 123.17.

C. *chaste union:* according to tradition in late antiquity and the medieval period, there were three types of chastity: for spouses, for widows, and for virgins. See, for example, Ambrose of Milan, *Vid.* 23; Augustine, *Bon. conj.* 27 and 34; Jerome, *Tract. Ps.* 95.8. For spouses, chastity did not mean total abstinence from sex, but that it was meant only for procreation; see Augustine, *Bon. conj.* 12 and 29. According to *Nat. Mary* (as in *Prot. Jas.* and *Ps.-Mt.*), Anna and Joachim did not practice total abstinence, since they promise to dedicate any children to the service of God. However, *Nat. Mary* does emphasize their chastity within the same framework discussed by Augustine and other patristic authors.

D. *Feast of Dedication:* the exact feast is not named in *Prot. Jas.* (where it is called "the great day of the Lord") nor in *Ps.-Mt.* ("at the time of the feast"), but the author here equates Joachim's offering with Hanukkah, also called the "Feast of Dedication." The reference in *Ps.-Mt.* was likely to either Passover or Shavuot, both Jewish pilgrimage festivals ordained in the Torah in which sacrifices were made: the Paschal Lamb for Passover and the First Fruits for Shavuot. However, no pilgrimage or sacrifice was made for Hanukkah. Given that the feast of Mary is on September 8 (celebrated in the West from the sixth or seventh century onward), there is a certain logic to the author identifying the feast with Hanukkah, since the date of Mary's conception would have needed to occur in early December—in line with the official observance of the Feast of the Conception of the Virgin in the West on December 8.

E. *Issachar:* in *Prot. Jas.* 1 and *Ps.-Mt.* 2, Joachim is confronted by a scribe named Reubel or Ruben, not the high priest. In *Ps.-Mt.*, the high priest (*pontifex*) is later identified with Abiathar (8:17, 20, 26; 12:6) and, in one textual crux in the A-text, Issachar (8:3). In *Nat. Mar.*, Issachar is the name of the high priest throughout.

1 Sam 10:27;
Pss 21:25 LXX;
101:18 LXX
offering, he despised him and spurned his gifts, asking why he would presume to stand among the fertile while infertile, saying that his gifts would be unworthy to God's sight, since he himself had been judged unworthy of offspring, as the scriptures said that all who did not produce a male in Israel were cursed. ³First he should loosen the curse with offspring, and therefore he could not come before the Lord with his offerings until then. ⁴For that reason, filled with shame at the reproach cast upon him, Joachim withdrew to the shepherds who were with their flocks in the pastures. Thus he did not return to his home, in case his family, who also were present and had heard this from the priest, might reprimand him with reproach.

cf. Prot. Jas. 1:4–11;
Ps.-Mt. 2:1–3

3 ¹But when he had been there for some time,^A on a certain day when he was alone, an angel of the Lord appeared with him in a great light. ²Therefore, he was disturbed by the vision, but the angel who appeared to him calmed his fear saying,^B "Do not be afraid, Joachim, nor be disturbed at the sight of me. For I am an angel of the Lord, sent to you to announce that your prayers are heard and your alms have ascended before him. ³For he observes and saw your shame and heard the reproach of barrenness unjustly cast upon you. For the punisher of sin is God, not nature. ⁴And therefore he who closes a womb, he will make it open again miraculously and so we might know that what is produced is not of lust, but is of a gift of God. ⁵Was not the first mother of your people, Sarah, infertile even until she was eighty years old? And yet in her old age she gave birth to Isaac, to whom was promised the blessings of all peoples. ⁶And Rachel, so pleasing to the Lord, so loved by holy Jacob, was sterile for a long time, and yet gave birth to Joseph, not only the lord of Egypt but also liberator of a great many peoples from hunger. Who from the leaders was

cf. Acts 12:7
cf. Luke 1:19
cf. Gen 15:1; 21:17;
Luke 1:13
cf. Acts 10:4
cf. Gen 11:30; 16:1
cf. Gen 21:2
cf. Gen 22:18;
2 Cor 9:5
cf. Acts 7:20
cf. Gen 30:1–24
Gen 37–50

A. *when he had been there for some time:* Nat. Mary has eliminated details from *Ps.-Mt.* about Joachim's self-exile in the wilderness as a shepherd, his interactions with other shepherds, and the visitations of the angel to him on multiple occasions.

B. Both this speech to Joachim (3:2–11) and the next speech to Anna in chap. 4 align in details (even verbal phrases) with the Annunciation in Luke 1. The author thus uses the biblical narrative to situate Mary as a precursor to Jesus in her conception and birth.

stronger than Samson or holier than Samuel?[A] And yet they both had sterile mothers.[B]

cf. Judg 13:2–24;
1 Sam 1:1–20

⁷If reason does not convince you to believe my words, certainly you must believe that examples of delayed conception and sterile births are usually miraculous. ⁸Therefore your wife Anna will give birth to a daughter for you and you will call her name Mary.[C] She will be, as you have vowed, consecrated to the Lord from childhood, and she will be filled with the Holy Spirit even from her mother's womb. ⁹She will neither eat nor drink anything unclean, nor will she live publicly among the people, but in the temple of the Lord, so that no one will ever be able to suspect or speak of any wrongdoing. ¹⁰Thus as she advances in years, just as she herself will be born miraculously from a sterile woman, so she will give birth uniquely[D] as a virgin to the Son of the Most High, who will be called Jesus; his name means he will be Savior of all peoples. ¹¹And this will be the sign that I declare to you: when you arrive at the Golden Gate in Jerusalem,[E] there you will

cf. Matt 1:21//
Luke 1:13;
Luke:31

cf. Judg 16:17

cf. Judg 13:4;
1 Sam 1:22

cf. 1 Macc 1:62;
Acts 10:14;
cf. Luke 1:15

cf. Isa 7:14; 38:7;
Jer 44:29; Luke 2:12

A. *Samson . . . Samuel*: in his *Epist.* 107.3 (*Ad Laeta*), Jerome uses the same examples of Samson and Samuel.

B. *Was not the first mother . . . both had sterile mothers* (3:5–6): this passage, with details that are not found in *Ps.-Mt.*, draws on the most famous of biblical women to experience infertility and miraculous births as exempla. The combination of examples resembles medieval sermons that drew on the Bible for lessons appropriate to contemporary audiences.

C. The use of the biblical phrasing here emphasizes the orthodoxy of this explanation of Anna's conception. The name Mary is placed here (it is not given in *Ps.-Mt.* before her birth) as a means of foreshadowing her place in the divine plan; this is similar to the naming of John the Baptist and Jesus in the gospels. Echoes of this narrative detail may be found in two eleventh-century liturgical prayers for the Feast of the Conception of the Virgin: the Benedictional of Canterbury (after 1023) and the Pontifical of Leofric, the first bishop of Exeter (1050–1073). These two texts are among the oldest witnesses to the Feast of the Conception in the West, which developed in the eleventh century and enjoyed immense popularity through the late Middle Ages.

D. *uniquely*: the Latin adverb *incomparabiliter* is postclassical; it developed in the fourth century and became prominently used by Carolingian theologians.

E. *Golden Gate*: as in *Ps.-Mt.*, this reference to "the Golden Gate" alludes to the eastern entrance into the old city of Jerusalem in premodern times. It is known as the Gate of Mercy in Hebrew and the Golden Gate in Christian literature, and it has also been equated with the gate through which Jesus entered Jerusalem on Palm Sunday (Mark 11:1–11 par.; John 12:12–19) as

cf. Gen 32:17;
1 Sam 10:5

cf. Luke 1:38;
Prot. Jas. 4:4;
Ps.-Mt. 3:1–6,
20–21

cf. Matt 14:26;
Mark 6:49

cf. Tob 12:14

cf. Luke 1:28

cf. Luke 2:37

meet your wife Anna, who is very anxious about the delay of your return, and then she will rejoice at seeing you." With these words the angel departed from him.

cf. Tob 11:8
Vul.

4 ¹Then he appeared to his wife Anna saying,ᴬ "Do not fear, Anna, nor think that what you see is a ghost. For I am the angel who has brought your prayers and offerings before the Lord. ²And now I am sent to you to announce that you will give birth to a daughter, who will be called Mary, blessed above all women. Immediately full of the grace of the Lord from her birth,ᴮ she will stay at home for three years of nursing. ³Afterward, dedicated to the service of the Lord, she will not depart from the temple until her adult years, serving God in fasting and in prayer night and day, abstaining herself from anything unclean. She will never know a man, but alone without example,ᶜ without stain, without corruption, without intercourse with a man, as a virgin she will give birth to a son; as a servant of God, she will give birth to the Lord; excellent in name and in deed, she will give birth to the Savior of the world.ᴰ ⁴Therefore, arise, go to Jerusalem,ᴱ and when

cf. Tob 12:12

---

well as the Beautiful Gate in Acts 3.

A. As with Joachim in chap. 3, *Nat. Mary* omits much in the narrative concerning Anna, her interactions with a maidservant, and the visitations of the angel to her on multiple occasions. This includes reducing the number of appearances, as well as the drama of Anna's lament and prayer about her infertility. In her note on this passage, Beyers suggests that these adaptations are to simplify the story's structure and add more historical coherence to the narrative (292 n. 1).

B. *full of the grace of the Lord:* the author emphasizes Mary's fullness of grace (*gratia plena*) as part of her identity from birth, long preceding the Annunciation. Like other details, this characteristic aligns with the author's use of the angel's speeches to foreshadow Mary's election. This passage also acts as an exegetical comment on Luke 1:28 as a theological point about Mary's nature, in line with developments of the cult of Mary in the medieval period.

C. *alone without example:* this formulaic phrase (*sola sine exemplo*) derives from Sedulius's *Carmen Paschale* 2.69 and became popular in the liturgy.

D. In lieu of narrative exposition, the author of *Nat. Mary* greatly expands the angel's speeches (4:2–3) to Joachim and Anna about Mary's birth and life. Here, Mary's life in the temple is foreshadowed, while the author omits the longer narrative details about this (from *Ps.-Mt.* 6) later in the text. As with Mary's name above, the details about her life are given to emphasize that she is part of the divine plan.

E. *go to Jerusalem:* because of the author's change of the location of Anna

cf. Gen 32:17;
1 Sam 10:5

you arrive at the gate that is called 'golden' because it is gilded, there as a sign you will meet your husband, about whose safety you are very anxious. When it has happened in this manner, know that what I declare to you will be fulfilled without a doubt."

cf. Prot. Jas. 4:1, 3;
Ps.-Mt. 2:8, 3:5–6,
21, 24–25

5 ¹Therefore, according to the commands of the angel, both of them went from the places where they had been and went up to Jerusalem. And when they arrived at the place designated by the angel's prophecy, they met each other. ²Then, mutually joyful at seeing each other and comforted by the certainty of the promise of offspring, they gave thanks owed to the Lord, the Uplifter of the lowly. ³Therefore, having worshiped the Lord, they returned home and awaited the divine promise in certainty and joy. So Anna conceived and gave birth to a daughter and, according to the angel's command, the parents called her name Mary.

cf. Luke 1:52;
Prot. Jas. 8–9;
Ps.-Mt.
3:26–29

cf. 1 Sam 1:20;
Judg 13:24;
cf. Prot. Jas. 4:10;
5:5–10; Ps.-Mt. 4:1

6ᴬ ¹When three years had passedᴮ and the time of her nursing was complete, they brought the Virgin to the temple of the Lord with offerings. ²But around the temple rose fifteen steps according to the fifteen Gradual Psalms.ᶜ Because the temple was set on a mountain, no one could approach the Altar of Offerings, which was on the outside, except by the steps.ᴰ Therefore, they set the

---

and Joachim's home in Nazareth, Anna must travel to Jerusalem to join Joachim at the Golden Gate.

A. The author of *Nat. Mary* omits Anna's song from *Ps.-Mt.* 5.

B. *When three years had passed:* the author uses a phrase (*Cumque trium annorum circulus uolueretur*) that echoes biblical passages, such as Lev 25:30 and 2 Chr 36:10.

C. *fifteen Gradual Psalms:* extending the imagery of Mary ascending the steps of the temple in *Ps.-Mt.* 4, the author more explicitly relates this episode to the fifteen Gradual Psalms (119–33 LXX, or 120–34 in the Hebrew psalter), a group of psalms all containing the ascription *canticum graduum* ("Shir Hama'aloth," or "Song of the Ascents," in Hebrew). In Benedictine monasticism, these psalms were given their own special category and status. In some Jewish and Christian traditions, the fifteen Gradual Psalms are meant to be recited while ascending the steps of the temple; see, for example, *t. Sotah* 7.7. In the Middle Ages, this became a common belief about the origin and use of this group of psalms. In his *Tract. Ps.*, Jerome allegorizes the fifteen Gradual Psalms with the fifteen stages of a Christian seeking to attain perfection.

D. *Altar of Offerings:* this detail about the Altar of Offerings being on the outside of the temple (not included in *Ps.-Mt.*) does not accord with the actual structure of the temple complex on the mount. The author seems to

Virgin on the lowest of them. ³While they took off the clothing that they had for traveling, according to custom, and put on more refined and elegant clothing,ᴬ the Virgin of the Lord ascended all the steps one at a time without a hand to guide and lift her,ᴮ so that for this reason someone watching might believe her to be not less than a mature age. ⁴Already in the Virgin's infancy the Lord worked a great deed and presaged how great she would be in the future by the evidence of this miracle. ⁵When they had celebrated with a sacrifice according to the custom of the Law and had completed their vow, they sent the Virgin into the enclosure of the temple with the other virgins raised in that place, and they returned home.

7 ¹But the virgin of the Lord advanced in age every day and progressed in virtue, because, according to the psalmist, "her father and mother left her, the Lord adopted her."ᶜ ²For every day she was visited by an angel, every day she delighted in a divine vision, which protected her from all evil and made her overflow in all goodness.ᴰ ³Thus she arrived at fourteen years old in such a way that none but the wicked were able to find anything worthy of reproach in her, and yet all the good people who knew her judged her life and conduct as worthy of admiration.

cf. Ruth 3:3

cf. Luke 2:27

cf. Prot. Jas. 7:4–9; Ps.-Mt. 4

cf. 1 Sam 2:26; Luke 2:41–52

Ps 26:10 LXX

cf. Prot Jas. 8:1–2; Ps.-Mt. 6:1–2, 7

---

be confused about the architecture of the temple and the organization of its parts.

A. *refined and elegant clothing:* Anna and Joachim needing to change clothes is new to *Nat. Mary.* There are no prescriptions for the types of clothes that must be worn when approaching or entering the temple, but the author seems to be alluding to Ruth 3:3 (even in verbal echoes) as a custom. Also possibly relevant are Paul's comments about garments and head-coverings in 1 Cor 11:3–15.

B. *without a hand to guide and lift her:* Mary taking the initiative to climb the steps is new to *Nat. Mary.*

C. The author does not use the standard Vulgate reading for Ps 26:10 ("For my father and my mother have left me: but the Lord hath taken me up," *Pater enim meus et mater mea dereliquerunt me Dominus autem collegit me*), but an Old Latin variant (based on LXX) that aligns this episode more closely with the psalm as a prophecy.

D. *visited by an angel:* the image of the angel visiting Mary ultimately derives from *Prot. Jas.* 8:1, and it appears in *Ps.-Mt.* 6:7. As a biblical motif (cf. 1 Kgs 19:5–7; Ps 77:25; and Wis 16:20) that was taken up by early Christian hagiographers, this detail emphasizes Mary's virtue as well as her ascetic lifestyle, which would have appealed to a monastic author and audience.

⁴Then the high priest announced that the virgins who had been placed in the temple and had fulfilled that time of years should return home for marriage according to the custom of the people and the age of maturity given in service (in the temple). ⁵While the others obeyed this command eagerly, only Mary the Virgin of the Lord responded that she was not able to do this, because her parents had dedicated her to the service of the Lord, and since she had vowed herself in virginity to the Lord, she could never violate that by knowing a man through intercourse.

cf. Prot. Jas. 8:3–5;
Ps.-Mt. 7, 8:1

⁶The high priest was set in anguish, for other than opposing Scripture, which says, "Vow and pay (to the Lord)," he knew that no one could break a vow, nor would he dare to introduce an unknown custom to the people. He ordered that at the upcoming feast all the elders from Jerusalem and the neighboring places should be present, so that he might learn from the council what should be done in such a doubtful matter.

Ps 75:12 Vul.

cf. Prot. Jas. 8:6–9;
Ps.-Mt. 8:2

⁷It happened in that manner, and everyone agreed together that the Lord should be consulted on this matter. While the others prostrated in prayer, according to custom the high priest sought counsel. ⁸Without delay, everyone heard a voice from the oracleᴬ and the place of the mercy seatᴮ to follow the prophet Isaiah to learn to whom the virgin should be entrusted and given in marriage, as Isaiah says, "There shall come forth a rod out of the root of Jesse, and a flower shall rise up out of his root. And

cf. Exod 25:18–20;
37:6–9

A. *oracle*: although this Latin term (*oraculum*) is often used of pagan divination in Classical literature, it became used in post-classical Christian texts with the sense of a divine announcement from God; for example, Jerome uses it with this meaning throughout the Vulgate.

B. *mercy seat*: the Latin phrase (*propitiatorii loco*) is translated in the Douay-Rheims as "propitiatory," but the more prevalent contemporary English term is "mercy seat," as used here. Latin *propitiatorius* is post-classical and appears throughout patristic writings, such as those by Ambrose, Jerome, and (later) Isidore of Seville, who mentions it as a place for prayers. Neither the oracle nor the mercy seat are mentioned in *Ps.-Mt.* The image and phrasing echo the biblical passages in which God gives commands for the creation of the Ark of the Covenant (Exod 25:18–20) and its later production (Exod 37:6–9), specifically in relation to the golden cover with two cherubim on top. The early medieval author Bede discusses this imagery in his commentary on the temple and its contents, in his *De tabernaculo* 1. The Ark, however, would not have resided in the temple during the Second Temple period (the time of the action of *Nat. Mar.*), since it disappeared during the Babylonian Conquest in 587 BCE.

the spirit of the Lord shall rest upon him: the spirit of wisdom, and of understanding, the spirit of counsel, and of fortitude, the spirit of knowledge, and of godliness. And he shall be filled with the spirit of the fear of the Lord." [9]So, according to this prophecy, everyone unmarried in the house and family of David suitable for marriage took his rod to the altar;[A] and for the one to whom a flower would blossom after taking the rod, the Spirit of the Lord would descend in the form of a dove onto the point,[B] and this would be the one to whom the virgin should be entrusted and given in marriage.

Isa 11:1–3

cf. Mark 1:10 par.

cf. Num 17

cf. Prot.
Jas. 9:1–4;
Ps.-Mt.
8:3–18

8 [1]Among the citizens was Joseph, a man from the house and family of David, whose wife was dead and who had grown children. [2]Because he thought it unsuitable that he might take such a young virgin as his wife since he had sons of greater age, when the others offered their branches according to the prophecy, only he withdrew his. [3]Since he appeared not to agree with the divine voice, the high priest thought that he must consult with the Lord again. He (the Lord) responded that only he who had not brought his rod was the chosen one for whom the Virgin should be given in marriage. [4]Therefore Joseph came forward, brought his rod with him, and a flower blossomed there, and a dove coming from

cf. Luke 2:4

A. *everyone . . . took his rod to the altar*: this scene is highly abbreviated from that in *Ps.-Mt.*, in which the high priest takes the rods into the temple overnight and emerges the next day to redistribute them to the men of Israel. It is also unclear which altar is meant by this reference, since both the Altar of Burnt Offering and the Altar of Incense are mentioned throughout the Hebrew Bible. The ambiguity suggests that the author was unconcerned with the details, although this is curious given the more general concern with details about the temple elsewhere in this text. Presumably, the altar mentioned here is the Altar of Burnt Offerings, since this is the only altar mentioned elsewhere (see 6:2).

B. *descend in the form of a dove*: in this instance, *Nat. Mary* both creates a more explicit link between Isaiah and the selection of Joseph and offers an innovative exegetical reading of the prophecy as typologically fulfilled in this episode. Neither *Prot. Jas.* nor *Ps.-Mt.* make the connection with Isaiah explicit, although it is implied in both texts. Here, the link with the line of Jesse and Joseph's Davidic genealogy is highlighted, aligning with the author's concern for this theme elsewhere. Beyers notes that this is a somewhat surprising interpretation, since it differs from the standard Mariological and Christological exegesis of Isa 11:1–3 (308 n. 1). The effect, however, is to raise the status of Joseph's role as one who fulfills prophecy in the Hebrew Bible, as do Mary and Jesus.

heaven descended on the point, so it was made clear to everyone that he was the one to whom the virgin should be given in marriage.

cf. *Prot. Jas.* 9:5–11;
Ps.-Mt. 8:19–22

⁵After marriage vows according to the usual custom, Joseph, in fact, stayed in the city of Bethlehem, to put his home in order and to attend to the necessary marriage arrangements. ⁶Mary, the true Virgin of the Lord, together with seven other virgins of the same age, whom she had received from the priest, returned to her parent's home in Galilee.^A

cf. 2 Sam 17:23;
Isa 38:1

cf. Luke 2:39;
Prot. Jas. 9:12;
Ps.-Mt. 8:31

9^B ¹At that time, that is at the time she first arrived in Galilee, the angel Gabriel was sent to her from God, who related to her the conception of the Lord and explained the matter and the means of the conception. ²When he had come into the bedroom in which she stayed, he filled it with great light, and truly greeted her with great joy saying, "Hail Mary, most pleasing to the Lord, virgin full of grace, the Lord is with you; blessed are you among all women, blessed are you among all humans born until now."^C

cf. Luke 1:26

cf. Luke 1:28

A. In addition to condensing the narrative, *Nat. Mary* introduces some radically different details in this verse. For example, in *Ps.-Mt.*, Mary takes with her seven virgins (who are named), not five, and they go to Joseph's home, not Galilee (although Joseph himself then departs while they live there).

B. Because of the author's greater reliance on the canonical Gospels as direct sources throughout the rest of this text, a number of complexities appear in the manuscript tradition, with various witnesses differing in specific readings (see Beyers's apparatus). This translation follows the main text of Beyers's critical edition. From this point forward, the author's dependence on *Ps.-Mt.* is difficult to discern, as the narrative more closely relies on and corresponds with the Matthew and Luke. Such distance from the apocryphal source is especially evident in the depiction of the Annunciation and the brief mention of Jesus' birth at the very end (10:8), without any of the characteristic features of *Ps.-Mt.*, such as the midwives. The story, in fact, becomes more like the author's own expansion or commentary on the canonical Gospels—a type of gospel harmony—rather than an adaptation of the apocryphal source. This is evident from the many borrowings of biblical passages, woven together with the author's own exposition for coherence. The author also draws on a wide range of commentaries on the gospels from the patristic and early medieval periods, as several of the passages connecting together the biblical materials rely on such traditions.

C. *Hail Mary . . . until now*: while this speech relies on Luke 1:28, it also demonstrates a type of exegetical expansion on the well-known biblical greeting.

³The Virgin, who already knew the faces of angels well and was not unfamiliar with heavenly light,ᴬ was neither afraid at the vision of the angel nor astonished at the greatness of the light, but was disturbed only at his speech, and she began to think to herself what manner such an unfamiliar greeting might be, what meaning it might have or what end it might have.ᴮ ⁴Inspired by God, the angel met this thought, "Do not fear, Mary, that this greeting might mean something contrary to your chastity. ⁵You have found favor with God. Because you chose the chastity of a virgin,ᶜ you will conceive without sin, and give birth to a son. ⁶He will be great, because he will have dominion from sea to sea and from the river to the ends of the earth, and he will be called the Son of the Most High, because he who is born on the earth in humility reigns in heaven exalted with the Father. ⁷And the Lord God will give him the throne of David his father, and he will reign in the house of Jacob forever and of his kingdom there will be no end. For he is King of kings and Lord of lords and his throne will be forever and ever."

⁸To the angel's words the virgin replied, not because she was unbelieving but she wanted to know the means,ᴰ "How will this

cf. 2 Tim 3:16

cf. Ps 71:8 Vul.

cf. Deut 10:17;
1 Tim 6:15;
Rev 17:14, 19:16

cf. Tob 9:11
Vul.; Ps 9:37
LXX;
Heb 1:8; cf.
Luke 1:28–33

A. *knew the faces of angels . . . not unfamiliar with heavenly light*: details about Mary's familiarity with angels and heavenly light (not in any of the author's sources for this section) are meant to remind readers of the angels who daily delivered food to her and to emphasize her virtue through communion with God's messengers.

B. *neither afraid . . . nor astonished*: contrary to the obvious sense given in Luke 1 (and by the angel's command not to fear), the author explicates Mary's anxiety not at the angel's presence but at the message and its implications. This interpretation (in light of the previous note that Mary was familiar with angelic presence) is made all the more striking by the use of the phrase "such an unfamiliar greeting" (*salutatio tam insolita*), meant to indicate that this speech was unlike any other Mary had encountered from an angel before. This phrasing seems to derive from early medieval literature: for example, concerning the angel's speech in Luke 1:28, Bede uses the term *insolita* ("unfamiliar") in his *In Lucae euangelium* 1; and Paschasius Radbertus uses *non consueta* ("not usual") in his *De assumption sanctae Mariae Virginis* 32.

C. *chastity of a virgin*: this phrase (*castitatem . . . uirginitatis*) and variants were widespread in early medieval literature, but especially in commentaries concerning Mary and the gospels: see, for example, Bede, *Homelia* 1.3 and 1.5; Hrabanus Maurus, *Commentaria in Matthaeum* 1:1; and Paschasius Radbertus, *De partu Virginis* 1.

D. *she wanted to know the means*: along with earlier exegesis on Mary's

be possible? Since I myself have not known a man according to my vow, how can I conceive except by human manner, or bear a child to birth without the seed of a man?" [9]To this the angel responded, "Do not think, Mary, that you will conceive in the human manner, for as a virgin you will conceive without intercourse with a man, as a virgin you will give birth, as a virgin you will nurse.[A] [10]For the Holy Spirit will come upon you and the power of the Most High will overshadow you against all flames of lust.[B] And therefore also the holy one born only of you, who alone is conceived and born without sin, will be called the Son of God.

cf. Luke 1:34–35

[11]Then, with hands outstretched and eyes uplifted to heaven, Mary said, "Behold, the handmaid of the Lord, although I am not worthy of the name mother.[C] May it be done according to your word." [12]It would be too much if we wanted to introduce in this little work all that we read about what preceded or followed the birth of the Lord. Therefore, let us omit what is fully written in the Gospel,[D] and come to what has been less fully narrated there.

cf. Luke 1:38

cf. John 21:25

cf. Prot. Jas. 11;
Ps.-Mt. 9

---

response to the Annunciation, the author is careful to note that her question was not out of doubt but was an act of curiosity from faith. This was in stark contrast to Zechariah's doubt in Luke 1:18. For earlier instances of similar comments on Mary and in contrast to Zechariah, see, for example, Ambrose, *Exp. Luc.* 1:34; Augustine, *Enarrat. Ps.* 67:21, *Serm.* 290.5, and *Serm.* 291.5; Bede, *In Lucae euangelium* 1 and *Homelia* 1.1; Beatus of Liébana, *Contra Elipandum*; Heiric of Auxerre, *Homilia* 1.5; and Milo of Saint-Amand, *Carmen de sobrietate* 2.30.

A. *as a virgin:* the repetition in this sentence offers a continual emphasis on Mary's perpetual virginity, as already highlighted throughout this text.

B. *flames of lust:* for this note about the Holy Spirit's protection of Mary's chastity against lust, the author drew on a widespread idea in earlier commentaries concerning Mary and the Gospels. For example, see Augustine, *Enarrat. Ps.* 67:21 (where he uses a phrase parallel to this text, *obumbrare contra*) and *Serm.* 291.5; Bede, *In Lucae euangelium* 1; Paschasius Radbertus, *De partu Virginis* 1; and Heiric of Auxerre, *Homilia* 1.5.

C. *handmaid . . . mother:* the epithets *ancilla* and *mater* are logically paired, though in juxtaposition to each other, drawing on a prominent understanding of Mary's role as both chosen by God and mother of Jesus. See, for example, Ambrose, *Exp. Luc.* 1:38; Bede, *In Lucae euangelium* 1; Ildefonso of Toledo, *De uirginitate perpetua sanctae Mariae* 12; Hincmar of Rheims, *Explanatio in ferculum Salomonis*; Paschasius Radbertus, *Sermo 3* and *De assumptione sanctae Mariae Virginis* 104; and Heiric of Auxerre, *Homilia* 1.4.

D. *let us omit . . . in the Gospel:* here the author explicitly mentions the various stories about Mary, Joseph, and Jesus' birth, possibly with a nod to non-canonical traditions such as those found in *Ps.-Mt.* The author

10 ¹Then Joseph, coming from Judea to Galilee, intended to marry the betrothed Virgin to himself as his wife. For three months had gone by and the fourth had begun from the time when she had become his betrothed. ²Meanwhile, the womb of the woman to give birth gradually grew as the child to be born began to show. Nor could it be concealed from Joseph. As is customary for betrothed men, he freely entered into the virgin's home and spoke with her, and realized that she was pregnant.[A] ³His spirit was enraged and he began to doubt[B] because he was ignorant about what he should do. For he did not want to expose her publicly because he was just, nor to defame her on suspicion of fornication because he was pious. Therefore, he considered privately dissolving the marriage and sending her away secretly.

cf. Matt 1:19;
Prot. Jas. 13; 14:1–4;
Ps.-Mt. 10

⁴But while he considered these things, behold an angel of the Lord appeared to him in his sleep, saying, "Joseph, son of David, do not be afraid, nor have suspicion of fornication by the Virgin, nor consider any wrongdoing by her, nor fear to take her as a wife. ⁵For what is produced in her, which now distresses your spirit, is not the work of a man but of the Holy Spirit. And she alone among virgins will give birth to a son and you will call his name Jesus, which is Savior.[C] For he will save his people from their

---

simultaneously indicates the previous divergence from *Ps.-Mt.* and reliance on the canonical Gospels, specifically Luke and Matthew (the main sources of chaps. 9–10), as well as the characteristic adaptation at work in *Nat. Mary* as the author condenses, comments on, and combines various sources from the Bible and exegetical tradition. In specifically mentioning "what is fully written in the Gospel" (*quae in euangelio plenius scripta sunt*), the author seems to be referring to the full story leading up to and including Jesus' Nativity in Luke 1–2, since that is the main source for the Annunciation in chap. 9.

A. *Then Joseph . . . realized that she was pregnant:* the image of Joseph visiting his betrothed seems to derive from Jerome, *Comm. Matt.* 1, and was widespread in commentaries on Matthew reliant on Jerome's exegesis—for example, by authors like Bede, Hrabanus Maurus, Smaragdus of Saint-Mihiel, Sedulius Scotus, Christian of Stavelot, and Remigius of Auxerre.

B. *enraged . . . doubt:* the terms for indicating that Joseph's "spirit was enraged" (*aestuare. . . animo*) and "he began to doubt" (*fluctuare coepit*) echo similar biblical phrases. See, for example, Jdt 13:29 (*aestuavit anima eius*), Ps 37:11 (*cor meum fluctuabat*), and Isa 29:9 (*fluctuate et vacillate*).

C. *which is Savior:* this phrase (*id est saluatorem*)—which does not appear in Matthew nor in *Ps.-Mt.*—emphasizes the Latin translation of the Greek term σωτήρ (*saluator*). In medieval commentaries, the phrase *id est* is commonly used to indicate an interpretive comment, just as the author presents

sins." [6]Therefore Joseph took the Virgin as his wife according to the angel's command, yet he did not know her, but protected and cared for her chastity.

cf. Matt 1:20–25;
1 Tim 5:22

cf. *Prot. Jas.* 14:5–8;
Ps.-Mt. 11

[7]And when the ninth month from the conception arrived, Joseph took his wife and whatever else was necessary to the city of Bethlehem, from which he himself had come. [8]And it came to pass that, when they were there, the days were fulfilled so that she should deliver, and she gave birth to her firstborn—just as the holy Evangelists taught[A]—our Lord Jesus Christ, who lives and reigns forever and ever. Amen.

cf. Luke 2:6–7;
Prot Jas. 17–20;
Ps.-Mt. 13

---

it here, in the form of an exegetical gloss on Jesus' name. This addition also creates a paronomastic instance of wordplay between *saluator* and *saluus* ("save") in the following sentence.

A. *just as the holy Evangelists taught*: while the prefatory material seems to raise the issue of the status of this text as an apocryphon, this phrase (*sicut sancti euangelistae docuerunt*) at the end of the narrative (as with the lack of reliance on *Ps.-Mt.* from 9:1 onward) sets the text in closer relation to the canonical Gospels and their authority.

Bibliography

Texts and Translations

Amann, Émile. *Le Protévangile de Jacques et ses remaniements latins*. Paris: Letouzey et Ané, 1910. (*Nat. Mary*, 240–64; *Ps.-Mt.*, 272–339)

Bergua, Juan Bautista, and Edmundo González-Blanco, eds. and trans. *Los Evangelios apócrifos*. 2 vols. Madrid: Ediciones Ibéricas, 2012. (*Nat. Mary*, vol. 1:414–23)

Beyers, Rita, ed. "Latin Translation of the *Protevangelium of James* in MS. Paris, Sainte-Geneviève, 2787." In *Apocrypha Hiberniae I. Evangelia Infantiae*, edited by Martin McNamara et al., 2:881–957. 2 vols. CCSA 13–14. Turnhout: Brepols, 2001.

———, ed. *Libri de nativitate Mariae: Libellus de nativitate sanctae Mariae, textus et commentarius*. CCSA 10. Turnhout: Brepols, 1997.

———, trans. "Livre de la Nativitaté de Marie." In *Écrits apocryphes chrétiens*, vol. 1, edited by François Bovon and Pierre Geoltrain, 141–61. Bibliothèque de la Pléiade 442. Paris: Gallimard, 1997.

Bonaccorsi, Giuseppe, ed. and trans. *Vangeli apocrifi, I*. Florence: Libreria editrice fiorentina, 1961. (*Ps.-Mt.*, 152–231)

Cowper, Benjamin Harris, trans. *The Apocryphal Gospels and Other Documents Relating to the History of Christ*. 7th ed. London: David Nutt, 1910. (*Ps.-Mt.*, 27–83; *Nat. Mary*, 84–98)

Cullman, Oscar, trans. "Infancy Gospels: Later Infancy Gospels." In *New Testament Apocrypha*, edited by Wilhelm Schneemelcher, 1:456–65. Translation editor R. McL. Wilson. 2 vols. Rev. ed. Louisville: Westminster John Knox, 1991–1993 (*Ps.-Mt.* 14, 18–25 only).

Dimier-Paupert, Catherine, ed. *Livre de l'Enfance du Sauveur: Une version médiévale de l'Évangile de l'Enfance du Pseudo-Matthieu (XIIIe siècle)*. Paris: Cerf, 2006.

Ehrman, Bart D., and Zlatko Pleše, eds. and trans. *The Apocryphal Gospels: Texts and Translations*. Oxford: Oxford University Press, 2011. (*Ps.-Mt.*, 73–113).

Elliott, J. K., trans. *The Apocryphal New Testament: A Collection of Apocryphal Christian Literature in an English Translation*. Oxford: Oxford University Press, 1993. Rev. repr. 1999. (*Ps.-Mt.*, 84–99; prefatory letters and chaps. 13–14, 18–25, 35–36, 40, and 42)

———, ed. and trans. *A Synopsis of the Apocryphal Nativity and Infancy Narratives*. 2nd ed. NTTS 34. Leiden: Brill, 2016.

Erbetta, Mario, trans. *Gli Apocrifi del Nuovo Testamento*. Vol. I.2: *Vangeli: Infanzia e passione di Cristo, Assunzione di Maria*. Turin: Casale Monferrato, 1981. (*Ps.-Mt.*, 44–70; *Nat. Mary*, 71–77 (*Nat. Mary*)

Fabricius, Johann Albert, ed. *Codex apocryphus Novi Testamenti*. 2 vols. Hamburg: Benjamin Schiller, 1703, vol. 1:19–38 (*Nat. Mary*).

Gijsel, Jan, trans. "Évangile de l'Enfance du Pseudo-Matthieu." In *Écrits apocryphes chrétiens*, edited by François Bovon and Pierre Geoltrain, vol. 1, 105–40. Bibliothèque de la Pléiade 442. Paris: Gallimard, 1997.

————, ed. *Libri de nativitate Mariae: Pseudo-Matthaei Evangelium, textus et commentarius*. CCSA 9. Turnhout: Brepols, 1997.

Giles, John A., trans. *The Uncanonical Gospels and Other Writings, Referring to the First Ages of Christianity*. 2 vols. London: Nutt, 1852. (*Ps.-Mt.*, vol. 1:66–89).

Hone, William, ed. *The Apocryphal New Testament*. London: Hone, 1820. (*Nat. Mary*, 17–24).

James, M. R., trans. *The Apocryphal New Testament*. Oxford: Oxford University Press, 1924. (*Ps.-Mt.*, 70–80).

Jones, Jeremiah, trans. *A New and Full Method of Settling the Canonical Authority of the New Testament*. 3 vols. London: Clark and Hett, 1726–1727. 3rd ed. Oxford: Clarendon, 1827. (*Nat. Mary*, vol. 2:69–81; *Ps.-Mt.*, 81–84; prefatory letters only).

Migne, Jacques-Paul, trans. *Dictionnaire des Apocryphes*. 2 vols. Paris: Migne, 1856. (*Ps.-Mt.*, vol. 1:1059–88).

Moraldi, Luigi, ed. and trans. *Apocrifi del Nuovo Testamento*. 2 vols. Turin: Piemme, 1971. (*Nat. Mary*, vol. 1: 95–104; *Ps.-Mt.*, 195–239).

Michel, Charles, ed. *Évangiles apocryphes*. Vol. 1. 2nd ed. Textes et documents pour l'étude historique du Christianisme 13. Paris: A. Picard, 1924. (*Ps.-Mt.*, 54–158).

Otero, Aurelio de Santos, ed. and trans. *Los Evangelios apócrifos*. 6th ed. Madrid: Editorial Católica, 1988, 171–216 (*Ps.-Mt.*), 243–58 (*Nat. Mary*).

Pistelli, Ermenegildo, trans. *Il Protevangelo di Jacopo*. Lanciano: R. Carabba, 1919, 105–25. (*Ps.-Mt.* 14, 18–24 only).

Schade, Oscar, ed. *Liber de infantia Mariae et Christi Salvatoris ex codice Stuttgartensi*. Halle: Libraria Orphanotrophei, 1869. (*Ps.-Mt.*).

Schneider, Gerhard, ed. *Apokryphe Kindheitsevangelien*. New York: Herder, 1995. (*Ps.-Mt.*, 213–55)

Thilo, Johann Karl, ed. *Codex apocryphus Novi Testamenti*. Leipzig: Vogel, 1832. (*Nat. Mary*, 317–36; *Ps.-Mt.*, 337–400).

Tischendorf, Constantin von, ed. *Evangelia Apocrypha*. Leipzig: Hermann Mendelsohn, 1853. 2nd ed., 1876. (*Ps.-Mt.*, 52–112; *Nat. Mary*, 113–21)

Walker, Alexander, trans. *Apocryphal Gospels, Acts and Revelations*. Edinburgh: T. & T. Clark, 1870. (*Ps.-Mt.*, 16–52, with the *pars altera*).

Studies and Other Works Cited

Berthold, Michael. "Zur Datierung des Pseudo-Matthäus-Evangeliums." *Wiener Studien* 102 (1989) 247–49.

Beyers, Rita. "De nativitate Mariae. Problèmes d'origine." *Revue de théologie et de philosophie* 122 (1990) 171–88.

————. "La réception médiévale du matériel apocryphe concernant la naissance et la jeunesse de Marie: Le *Speculum historiale* de Vincent de Beauvais et la *Legenda aurea* de Jacques de Voragine." In *Marie dans les récits apocryphes chrétiens*, Tome 1: *Communications présentées à la 60e session de la Société Française d'Etudes mariales: Sanctuaire Notre-Dame-du-Chêne, Solesnes 2003*, edited by Édouard Cothenet et al., 179–200. Paris: Médiaspaul, 2004.

————. "La règle de Marie: caractère littéraire et inspiration monastique." *Apocrypha* 22 (2011) 49–86.

————. "The Transmission of Marian Apocrypha in the Latin Middle Ages." *Apocrypha* 23 (2012) 117–40.

Bieler, Ludwig. "Exagellia." *AJP* 69 (1948) 309–12.

Biggs, Frederick M., ed. *Sources of Anglo-Saxon Literary Culture: The Apocrypha*. Instrumenta Anglistica Mediaevalia 1. Kalamazoo, MI: Medieval Institute, 2006.

Boulton, Maureen Barry McCann. *Sacred Fictions of Medieval France: Narrative Theology in the Lives of Christ and the Virgin, 1150–1500*. Gallica 38. Cambridge: Brewer, 2015.

Burke, Tony. *De infantia Iesu euangelium Thomae graece*. CCSA 17. Turnhout: Brepols, 2010.

Cain, Andrew. *Jerome and the Monastic Clergy: A Commentary on Letter 52 to Nepotian, with an Introduction, Text, and Translation*. Supplements to Vigiliae Christianae 119. Leiden: Brill, 2013.

Canal, José M. "Antiguas Versiones Latinas del Protoevangelio de Santiago." *Ephemerides Mariologicae* 18 (1968) 431–73.

————. "En torno al Evangelio del Pseudo-Mateo." *Marianum* 60 (1998) 197–237.

————. "Los sermones marianos de San Fulberto de Chartres. Adición." *RTAM* 30 (1963) 329–33.

————. "Los sermones marianos de San Fulberto de Chartres. Conclusión." *RTAM* 30 (1963) 139–47.

————. "Texto crítico de algunos sermons marianos de San Fulberto de Chartres o a él atribuibles." *RTAM* 30 (1963) 55–87.

Cartlidge, David R., and J. K. Elliott. *Art and the Christian Apocrypha*. London: Routledge, 2001.

Caxton, William. *W. Caxtons Infantia salvatoris*. Edited by Ferdinand Holthausen. Halle: Niemeyer, 1891.

Chisholm, John Edward, ed. *The Pseudo–Augustinian Hypomnesticon Against the Pelagians and Celestinans*. 2 vols. Paradosis: Beiträge zur Geschichte der altchristlichen Literatur und Theologie 20–21. Fribourg: University of Fribourg Press, 1967–1980.

Clayton, Mary. "De Nativitate Mariae." In *Sources of Anglo-Saxon Literary Culture: The Apocrypha*, edited by Frederick M. Biggs, 30–31. Instrumenta Anglistica Mediaevalia 1. Kalamazoo, MI: Medieval Institute, 2006.

————. *The Apocryphal Gospels of Mary in Anglo-Saxon England*. Cambridge Studies in Anglo-Saxon England 26. Cambridge: Cambridge University Press, 1998.

————. *The Cult of the Virgin Mary in Anglo-Saxon England*. Cambridge Studies in Anglo-Saxon England 2. Cambridge: Cambridge University Press, 1990.

Donahue, Charles. *The Testament of Mary: The Gaelic Version of the Dormitio Mariae Together with an Irish Latin Version*. Fordham University Studies, Language Series 1. New York: Fordham University Press, 1942.

Dzon, Mary. "Cecily Neville and the Apocryphal *Infantia salvatoris* in the Middle Ages." *MS* 71 (2009) 235–300.

———. "Jesus and the Birds in Medieval Abrahamic Traditions." *Traditio* 66 (2011) 189–230.

———. *Middle English Poems on the Apocryphal Childhood of Jesus*. Forthcoming.

———. "Out of Egypt, Into England: Tales of the Good Thief for Medieval English Audiences." In *Devotional Culture in Late Medieval England and Europe*, edited by Stephen Kelly and Ryan Perry, 147–241. Medieval Church Studies. Turnhout: Brepols, 2014.

———. *The Quest for the Christ Child in the Later Middle Ages*. Philadelphia: University of Pennsylvania Press, 2017.

Elliott, J. K. "Christian Apocrypha and the Developing Role of Mary." In *The Oxford Handbook of Early Christian Apocrypha*, edited by Andrew Gregory and Christopher Tuckett, 269–88. Oxford: Oxford University Press, 2015.

Fassler, Margot. "Mary's Nativity, Fulbert of Chartres, and the *Stirps Jesse*: Liturgical Innovation circa 1000 and Its Afterlife." *Spec* 75 (2000) 389–434.

———. *The Virgin of Chartres: Making History Through Liturgy and the Arts*. New Haven: Yale University Press, 2010.

Gijsel, Jan. *Die unmittelbare Textüberlieferung des sogenannten Pseudo-Matthäus*. Verhandelingen van de Koninklijke Academie voor Wetenschappen, Letteren en Schone Kunsten van België, Klasse der Letteren 96. Brussels: Paleis der Academiën, 1981.

———. "Nouveaux témoins du pseudo-Matthieu." *SacEr* 41 (2002) 273–300.

Ginzberg, Louis. *The Legends of the Jews*. Translated by Henrietta Szold. 7 vols. Philadelphia, PA: The Jewish Publications Society of America, 1909–1938.

Hall, Thomas N. "The Earliest Anglo-Latin Text of the *Trinubium Annae* (*BHL* 505zl)." In *Via Crucis: Essays on Early Medieval Sources and Ideas in Memory of J. E. Cross*, edited by Thomas N. Hall, with assistance from Thomas D. Hill and Charles D. Wright, 104–37. Medieval European Studies 1. Morgantown: West Virginia University Press, 2002.

———. "The Miracle of the Lengthened Beam in Apocryphal and Hagiographic Tradition." In *Marvels, Monsters, and Miracles: Studies in the Medieval and Early Modern Imagination*, edited by Timothy S. Jones and David A. Sprunger, 109–39. Kalamazoo, MI: Medieval Institute, 2002.

Hawk, Brandon W. "'Cherries at Command': Preaching the *Gospel of Pseudo-Matthew* in Anglo-Saxon England." In *Fakes, Forgeries, and Fictions: Writing Ancient and Modern Christian Apocrypha, Proceedings from the 2015 York University Christian Apocrypha Symposium*, edited by Tony Burke, 207–30. Eugene, OR: Cascade Books, 2017.

———. "Gospel of Pseudo-Matthew in Images." Online: https://brandonwhawk.net/gospel-of-pseudo-matthew-in-images/.

———. "The *Gospel of Pseudo-Matthew*, the *Rule of the Master*, and the *Rule of Benedict*." *RBén* 128 (2018) 281–93.

———. *Preaching Apocrypha in Anglo-Saxon England*. Toronto Anglo-Saxon Series 30. Toronto: University of Toronto Press, 2018.

Herbert, Maíre, and Martin McNamara, trans. *Irish Biblical Apocrypha*. Edinburgh: T. & T. Clark, 1989.

Heyden, Katharina, trans. "The Legend of Aphroditianus." In *New Testament Apocrypha: More Noncanonical Scriptures*, vol. 1, edited by Tony Burke and Brent Landau, 1–16. Grand Rapids: Eerdmans, 2016.

Hock, Ronald F., ed. and trans. *The Infancy Gospels of James and Thomas.* The Scholars Bible 2. Santa Rosa, CA: Polebridge, 1995.

Jerome. *Epistolae et Tractatus.* Edited by Giovanni Andrea Bussi. 2 vols. Rome: Conradus Sweynheym and Arnoldus Pannartz, 1468.

Junod, Éric and Jean-Daniel Kaestli. *L'histoire des actes apocryphes des apôtres du IIIe au IXe siècle: Le cas des Actes de Jean.* Cahiers de la Revue de théologie et de philosophie 7. Lausanne: La Concorde, 1982.

Kaestli, Jean-Daniel. "Mapping an Unexplored Second Century Apocryphal Gospel: The Liber de Nativitate Salvatoris (CANT 53)." In *Infancy Gospels: Stories and Identities*, edited by Clare Clivaz et al., 506–59. WUNT 281. Tübingen: Mohr/Siebeck, 2011.

———. "Recherches nouvelles sur les 'Évangiles latins de l'enfance' de M. R. James et sur un récit apocryphe mal connu de la naissance de Jésus." *ETR* 72 (1997) 219–33.

Kaestli, Jean-Daniel and Martin McNamara, eds. "Latin Infancy Gospels: The J Compilation, Introduction and Edition." In *Apocrypha Hiberniae I. Evangelia Infantiae*, edited by Martin McNamara et al., 2:621–880. 2 vols. CCSA 13–14. Turnhout: Brepols, 2001.

Lambot, Cyrille. "L'homélie du pseudo-Jérôme sur l'Assomption et l'Evangile de la Nativité de Marie d'après une lettre inédite d'Hincmar." *RBén* 46 (1934) 265–82.

Lillis, Julia Kelto. "Paradox *in Partu*: Verifying Virginity in the *Protevangelium of James*." *JECS* 24 (2016) 1–28.

McNamara, Martin. *Apocrypha in the Irish Church.* Dublin: Dublin Institute for Advanced Studies, 1975.

———. *The Bible and the Apocrypha in the Early Irish Church (A.D. 600–1200): Collected Essays.* Instrumenta Patristica et Mediaevalia: Research on the Inheritance of Early and Medieval Christianity 66. Turnhout: Brepols, 2015.

McNamara, Martin, and Jean-Daniel Kaestli. "The Irish Infancy Narratives and Their Relationship with Latin Sources." In *Apocrypha Hiberniae I. Evangelia Infantiae*, edited by Martin McNamara et al., 1:41–134. 2 vols. CCSA 13–14. Turnhout: Brepols, 2001.

McNamara, Martin, et al., ed. *Apocrypha Hiberniae I. Evangelia Infantiae.* 2 vols. CCSA 13–14. Turnhout: Brepols, 2001.

McNamara, Martin, et al., eds. "The Infancy Narratives of the *Leabhar Breac* and Related Manuscripts." In *Apocrypha Hiberniae I. Evangelia Infantia*, edited by Martin McNamara et al., 1:247–439. 2 vols. CCSA 13–14. Turnhout: Brepols, 2001.

Mingana, Alphonse. "The Vision of Theophilus, Or the Book of the Flight of the Holy Family into Egypt." *BJRL* 13 (1929) 383–474. Reprinted in Mingana, *Woodbroke Studies.* Fascicle 3. Cambridge: Heffer, 1931.

Ó Cuív, Brian, ed. "A Thirteenth-Century Irish Poem Containing Elements from Infancy Narratives." In *Apocrypha Hiberniae I. Evangelia Infantiae*, edited by Martin McNamara et al., 2:489–513. 2 vols. CCSA 13–14. Turnhout: Brepols, 2001.

Reinsch, Robert. *Die Pseudo-Evangelien von Jesu und Maria's Kindheit in der romanischen und germanischen Literatur.* Halle: Niemeyer, 1879.

Reynolds, Joyce. "Aphrodisias." In *The Oxford Classical Dictionary*, edited by Simon Hornblower et al., 116. 4th ed. Oxford: Oxford University Press, 2012.

Schäferdiek, Knut. "The Manichean Collection of Apocryphal Acts Ascribed to Leucius Charinus." In *New Testament Apocrypha*, edited by Wilhelm Schneemelcher, 2:87–100. Translation editor R. McL. Wilson. Rev. ed. 2 vols. Louisville: Westminster John Knox, 1991.

Sheingorn, Pamela. "Reshapings of the Childhood Miracles of Jesus." In *The Christ Child in Medieval Culture: Alpha es et O!*, edited by Theresa M. Kenney and Mary Dzon, 254–92. Toronto: University of Toronto Press, 2012.

Shoemaker, Stephen J. *Ancient Traditions of the Virgin Mary's Dormition and Assumption*. OECS. Oxford: Oxford University Press, 2002.

Spittler, Janet E. *Animals in the Apocryphal Acts of the Apostles: The Wild Kingdom of Early Christian Literature*. WUNT 2/247. Tübingen: Mohr/Siebeck, 2008.

"The Tring Tiles." Museum Number 1922,0412.1.CR, *The British Museum*. Online: http://www.britishmuseum.org/research/collection_online/collection_object_details.aspx?objectId=20765&partId=1.

Vogüé, Adalbert de, and Jean Neufville, ed. and trans. *La Règle de Saint Benoît*. 6 vols., Sources chrétiennes 181–86. Paris: Cerf, 1971–1977.

Voicu, Sever J. "La tradition latine des *Paidika*." *Bulletin de l'AELAC* 14 (2004) 13–21.

———. "Verso il testo primitivo dei Παιδικά τοῦ Κυρίου Ἰησοῦ 'Racconti dell'infanzia del Signore Gesù." *Apocrypha* 9 (1998) 29–34.

Vuong, Lily C. *Gender and Purity in the Protevangelium of James*. WUNT 2/358. Tübingen: Mohr/Siebeck, 2013.

Whatling, Stuart. "Bay 28—The Life of the Virgin." *Chartres Cathedral: Various Windows*. Online: http://www.medievalart.org.uk/chartres/28b_pages/Chartres_Bay28b_key.htm.

Index of Ancient Sources

John

Acts of the Apostles

1 Corinthians

2 Corinthians

Galatians

1 Thessalonians